CARYL PHILLIPS

The Right Set

Caryl Phillips was born in St. Kitts, West Indies. Brought up in England, he has written for television, radio, theater, and cinema. He is the author of one book of nonfiction, *The European Tribe,* and six novels, *The Final Passage, A State of Independence, Higher Ground, Cambridge, Crossing the River,* and *The Nature of Blood,* and has edited one previous anthology, *Extravagant Strangers.* His awards include the Martin Luther King Memorial Prize, a Guggenheim Fellowship, and a James Tait Black Memorial Prize. He divides his time between London and New York.

Also by CARYL PHILLIPS

Fiction
The Final Passage
A State of Independence
Higher Ground
Cambridge
Crossing the River
The Nature of Blood

Nonfiction
The European Tribe

Plays
Strange Fruit
Where There Is Darkness
The Shelter

Screenplay
Playing Away

Anthology
Extravagant Strangers (editor)

The Right Set

THE RIGHT SET

A Tennis Anthology

Edited and with an Introduction by

CARYL PHILLIPS

VINTAGE BOOKS

A Division of Random House, Inc.

New York

A VINTAGE ORIGINAL, JUNE 1999

Anthology copyright © 1999 by Caryl Phillips

All rights reserved under International and Pan-American Copyright
Conventions. Published in the United States by Vintage Books,
a division of Random House, Inc., New York, and simultaneously in
Canada by Random House of Canada Limited, Toronto.
Originally published in paperback in Great Britain by
Faber and Faber Limited, London.

Pages 315–318 constitute an extension of this copyright page.

Vintage Books and colophon are registered trademarks of
Random House, Inc.

Library of Congress Cataloging-in-Publication Data
The right set : a tennis anthology / edited and with an introduction by
Caryl Phillips. — 1st Vintage Books original ed.
p. cm.
Includes bibliographical references and index.
ISBN 0-375-70646-1
1. Tennis. 2. Tennis—History. I. Phillips, Caryl.
GV991.2.R54 1999
796.342—dc21   99-17240
CIP

www.vintagebooks.com

Printed in the United States of America
10 9 8 7 6 5 4 3 2 1

for John Biggins

Editor's Note

During the two years that I found myself reading about tennis and thinking about the shape of this anthology, I was helped and encouraged by a number of people. Among them Helen Anglos, Chris Benfy, Richard Cody, Anne Elletson, Allen Guttmann, Ming Nagel and Bill Pritchard. However, my greatest debt is to Cordelia Lawton, who worked tirelessly with me on the final version of the anthology. Her skill as a researcher, her keen editorial eye, and her patience with my often vague explanations and suggestions, leave me deeply in her debt. Her good humour and fine judgement made *The Right Set* a pleasure to work on, and I thank her most sincerely.

C.P.

Contents

CONTENTS

Introduction

As a young boy growing up in Britain, I remember my three brothers and I being captivated by the 'bad boy' antics of the Romanian tennis star, Ilie Nastase. In 1972 he played the unsmiling, stern-looking Stan Smith in the Wimbledon final and, against all the odds, he lost. My brothers and I were dismayed. However, we immediately picked up our cheap wooden racquets, raced out to the square of concrete that was our 'tennis court', and began thumping a worn-out grey ball back and forth. And, of course, being brothers we argued. 'I want to be Nastase!' 'No, I'm Nastase!'

Thinking back to this moment I find myself asking a couple of questions. First, why did we root so hard for Nastase? After all, we shared a language with Smith, and Nastase was from a world which, although geographically closer, was culturally and politically alien to our own. Second, although we had all played soccer on a soccer pitch, and cricket on a cricket field, and run around a 400-metre track, we had never been formally introduced to a tennis court. Why then did we possess this enthusiasm for the game, and furiously bang the ball within the imaginary tram lines and over the imaginary net? In the attempt to answer these questions I discovered the impulse to edit this anthology.

Tennis has its origins in the Middle Ages, and from the beginning the game has been wedded to traditions that are more country than city, more patrician than plebeian. In 1874 the modern form of tennis began to evolve, and almost immediately the middle classes on both sides of the Atlantic took to the game. The twentieth century has witnessed a remarkable growth in the popularity of tennis, but alongside this growth the game has had to accommodate the 'outsider', whether one wishes to define 'outsider' in terms of class, race, gender or nationality. As the century draws to a close, the 'barbarians' have not only begun to gather inside the gates, but some of these gates and at least one grand-slam stadium have been named after them.

This century has witnessed the movement of tennis away from the lawns of the country estates to the asphalt courts of the inner city. Who calls the game 'lawn tennis' any more? To play this 'new' game of tennis one simply needs to beg, steal or borrow a racquet, and, in the absence of a partner, find a brick wall against which one can slap the ball. Then, of course, one must hope to be discovered by someone who will begin to hone that natural talent into something purposeful and wedded to skill.

In our case there was no one to discover what modicum of talent either my brothers or I might have possessed. However, during Wimbledon fortnights we continued to race out of the house and appropriate the shots, mannerisms and behaviour of whoever happened to be our favourite players that particular year. And then came the great year of 1975, when Arthur Ashe, a cerebral black man who was clearly nobody's fool, won the men's championship, and Billie Jean King, who had always spoken out on the subject of women's rights, won the women's title. From that moment I became a firm devotee of the game, and I have subsequently tried to understand some of the complex history and psychology of this wonderful sport called Tennis.

The Right Set is divided into nine sections which address various aspects of tennis since its modern incarnation in 1874. 'The History of the Game' examines Major Walter C. Wingfield's controversial 'invention' of tennis, having first obtained a provisional patent on the game. Various accounts of the rapid evolution of the sport in Britain and the United States follow, including a fascinating description of the very first Wimbledon tournament.

At 11.15 a.m. on 16 February 1926, one of the most remarkable sporting events of the twentieth century took place. 'The Great Match' between the Frenchwoman, Suzanne Lenglen, and the American, Helen Wills, captured the attention of the world. In an age before television, it is difficult for the modern sports fan to fully comprehend the grip that this single tennis match exerted on the world's imagination. Perhaps the closest equivalent would be the 1974 Ali–Foreman 'Rumble in the Jungle', but 'The Great Match' probably outdoes even this event in terms of the reams of reportage and the number of imaginative reconstructions that have been published since this historic encounter.

It is impossible to know who was the greatest player of all time, but we can have fun speculating. How would Tilden have fared against Borg? Or Lacoste against Laver? Or Helen Wills against Martina Navratilova? 'The Old Guard' may have been amateurs sailing across oceans to play tournaments in exchange for a handshake and an occasional envelope under the counter, but the literature devoted to extolling their virtues, both on and off the court, suggests that, in terms of ability, there is precious little to choose between them and the modern players with their private jets and multi-million-dollar contracts.

These days 'Money and Tennis' go together like 'Television and Basketball' or 'Las Vegas and Boxing'. Tennis players are among the highest paid athletes in the world, and for top-ranked players, whether they win or lose makes precious little difference to their income, underpinned as it is by appearance guarantees and endorsement contracts. But this was not always the case. Only a couple of generations ago, any player who accepted money in exchange for playing tennis was barred from Wimbledon and all the major championships. This was a gentlemen's sport, and gentlemen did not play for money.

Questions of 'Race and Nationality' only served further to complicate the situation with regard to tennis being a 'gentleman's' game. After the Second World War, players with names like Drobny, Medvedev and Lendl began to appear. Latin Americans and black Americans also began to stake a claim to tennis. Alongside the emergence of these 'new' gentlemen came the development of the women's game. 'Women and Tennis' were originally somewhat tentative partners, but as women in society at large became authors of their own destiny, demanding equal pay and no longer happy to dwell in the twilight, the same movement for equality began to affect tennis.

While the players may have become fitter, and the equipment increasingly sophisticated, and the surfaces more diverse, tennis essentially remains a game of 'Artistry and Psychology' between two individuals that must be won with the brain as well as with the body. Perhaps what has really changed is the insistence of 'The Modern Personalities' that they be allowed to behave in ways that hitherto would have been deemed unacceptable. Today there is so much money at stake, and the pressure of the media is so intense, that players often gravitate to the very limits of sportsmanship in order that they might achieve an advantage.

All games must evolve; cricketers now wear helmets, soccer players have pants that stop above the knees, sprinters wear featherlight shoes with plastic spikes, and golfers have a variety of highly crafted clubs from which to choose. So it is with tennis; there has been palpable change, not only technologically but socially and culturally. However, decent behaviour on court, respect for one's opponent and the acceptance of 'bad', or even ludicrous, line-calls will help to prevent tennis from totally capitulating to the lure of the entertainment industry. A respect for 'Tradition and the Game' is needed now, more so than ever before.

Luckily, enough of the old traditions remain in place to make one confident that, at least in the near future, there will be no surrender to the 'anarchy' of unsportsmanlike behaviour which prevails in other major sports. Paradoxically these traditions, vigorously sponsored as they are by 'The Right Set' – the establishment – will always ensure the emergence of an Ilie Nastase, or a John McEnroe, or an Andre Agassi, or a Martina Navratilova, players who will always make the public sit up and pay attention. When the 'bully' is tennis and its sometimes *too* rigid traditions, then an audience is guaranteed. After all, so many of us still love to root for the 'outsider' or the rebel.

These days, when Venus Williams thumps the ball past Martina Hingis, or Andre Agassi swaggers lazily on to court, I still feel like grabbing my racquet and racing out for a game. This time I am not playing on a concrete square, but on a court in the park. However, through the chain-link fence I can already see countless numbers of young children busily marking their imaginary tram lines and visualizing their imaginary net, and they are shouting at each other, 'I want to be Venus Williams!' 'I want to be Andre Agassi!' Modern tennis, having grown out of a privileged tradition, still has its spirit anchored deeply enough in the patrician past for the game to remain capable of producing successive generations of 'outsiders'. 'The Right Set' will continue to determine who belongs and who is to be regarded as an interloper. Herein lies a large part of the enduring appeal of tennis.

Caryl Phillips
August 1998

1 The History of the Game

Lawn Tennis: The Sturdy Bastard
HEINER GILLMEISTER

The eighteenth and nineteenth centuries had witnessed the steady decline of the ancient game of tennis. What had remained of the pastime of the aristocrats, was at last swept away by the insurgent populace of the French Revolution. In this situation there appeared, on 7 March 1874, in the London *Court Journal*, the favourite reading of English court circles, a truly remarkable note. Sandwiched between notable instances of a fisherman's yarn and a report about top-flight hunts that had gone to rack and ruin because of some uninvited second fox, the following announcement caught the curious reader's eye:

> We hear of a new and interesting game coming out, which is likely to attract public notice, now blasé with croquet and on the *qui cire* for novelty. It has been patented under the name of 'Sphairistike or lawn tennis'. It has been tested at several country houses, and has been found full of healthy excitement, besides being capable of much scientific play. The game is in a box not much larger than a double gun case, and contains, besides bats and balls, a portable court, which can be erected on any ordinary lawn, and is ornamental as well as useful.

The publication of this item was of service to a man the court considered to be a friend. The author of these lines, Major Walter Clopton Wingfield, was a personal acquaintance of the Prince of Wales, later to become Edward VII. Only a few days previously, on 23 February 1874, he had obtained a provisional patent on a 'New and Improved Court for Playing the Ancient Game of Tennis'. In June, the patent became valid. Six months had elapsed during which it might have been challenged, but nobody had cared to.

In the patent itself it was stated that the purpose of the invention was to create a portable court by which the game of old might be played in a 'much simplified' manner, in the open air, and with complete disregard for special courts which had always been considered an indispensable requisite. In principle, the inventor argued, only two posts were needed, to be erected at a distance of about twenty-one feet, and an oblong net, stretched between them and dividing the court into two halves. By means of paint, a coloured line or tape, an in-court and out-court had to be marked, a right and left service-court (at the base-line of the out-court), a service crease and the side boundaries. In this way, the ancient game of tennis, a pastime requiring covered courts and therefore, because of the high costs, the preserve of a privileged few, would be within the means of everybody; a highly democratic view, no doubt. Such a court could be erected within a few minutes, on any appropriate surface, indoors as well as outdoors, and even on ice.

On 25 February 1874, two days after the patent had been granted, Wingfield's Rules of the Game appeared in print. In this pamphlet, the Major proudly referred to the legal document in his possession. It was the last piece to be added to the boxed tennis sets that had been ready for delivery at Messrs French and Co. in Churton Street, London, from where they were now dispatched in large numbers. French and Co. were the sole distributors of the Wingfieldian monopoly.

On the title page of the small booklet (no more than eight printed pages) the game was referred to (as in the *Court Journal*) as '*Sphairistikè* or Lawn Tennis'. The Greek name appeared in Greek letters on top of the page whereas Lawn Tennis was printed onto a Wingfieldian tennis net running diagonally across it in the form of a band.

Inside, the game was called 'The Major's Game of Lawn Tennis', and it was dedicated to the members of the glorious party which had gathered, in December 1873, at Nantclwyd, a stately mansion in Wales. A short description of the court, said to measure twenty by ten yards, was then given, and an illustration showed, against the background of an English country-house park, a mixed doubles 'à la Wingfield' in progress. Two more pages contained the rules, six in all. Of the complex rules of the tennis game of old (which, as we have seen, Wingfield expressly mentioned), only two had been allowed to stay: the ball had to be played over the net, and hit either on the volley or after its first bounce (Rule III). Another relic of the past was the rule envisaging a service from one side of the court only. In Wingfield's system, however, there was an additional constraint in that it had to be executed from a fixed point, a diamond-shaped service crease. Curiously enough, the server's camp was still referred to as the 'in-side', although there was no longer a *dedans* (an open gallery at the server's end of the court) which had to be defended. Goals were notably absent from Wingfield's invention, and, of course, the age-honoured chase rule had also been abandoned at last. Points (called *aces*) could be scored by the serving party only, and, as in modern volleyball, their opponents (Wingfield provides for a singles as well as a doubles game) could score only after the right to serve had been wrenched from them. Fifteen aces were needed to win a game.

The English Major had launched his game at the best of times. England's sporting public virtually craved, as Wingfield rightly observed in his *Court Journal* note, some newfangledness. Croquet which had boasted of a vast following only a few years before had for some become too complicated by the introduction of new complex rules; to others, it was either too simple or too sissy, a girls' pastime at best. Nevertheless there were, as a consequence of the croquet mania, vast areas of well-trimmed croquet lawns available throughout the country. Such spare land, from a sportsman's point of view, was badly in need of exploitation. It has often been claimed that lawn tennis owes its existence to the invention of the lawn mower, but this is only partly true. Before England, Ireland, and, to a less degree, Scotland, could become 'white with lines of lawn-tennis courts' (as H. W. W. Wilberforce at the beginning of the 1890s once put it), the lawn mower had earlier produced surfaces that allowed the smooth run of croquet bowls. Lawn tennis courts were the by-product of the croquet lawn.

As a result of another invention, the discovery of vulcanization by Charles Goodyear, it had been possible for some time to manufacture rubber balls filled with air which proved to be real bouncing bombs even on turf. It was therefore not only the solid walls encompassing the ancient tennis court, and the shelter of its roof that could be dispensed with, but also its hard tiled floor which alone had prompted a reaction from the stuffed tennis-balls of old. Those who had learned Goodyear's lesson best were the Germans. Little wonder, therefore, that Wingfield ordered his first assortments of balls from Germany. They were naked little featherweights, greyish or red and without the flannel cover which was later to become their hallmark.

The huge success which the Major's game enjoyed, at least in the beginning, was the result of careful planning. Apart from the note in the *Court Journal*, there had been eulogies in advance in the *Army and Navy Gazette* as well as in the journal *The Field*, of which the former had recommended the new game for no less than every barrack square in the entire United Kingdom. *The Field*, the country gentleman's journal the English-speaking world over, had gone so far as to print Wingfield's rule book almost in full in its sporting section. As a result, the journal in the months to follow abounded with contributions devoted to the new game. In this manner, lawn tennis managed to command the attention of a large readership for a long time.

Tennis: A Cultural History, 1997

The First Wimbledon
A. WALLIS MYERS

The salient fact about lawn tennis, and therefore about Wimbledon, which is its capital, is not its age but its youth. Compared with the veteran of cricket and the patriarch of golf, lawn tennis is a mere stripling. No legends of its precocious infancy are chronicled; no daily newspapers championed its future. Many people, indeed, derided the game; none of its early disciples trained to excel at it; its introduction was an accident in the social life of placid Victorianism, and, but for the faith and fortitude of a few zealots, who nursed the weakling, lawn tennis might have enjoyed no greater fame or fashion than rinking.

Fifty years ago, on a croquet lawn at Wimbledon, a company of sober-minded gentlemen, divided in their allegiance to racquets and tennis, both indoor games, launched a ship to which they attached the name of 'The Lawn Tennis Championship.' The mariners were sailing on uncharted seas; their Eldorado was nothing more dazzling than a desire to bestow permanence on a pastime the potentialities of which had only been vaguely visualized. Buffetings, and satire from larger craft, befell them. If their land of promise was revealed in the 'eighties, it was to recede in the 'nineties; not until the new century was its rich outline really exposed. Of the fertility of this realm, its rapid growth in population and power, the interest which its life would excite in all parts of the world, and, above all, in the proof it would furnish of women's athletic emancipation – that dream, realized today, had but few portents in 1877.

Round numbers, Dr Johnson declared, are false. Lawn tennis had been invented before 1877, but the first Wimbledon founded in that year gave the new pastime a style and status of its own. It clarified conflicting codes, lent form and substance to conditions of play that had been primitive and crude, invested lawn tennis with the dignity of corporate life.

The game is young enough for its early struggles and vicissitudes to be remembered by many living men. It is old enough to have reached a prosperity and a permanence that entitle it to be called the pastime of all peoples. It has a larger army of disciples than any ball game in the world. Whether lawn tennis was an adaptation of the ancient game of [court] tennis to the needs of society – a claim urged by Major Wingfield when he deposited a specification in 1874 with a view of patenting his 'new and improved portable court'; whether lawn tennis assumed a vogue in England because it demanded more violent exercise than croquet, the province of which it usurped in the private garden; whether its early appeal was due to the fact that women could pursue it as diligently as, and in company with, men – these speculations do not affect its commanding position today. They only serve to demonstrate that, in spite of obscure origin, initial privation and public ridicule, lawn tennis occupies today a unique place in the physical and social life of the world's inhabitants.

Popular as it is in England, the land of its birth, lawn tennis has even greater vogue in other lands. It is the summer game of America's youth; the Continent of Europe pays it universal homage; every French boy and French girl of athletic tendency has been inspired by the prowess of French champions; it holds the Oversea Dominions in a firm and strengthening grip; its recent development in the prosperous countries of South America has been extraordinary; it is pursued throughout India and the Orient; the Japanese have embraced it fervently; from China to Peru the net has been spread.

In this great development the share of Wimbledon needs no advertisement. Wimbledon was the nursery of the game; it bred the giants of the past, men who, by the exercise of their art, the vigor of their physique and the force of their personality, inspired countries beyond to accept and pursue the cult of lawn tennis. As and when this oversea talent ripened, Wimbledon became the clearing-house of the world's skill, the final assessor of form, the standard by which championship mettle was measured. It has long ceased to be a national tournament; time, competition and sentiment have made it international. As such, its prestige is unique and its educational value incalculable. It unites on common ground players of all nationality. It provides for the champions of other lands a neutral court on which, with conditions equitable to each side, the question of supremacy may be decided.

'On the Lawns of the All-England Club,' the words of Mr Rudyard Kipling, engraved over the portals of the Center Court – 'If you can meet with Triumph and Disaster, And treat those two Impostors just the same' – have their meaning understood.

There have been many matches of historic interest on those 'Lawns of the All-England Club.' . . . The championship meeting is greater than any champion. Wimbledon has given more to the world than a register of skilful men and women. It has founded and permeated beyond its boundaries a spirit of camaraderie and fair play that has oiled the wheels of sport in every land. It may justly claim to have 'set the cause above renown.'

Croquet, racquets and [court] tennis (the ancient and royal game) were all associated, in greater and less degree, with the first Lawn Tennis Championship Meeting. Disciples of these games were its founders; they swaddled the then infant game of lawn tennis, took it out for its public airing, so to speak, and offered it food and shelter in a cold and critical world. Croquet's sympathy, it is true, may have been a species of cupboard love. The All-England Croquet Club, which had been founded in 1868, discovered after a rather precarious life of seven years that croquet had its limitations; the club exchequer was almost empty. The sacred lawns at Worple Road, Wimbledon, had been invaded by a few members who preferred to hit a moving ball with a racket rather than tap a stationary ball with a mallet. These heretics doubtless found that a neatly groomed surface free from bush or other obstruction, and permitting the ball to bound with some uniformity, offered new and alluring scope to a pastime which, in its common or garden form, had been pursued under crude and cramping conditions. They began, like youthful porridge eaters in a famous novel, to ask for more, and they got it, first by the addition of 'Lawn Tennis' to the title of the Club, and then, a few months later, by the institution of a Lawn Tennis Championship.

The honor of promoting and organizing the first Wimbledon must be given to four gentlemen, all of whom deserve the gratitude of lawn tennis players the world over. Three of them – Mr Julian Marshall, the eminent authority on [court] tennis; Mr Henry Jones (widely known and respected as 'Cavendish'); and Mr G. G. Heathcote, a tennis player of repute and stipendiary magistrate at Brighton – formed the subcommittee which, bringing order out of chaos and practical wisdom out of conflicting prejudice, framed not only the rules of the Championship, but virtually the rules of the game itself. The fourth was Mr J. H. Walsh, the editor of the *Field*, in whose office at 346 Strand (now the site of the *Morning Post* office) the All-England Club had been founded. It was Mr Walsh who introduced lawn tennis into the program at Wimbledon and who, with Mr B. C. Evelegh as seconder, carried the motion to hold a championship meeting. Mr Walsh induced the proprietors of the *Field* to offer for competition a silver challenge trophy of the value of twenty-five guineas – a cup won outright by the late William Renshaw and now in possession of his family.

'If of late years,' says Mr Heathcote, 'many a local committee has been able to offer more costly prizes, a special and almost sacred value will, in the opinion of lawn tennis enthusiasts, forever attach to the trophy which, in the infancy of the game and amid all the uncertainties which necessarily surround a new and difficult experiment, the generosity of the *Field* newspaper and the energy of Mr Walsh enabled the committee of the All-England Croquet and Lawn Tennis Club to offer to the lawn tennis players of England.'

Chief among these uncertainties and difficulties was the question of rules. No important match had hitherto been played and no tournament had been conducted under the code drawn up in 1875 by the Tennis Committee of the Marylebone Cricket Club. That code, valuable as it may have been at the time, had obvious imperfections. Its compilers adopted the hourglass-shaped court, claimed as part of his invention by Major Walter Wingfield, the author of *Sphairistikè*. It provided that the court should be divided into two equal parts by posts 7 feet in height and 24 feet apart, with a net 5 feet high at the posts and 4 feet high at the center. Baselines 30 feet in length were to be drawn at a distance of 39 feet, and service lines at a distance of 26 feet from the net. The players were to be distinguished as 'Hand-in' and 'Hand-out.' Hand-in alone could serve or score; and on losing a stroke he became Hand-out. The service was to be delivered with one foot outside the baseline, and was required to drop between the net and the service line of the court diagonally opposite to that in which the server stood. If he failed to serve the ball over the net, the player lost the stroke and became Hand-out, but it was a fault only if the ball bounded in the wrong court or over the service line. The balls were to be 2¼ inches in diameter and 1¼ ounces in weight. The game was 15–up, as in racquets ... In doubles matches the partner of the striker-out might take a service dropping in the wrong court.

The MCC code had excited controversy both by speech and written word among the adherents of the new game. Most of these had graduated in racquets and tennis; the rival methods of scoring these games had their advocates in lawn tennis. Nor was there more unanimity over the size of the court, the height of the net, the position of the service line and the question of faults. The subcommittee already mentioned might have been more discreet than valorous and based the Championship rules on the existing code. They took the bolder line and framed what was virtually a new set of conditions and rules. Their enterprise was criticized, even vehemently; history has proved that their instinct was sound; for, in the main, with amendments and adjustments rendered necessary by progress and the passage of time, their charter holds good today, not only at Wimbledon, where it was first interpreted, but on every court throughout the world. The unqualified success of the first championship meeting proved that revolution was demanded.

Three of the principles laid down in 1877 have stood the test of time and are still law – an adequate tribute to the original legislators. These three may be tabulated.

1 A rectangular court 26 yards long by 9 yards wide, the net being suspended from posts placed three feet outside the court.
2 The adoption of tennis [court tennis] scoring in its entirety.
3 The allowance of one fault without penalty, whether the service dropped in the net, in the wrong court, or beyond the service line.

In regard to the service line, that was still left at 26 feet from the net; the server had his feet *à cheval* the baseline, and a service which touched the net was declared to be good. In these three instances experience had dictated a change. The height of the net was 5 feet at the posts and 3 feet 3 inches at the center; the balls were prescribed to be of not less than $2\frac{1}{4}$ inches and not more than $2\frac{5}{8}$ inches in diameter, and $1\frac{1}{4}$ ounces to $1\frac{1}{2}$ ounces in weight. Here, too, there has been evolution.

The first intimation to the outside world of the championship meeting was given in a notice appearing in the *Field* of 9 June 1877. It was signed by Henry Jones, Hon. Secretary of the Lawn Tennis Subcommittee:

'The All England Croquet and Lawn Tennis Club, Wimbledon, propose to hold a lawn tennis meeting, open to all amateurs, on Monday, July 9th, and following days. Entrance fee 1 pound, 1 shilling. Two prizes will be given – one gold champion prize to the winner, one silver to the second player.'

It was added that 'Players must provide their own racquets and must wear shoes without heels,' while intending competitors were informed that balls could be obtained for practice by personal application to the gardener.

Twenty-two gentlemen sent in their names, which were duly drawn at the *Field* office two days before the meeting opened. The majority were more or less familiar with [court] tennis scoring, a circumstance which, says Mr Heathcote, 'was perhaps fortunate for the legislators, as it prevented any marked dissatisfaction with the rules.' One of the competitors – Mr Spencer W. Gore, who proved to be the winner – has, however, placed on record that the innovations (i.e., the new regulations imposed by the subcommittee) caused some dissatisfaction. 'We detested the tennis scoring, which was then for the first time introduced and which puzzled us "pretty considerable." The service line, under the new laws, was actually 5 feet farther from the net than it is at present, and the balls were smaller and lighter than those now in use.' But the first champion is careful to add that without the bold policy of the original championship committee 'we might still be grovelling in an hourglass court, with balls of all sorts and sizes, and governed by laws varying according to the size of the lawn and surrounding accidents of nature.' Such has ever been the tendency of the British citizen. He may croak a little in private; in public he upholds the laws which he himself, by elected representatives, has shaped. Well has it been for lawn tennis that a game so cosmopolitan in its future development should have had as its original legislators men of courage, foresight and character.

It must not be supposed, however, that the first championship meeting was held without hitch or hindrance. Laws had been laid down; the question was to provide implements which should subscribe to them. The balls, for example, had to be made for the occasion. They were required to be of certain weight and to be sewn in a particular way. The influence of the wind could not be overlooked. Their white cloth covers (in the earliest days the balls were uncovered) had to be sewn on like the cloth of a tennis ball, and not with cross stitches; the thread had to be unbleached carpet thread; the dyed thread, used by certain makers 'for the sake of prettiness,' was barred. Of the fifteen dozen used, according to the *Field*, there was 'not a bad one among them.' Wells, by the way, were used to hold the balls when not in flight; these were supplied specially by a firm in the Strand. As for the nets they were all of the 'right size and texture,' and the posts of the 'right height and stoutness.' The lines were marked very distinctly, the machine having been taken over them twice. The umpires, who sat in raised seats between the guy ropes supporting the net posts, had both score cards and measuring rods – for the net, even at Wimbledon in 1877, was pegged down in the middle. That the first umpires, like the last, sometimes sinned against the light was only too true. Even 'Cavendish,' the referee, wrote after the meeting: 'It is hopeless to expect exceptional umpires at Wimbledon; players must take the chance of a mistake, which, after all, is as fair to one side as to the other.' But he did not suggest that the umpires' seats should be raised two feet or three feet; they are nearly twice as high today.

The first Wimbledon proved that whatever the winning style at lawn tennis might ultimately become, the style of the real [court] tennis player was doomed. The graduate in real tennis had every advantage on this occasion. The net was high at the sides and low in the middle; he was encouraged to play his shots diagonally from corner to corner; the service line was so far from the net as to give his heavily cut service every scope. Yet the competition was won, and won comfortably, by a racquets player, Spencer W. Gore, an old Harrovian. He met and defeated several players who were proficient at real tennis, notably C. G. Heathcote and W. C. Marshall. Endowed with a natural aptitude for all games, possessing great activity, a long reach and a strong and flexible wrist, he went up to the net and volleyed the drives of his adversaries. His volleys, novel in their conception and in their effort, were no mere pat over the net. As Mr Heathcote says, he was 'the first to realize, as the first and great principle of lawn tennis, the necessity of forcing his opponent to the back line, when he would approach the net, and by a dexterous turn of the wrist would return the ball at considerable speed, now in the forehand and now in the backhand court, till, to borrow the expression of one of his best opponents of that year, his antagonist was ready to drop.' But if volleying was successful at the first championship meeting it was due to the fact that, with the net high at the sides, players did not attempt the drive down the line.

Nearly all the competitors used a service that was delivered from a point level with the shoulder. Some of these services were unplayable, doubtless because the lawns at Wimbledon at that time, employed exclusively for croquet, were smoother and softer than they afterwards became, but we know that many of them were faults. Indeed, Spencer Gore declared that at least one third of the services in the matches in which he participated were invalid. Of the 601 games contested in the 70 sets, 376 were won by the server and 225 by the striker-out, showing a preponderance of about 5 to 3. Spencer Gore's service was more varied than any other; he 'kept up his sleeve' an underhand service with a double dose of cut. Of course, if a modern overhead service had then been adopted the service superiority, having regard to the distance of the service line from the net, would have been overwhelming.

Two or three other points may be noted about the original Wimbledon. Sudden death was decreed after 'five-all.' Players changed courts after every set – a condition that placed a premium on the service, especially when the server had both the sun and the wind in his favor, as he often had. The layout of the old ground, doubtless because of its croquet origin, took no account of the sun's incidence, and even some of the greatest matches on the Center Court, as we shall see presently, suffered from this unconscionable penalty – the sun hitting the eyes of players on the pavilion side of the court. The tournament was adjourned over the Eton and Harrow match; indeed, for some years play was not continuous from day to day. About 200 spectators watched the final, paying one shilling each for the privilege. The weather was unfavorable and the court dead and slippery; the match was played, indeed, in order not to disappoint the 'crowd,' between heavy showers. Gore won the first set at 6–1 after fifteen minutes' play, the second set at 6–2 after thirteen minutes, and the third set at 6–4 after twenty minutes. It was a contest between Gore's racquet style and Marshall's tennis style, and the result was conclusive.

The championship was founded, but the game did not shake itself free from the shackles of tennis and racquets – that is, from the strokes of men who had grafted lawn tennis onto another game and were not young enough to create a style really applicable to the new pastime – for three years. The daring volley of Spencer Gore actually became obsolete – to be revived in another and more brilliant form by the youth and activity of the Renshaw twins... Meanwhile from 1878 to 1880, the patient baseliner, the player who made certainty of return his rule and the long rest his ambition, governed, and, by the monotony of his stroke, threatened the game. For the second meeting in 1878, by a new code framed jointly by the MCC and the All-England Club, the height of the net had been reduced to 4 feet 9 inches at the posts, and 3 feet at the center. The service line was brought 4 feet nearer to the net. The balls were increased in weight to 9 ounces. These changes, though they exerted their influence later and were a sign of progress, only served to emphasize the need for an independent style. The game was there: the men to exploit its possibilities of speed and counter-speed had not yet appeared.

Nevertheless P. Frank Hadow and J. T. (now Canon) Hartley, who held the title in 1878 and in 1879 and 1890 respectively, were both players of skill and fortitude. The first, like Spencer Gore, had been a Harrow boy and proficient at racquets. He had been in Ceylon, coffee planting for three years and, returning to England for a short holiday, left cricket and devoted his time to lawn tennis, first on a covered court at Maida Vale (the nursery of many fine players of the 'eighties, by the way) and then on turf. All June he went down to Wimbledon and practiced with H. F. Lawford, whose power was then developing in a massive frame, and with L. Erskine. Mr Hadow, who is now 71, has told of a sequel in a letter to the writer:

'I felt very fit and well up to the break-off for the Eton and Harrow match, when I somehow got a touch of the sun and was otherwise ill, with the result that the Saturday, Sunday and Monday I had to keep quiet with ice on my head. On the Tuesday I had to go down to play in the final against Erskine, but was fairly fit though feeling pretty cheap, and was glad when it was over and able to get to bed again with a horrible headache, where I remained all the next day. On the following day I had to play Spencer Gore, the previous year's champion. I confess I was not feeling even as well as when playing Erskine, taking a frantic headache with me in the train to Wimbledon, which got worse and worse.

'It was not easy to drive down the sidelines, like a racquet stroke down the sidewall, with the net sagging to the center from the posts and fastened below the top of each post, instead of being level. I was told the "lob" had not been introduced before – certainly I had never tried it before. It was only natural enough though, with a tall, long-legged and long-armed man sprawling over the net, ready to reach over at the ball before it had even reached the net. My attempts to pass Gore, I can remember, with a low, hard stroke, when he was at the net, usually failed.'

Mr Hadow left both England and lawn tennis after his victory. Nor has he ever been to Wimbledon nor seen first-class tennis since.

The entry rose to 34 in 1878. It was larger because the game was better known and understood. The agreement between the MCC and the AEC had cleared the air, and in a few weeks over 7,000 copies of the revised rules were sold. Whereas the previous year it had been the exception to find tennis scoring used (out of Wimbledon), this year it was considered rather an affront to ask an opponent whether he scored by that method. The lawns at Wimbledon had all been levelled in the winter; the courts were adjudged in excellent condition. Improved implements were used, and the famous Tate racket, with an oval face, made its appearance. There were complaints that the net cord was not stout enough and not the right color; also that the post came above the staple which fixed the rope. These were the shadows of coming improvements.

The match between Erskine and C. G. Hamilton in the fourth round deserves passing mention because it was the first in Wimbledon's history that yielded five sets and depended on its issue on one stroke. Hamilton had represented Cambridge University at tennis and employed a severe cut on both wings. Seven hundred spectators applauded a very evenly balanced contest. Hamilton led 5–3 in the last set and was twice within a point of winning; after 5–5 there were four deuces and a desperate finish. The winner put out H. F. Lawford quite easily in the next round – Lawford was then only distinguished for his accuracy; his speed was to come – but fell to Hadow in three sets in the final. The latter never let a ball pass him that was within reach. In the challenge round Spencer Gore's volleying propensities caused his racket on one occasion to be over the net before the ball crossed it. There was a halt and a discussion before it was decided that the rules did not bar him from holding his racket anywhere within reach. So Gore continued to commit an act that today is illegal. But more often than not when the holder ran in, the challenger tossed the ball over his head. Hadow won by lobbing; it was a revelation to the crowd. On the cruelly hot day the regulation enjoining vantage sets in the last stage – the first time they had been necessary – added to the strain of the competitors. After five-all in the third set there was talk of adjourning, but the volleyer and the lobber got together again and finished the sixteenth game. 'A terrific set' was the *Field*'s comment.

The volleying incident mentioned provoked a heated debate. The volleyer became a target for abuse. Not only, declared his enemies, were the best strokes of his adversary killed; he even invaded the latter's territory. 'It was proposed, on the one hand,' says Mr Heathcote, 'that a penalty should be imposed on touching the net in striking, while others wished to limit the possibility of volleying at the net by the addition of a volleying line within which the player was not to stand, while others even desired to prohibit the practice altogether.' It was argued that the umpire had enough burdens already, but the objection was overruled and players were forbidden to volley a ball before it had passed the net. The volleyer, as we have seen, retired for the time being.

The Fireside Book of Tennis, 1972

Lawn Tennis in America
HEINER GILLMEISTER

In 1890, Richard Dudley Sears, in his contribution to *The Badminton Library*, told the story of the lawn tennis ball's first bounce in the United States, and of the two players who had lent a helping hand in the process, his elder brother, Fred R. Sears, and Dr James Dwight who has been called the Father of American Lawn Tennis. Sears, seven-time US champion and record holder to date, could write with authority. Dick was the grandson of David Sears who had been left 'the largest fortune ever inherited in New England' and had then been 'the richest citizen of Boston'. David Sears, an ardent admirer of Napoleon, had named his country place 'Longwood', after the house on St Helena in which his hero had died. On a corner of the 600-acre Sears estate, at what now is Brookline and Longwood Avenue, twenty-five cricket enthusiasts had in 1877 organized the Longwood Cricket Club. One year later, a tennis court had been laid out on the club's premises, and by 1890, the Longwood Cricket Club had become essentially a lawn tennis club. Sears as well as his friend James Dwight were both members of the Longwood Cricket Club, and as a student Dwight had been in the habit of cycling over to Longwood several times a week in spring in order to play tennis. Early photographs show Sears and Dwight, tennis rackets in hand, in the cricket attire of the Longwood Cricket Club.

The story told by Dick about his brother and his friend Dwight was this. Not far from the very place where English tea had been thrown into the sea by angry colonists a hundred years earlier, the two boys had greeted another British commodity with enthusiasm. It was an original box with Wingfield's *Sphairistikè*. They had discovered it in the seaside summer house owned by a certain William Appleton at Nahant not far from Boston. Appleton's son-in-law, Mr J. Arthur Beebe, had only just brought the boxed set with him from London and had meant to present it to the Appletons themselves, but Sears and Dwight, out of youthful curiosity, had taken the gift, and with the impatience of youth, had marked out a court in the side yard of the house some time in August, 1874. After a few rallies they had become so enthusiastic about the new game that despite a pelting rain neither of them felt an urge to stop. Only after each of them had won a set did they abandon their game, having played in rubber boots and mackintoshes all the time. This 'Boston Tennis Party' remained a singular experience at the time. Only from the beginning of spring in the following year did lawn tennis begin to be played with any regularity – in Nahant, Newport and New York.

At the beginning of the 1930s, an attempt was made in the United States to deny to the two Nahant players their pioneering effort. In their place, a pioneering lady was enthroned, a certain Mary Ewing Outer-bridge, who, equipped with an original set of Wingfield's *Spharistikè*, was said to have disembarked in New York on 2 February 1874, after a cruise aboard the SS *Canima* to Bermuda where she had picked up her tennis paraphernalia. The campaign was conducted, among others, by Malcolm D. Whitman and by William Henderson, who had already advanced a highly speculative theory about the origin of tennis in the Old World. Knowing that Wingfield had been granted a patent no earlier than 23 February 1874, the two were compelled, in order to vindicate their theory, to again accuse Wingfield of highly dubious methods. Since Mary Outerbridge would hardly have acquired her *Sphairistikè* box without the rules, a rather indispensable prerequisite, the very same rules had, through rather mysterious agencies, to have reached the British dominion before her departure, on either 22 or 23 January 1874. That is why Whitman, the player, asserted that the booklet had appeared in print in December 1873. Henderson, the historian, who saw at once that even this early date was much too late, corrected him by opting for November 1873. On poor Wingfield, however, again fell the blame of having deliberately told a lie when he claimed, on the first page of his rules, to own a royal patent. Since 25 February 1874 has now and beyond all doubt been established as the date of the first printing of Wingfield's rules, Whitman's and Henderson's attempts to rewrite tennis history have turned out to be yet another unfortunate mission to the Bermuda Triangle. Mary Outerbridge, however, is not entirely without merits. On one of her many excursions to Bermuda (presumably in the spring of 1875) she actually bought a set of Wingfield's *Sphairistikè*. Having obtained the permission of her brother A. Emilius Outerbridge, director of the Staten Island Cricket and Baseball

Club, she rigged up the net in a remote corner of the cricket ground without much ado. It was thus for the first time that lawn tennis (in the States, at first, as much a game for private circles as in England) was given the attention of a sports club and thus attracted public notice. Mary's efforts will have to be rated higher even than those of Sears and Dwight who played the inaugural match at Nahant, for, without her, there would scarcely have been the notorious Staten Island tennis tournament, the first major event of its kind, which by an organizational scandal of the first order eventually set things going.

It was yet another Outerbridge, another of Mary's brothers, Eugenius H. Outerbridge, who came forward with the idea of holding, on the courts of the Staten Island Cricket and Baseball Club, a national championships. Eugenius Outerbridge was the club's secretary. The local press heralded the sporting event in the following way: 'It will no doubt furnish quite a good deal of amusement to Staten Islanders', the *Richmond County Sentinel* observed, 'to see able bodied men playing this silly game.'

The tournament began in fine weather on 1 September 1880, on a site very close to the bay and now buried under the parking lot of the ferry. The reporters of the New York newspapers who chose to write about the event were enamoured of the scenic view, the sunset over the bay, the elegant ladies in their colourful dresses and the gentlemen, coaches and horses which had brought the visitors, and the handsome silver cup worth a hundred dollars showing, on one side, the engraving 'The Champion Lawn-Tennis Player of America'. A nice sketch accompanying the report was meant to give the reader a visual impression of the ladies and gentlemen, the nearby bay and its sailing ships, and finally the game, lawn tennis. The papers were silent about results at first.

The subject of scores was eventually broached by the players themselves and reporters of *The New York Times* and the *Richmond County Gazette* which harked back to the event a week later. In the men's singles the victory had been carried off by an Englishman, O. E. Woodhouse. Woodhouse happened to be on a visit to the United States, and had learnt about the tournament from a Chicago daily newspaper. He won easily, a fact which caused no surprise. The Englishman had reached the final of the All Comers' event of the All England Championships in the same year, yielding to no less a player than the formidable Lawford.

In the doubles, R. D. Sears and Dr James Dwight gained prominence, though in a manner the two men from Boston (excellent players and members of the newly founded Beacon Park Athletic Association) had hardly anticipated. The organizers urged them to play with a brand of ball smaller by one-third than the one they were used to in Boston (and manufactured by Ayres of England) and much too light. Dwight later in life became a stickler for rules, enforcing them with a zeal little short of the obsessional. It must have been here that he experienced the traumatic shock that caused his obsession.¹ He voiced a vigorous protest, upon which the organizers, little impressed, brought to his notice the inscription 'Regulation' adorning the Staten Island ball, and nonchalantly suggested to him to pull out if a ball of such description did not please him. Dwight and Sears swallowed the decision made by the Staten Island management, but refused to play in the singles, and received a sound drubbing by the team from Morristown, New Jersey, in the early rounds of the doubles.

In the Staten Island tournament, three things had turned out to be a nuisance: the counting method up to 15 points as employed in rackets, the height of the net, and, above all, the type of ball used. A supreme court of appeal, this had become clear to everybody, was badly needed. That is why, on 5 May 1881, a notice appeared in the journal *American Cricketer*, signed by Clarence M. Clark, president of the All-Philadelphia Lawn Tennis Committee, James Dwight, representative of the Beacon Park Athletic Association, Boston, and E. H. Outerbridge, who had perpetrated the Staten Island ball trick, but seemed to have learnt a lesson after all. As a result, the inaugural meeting of the United States National Lawn Tennis Association (USNLTA) took place at the Fifth Avenue Hotel in New York on 21 May 1881. The thirty-six delegates, representing nineteen clubs and having a proxy to vote for another sixteen, agreed to adopt the rules of the All England Club for one year. A commission of three was entrusted with the organization of tournaments and a representative of the Albany Tennis Club, Robert S. Oliver, was elected first President of the USNLTA.

The assembly also resolved on holding an official championship, and as early as June the executive committee, on the question of the venue, decided in favour of the newly built Newport Casino, Rhode Island; the date for the event was set for 31 August 1881. This time the competitors from Boston were by far more successful, although the reason for their superiority was not so much the tennis ball that was now employed (the English Ayres' ball), but the tactics adopted by the first United States champion, Dick Sears. He, not unlike the English champion Gore, advanced to the net to a point well beyond the service line where his opponents' returns met his 16oz racket held rather short in the handle. The harder the balls were hit through the middle, the higher was the speed with which Sears sent them back, giving the right as well as the left side of his opponents' court a fair share. On the other side of the net, Sears' victims scrambled over the court in a manner resembling (to use Sears' own words) the course of the see-saw.

After his triumph over the uncomprehending baseliner, Sears and his partner Dwight had taken it into their heads that the tactics Dick had adopted in the singles would pave the way for success also in the doubles. In unison the two advanced to the net, only to realize that their opponents from Philadelphia, rather than clinging to the baseline, had divided up into a player who occupied the rear and one who positioned himself close to the net. The men from Boston failed miserably. So weak were their volleys that the man at the net had no difficulty placing them right and left near the side-line. Not until the following year did they succeed in seasoning their doubles game with the swift gracefulness of the Renshaw brothers whose method they had taken over, albeit inadvertently. Their play was now in a different class and simply too fast for the net man, and they won their first (out of five) championships. Fifty years later, in a commemorative publication of the USNLTA, Sears gave these recollections of the first US championships:

A large number of the players wore knickerbockers, with blazers, belts, cravats, and woolen stockings in their club colors. Their shoes were rubber-soled and generally of white canvas or buckskin. None of their sleeves were cut off, and while the large majority rolled them up, a few left them at full length. They all wore caps or round hats with a rolling brim that could be turned down in front to ward off the glare of the sun. The rackets were generally lopsided slightly as in the old court tennis bats.

The winners in both singles and doubles in this first championship were given medals instead of the usual cups, and the conditions were the best two of three sets until the finals, which was the best of five. No 'vantage sets were played and the players changed courts only at the end of each set.

The second year the championship found all of the players serving overhand with more or less speed, mostly less, with everyone coming in to volley as soon as any good opening presented itself; but as both

Dwight and I had taken up lobbing, a stroke, which, to be effective, requires a good deal of practice, a certain amount of discouragement appeared, and when these players also tried this stroke they generally lobbed much too short, giving us an easy kill. In addition, we no longer tapped our volleys, as in 1881, but hit them with a good deal of speed. I had discarded my 16 ounce racket and was using one of only 14 ounces.

Until 1915 the courts at Newport Casino where Sears and Dwight collected their numerous victories proudly hosted the US championships. Then they were transferred to Forest Hills in the Borough of Queens, New York. In 1978 they found a new home in Flushing Meadow, also in Queens, which derives its name from the Dutch town of Vlissingen from where the first settlers – English Non-Conformists who had ended up in The Netherlands – had come in the seventeenth century. In Newport, the International Tennis Hall of Fame and an annual men's tournament on grass are today the only reminders of a glorious past.

Tennis: A Cultural History, 1997

1 See Alexander, *Lawn Tennis*, *Tennis: A Cultural History*, 1997, p. 64f.:

Dr Dwight was a strict constructionist of rules and while not playing he circulated about courts seeing that officials were enforcing the rules, especially the foot-fault rule. He also was a stickler for proper balls, perhaps caused by his experience at the 1880 Staten Island tournament. Knowing this propensity, Willie Renshaw, when umpiring a match of Dwight's, boxed up the worst of the old balls, and when Dwight called for new balls he gave them those. The anticipated violent reaction caused great mirth among the knowing spectators.

The First American Championships
RICHARD D. SEARS

By the year 1880 quite a number of clubs had taken up lawn tennis, and, in addition to an open tournament at Staten Island, New York, there was an inter-club, four-handed match arranged between the Young America Club of Philadelphia and the Staten Islanders, which was played in Philadelphia. The Philadelphians had been playing over a net of different height, and with balls of a different size and weight than those used at Staten Island. At this time dealers here had been selling any sort of ball, stamping them, without any recognized authority, 'Regulation.' Hardly any two dealers used the same weight or size, and the various club committees were all at sea with their own particular balls.

This condition of affairs finally decided three clubs, one each in New York, Philadelphia and Boston, to send out an invitation to such other clubs as they knew were playing the game for a meeting in order to form a national association to bring order out of chaos. Thirty-three clubs met in New York on 21 May 1881, and the United States Lawn Tennis Association was formed. A date was set for the first championship, 31 August, the place chosen for this being Newport, Rhode Island, and, after some discussion, the English rules were adopted as well as the English ball made by Ayres.

When the time arrived, twenty-five players turned up to try their luck in the singles, and thirteen pairs entered for the doubles. Dr Dwight, who had been more instrumental than anyone else in the formation of the Association, did not enter for the singles, but with me as partner he entered in the doubles. The entrants knew about the various styles of play of their clubmates, but nothing whatever of the others.

As already mentioned, the Ayres ball was used and the nets were 4 feet at the posts and 3 feet at the center. This had led to a scheme of attack by playing, whenever possible, across court to avoid lifting the drives over the highest part of the net along the sidelines. This method just suited me, as I had taken up a mild form of volleying, in practice, and all I had to do was to tap the balls as they came over, first to one side and then to the other, running my opponent all over the court. My racket this year weighed 16 ounces!

All of the players entered came from the East and most of the doubles teams were made up on the spur of the moment, with the result that there was little teamwork and the partners were constantly interfering with each other. The ultimate winners of the pairs showed much better team play than anyone else, with the result that they won without much difficulty. These winners, Clarence Clark and Fred Taylor of Philadelphia, played one man close to the net with the other in the back court. Lobbing had not come in at this time and when this pair met Dwight (who also volleyed) and myself they won handily. Our volleying, as I have stated in my account of the singles play, did not have enough speed to worry their net man.

A large number of the players wore knickerbockers, with blazers, belts, cravats, and woolen stockings in their club colors. Their shoes were rubber-soled and generally of white canvas or buckskin. None of their sleeves were cut off, and while a large majority rolled them up, a few left them at full length. They all wore caps or round hats with a rolling brim that could be turned down in front to ward off the glare of the sun. The rackets were generally lopsided slightly as in the old court tennis bats.

There were no grandstands, the courts being roped off, and the gallery sat on camp stools or light chairs set out in two or three rows, and those who arrived late were obliged to stand. The nets were made of much lighter materials than today and were not reinforced at the center, and the center strap was made of iron. The flimsiness of the net did not make much difference at first because none of the services was particularly severe; in fact a few of the players served underhand, but I must confess without much success. There were no heavy rollers to keep the court surface in good condition, only hand rollers being in use.

The winners in both singles and doubles in this first championship were given medals instead of the usual cups, and the conditions were the best two of three sets until the finals, which were the best of five. No 'vantage sets were played and the players changed courts only at the end of each set.

The second year of the championship found all of the players serving overhand with more or less speed, mostly less, with everyone coming in to volley as soon as any good opening presented itself; but as Dwight and I had both taken up lobbing, a stroke which, to be effective, requires a great deal of practice, a certain amount of discouragement appeared, and when these players also tried this stroke they generally lobbed much too short, giving us an easy kill. In addition, we no longer tapped our volleys as in 1881, but hit them with a good deal of speed. I had discarded my 16-ounce racket and was using one of only 14 ounces. When it came to the doubles, Dwight and I had developed as good teamwork as any other pair, a condition of affairs quite different from the year before. This extra speed, together with our lobbing, when it seemed wise to use this stroke, put the formation used by Clark and Taylor in 1881, and this year copied by most of the other pairs, in a very difficult position, and we managed to carry off this championship.

This year also, in addition to a championship cup, another cup was put up to be won three times, but under rather severe terms, inasmuch as it not only required three years to win it, but these three years must be successive before it became the property of the champion. A change was also made in the playing rules instructing the referee to allow a change of court at the end of the first, third, fifth and each following odd game, providing the request for this was made before the toss; otherwise no change was allowed until the deciding set.

It was in this year, also, that Mr Horsman, a New York dealer in sporting goods, offered the so-called Diamond Racket. This was a full-sized racket made of various inlaid woods with a gold cap at the end of the handle, a gold band with places for ten names around the head, and another gold band around the throat, three diamonds being set here surrounded by small pearls. The strings were harp strings. The strings attached to this prize, however, were so absurd that I could not see my way to take it, and, upon my refusal, the Association also turned it down and returned it to the donor . . .

The only step in the development of the game in 1883 was a change in the rules introducing 'vantage sets in the final round, and in the following year the height of the net at the posts was lowered from 4 feet to 3 feet 6 inches, the champion was barred from the All-Comers and was to defend his title against the winner, and the Bagnall-Wilde system of the draw, which brought all the byes, if there were any, into the first round (which, for some unknown reason, we called the preliminary round), was adopted.

This was the year when steel points appeared for the first time. I do not speak of these points as spikes as I do not want to confuse them with the long spikes of the present time. I had been in England with Dwight in the early summer of this year and we found practically all the English players using these points. On our arrival at Newport we persuaded the governors of the Casino to mark out a court and let us play a set with some other pair; we to wear these points and they to play in rubber soles, and at the finish an inspection to be made of the condition of the turf on both sides of the net.

It was damp and the court was rather 'greasy.' The side that we had used showed hardly a scar, while the other court was in a terrible condition. The result was that the Casino management preferred to have these points worn rather than the rubber soles. Unfortunately, these points clogged up more or less with grass after a short time, and every once in a while a few seconds had to be taken out to clear them. These points were only one-eighth of an inch long and were too short to go down into the turf to any extent and naturally failed to hold one up as well as those in present use, but they held immeasurably better than the rubber soles in use at that time.

The championship this year brought out, for the first time here, the so-called Lawford stroke. I use the term 'so-called' in this connection because that was the name given to it by the press, but never by me. When asked where I had learned it, I replied that the idea came to me from watching Lawford and from playing with him. I do not think that anyone could have exactly copied Lawford. He was a heavily built man who had not taken up the game until he was twenty-six years old. He was not very light on his feet, and certainly not easy or graceful. In spite of these handicaps, however, he was one of the greatest players of his time. He seldom came up to the net, but when he did he generally killed the ball. His usual manner of playing his forehand stroke was to wait until the ball was dropping; his racket was almost perpendicular to the ground, with his wrist and hand slightly more forward than the head of his racket; then, hitting the ball with a great deal of force and at the same time pulling up on it, he gave it a tremendous over-spin, causing it to drop sharply after crossing the net and making it a very difficult stroke to volley successfully. By allowing the ball to drop a little before hitting it, the over-spin was considerably increased. When he was further forward in the court and hit the ball nearer the top of the bound, he hit with his racket more nearly horizontal with the ground, very much as the stroke is played today. This latter stroke was both much easier to play and much easier to volley well. The perpendicular method also had this advantage: the direction in which you meant to send the ball was more easily concealed, as the slightest little turn of the wrist at the last moment would change it from one corner to the other. I remember that I called this a lifting stroke, not a Lawford, as it felt to me as though I were lifting the ball. When I next saw Lawford he was very curious to know what we meant in America by the term 'Lawford' stroke, as he claimed that, except for his awkwardness, he hit the ball just the same as Renshaw or any other first-class player, and that any drop that took place was simply due to gravity. It was not until some time later that one could persuade even the English cricketers that a ball could be made to curve in the air.

As the first championship cup under the three successive winnings became my property this year, another cup, under the same conditions, was put up at the annual meeting of the Association in 1885, and 'vantage sets in the earlier best-two-in-three matches were decided upon. Another change was the adoption of the Peck and Snyder ball in place of the Ayres English ball. The reason for this change was due to the fact that the English balls varied quite perceptibly in both size and weight. At that time, in America, the committee did not test each individual ball as was done in England. There, outside the club house on the old Wimbledon grounds, could be seen a large mesh bag into which all the balls which varied from the regulation weight or size in the slightest degree were thrown.

No other changes were made this year, but in 1886 the number of sets in the early rounds was made the best of five instead of the best of three but no 'vantage sets were played in these rounds unless the score reached two sets-all, in which event the deciding set was 'vantage. In addition, the Peck and Snyder ball, not having proved as satisfactory as the Ayres ball which it had replaced the year before, was given up and a return was made to the English ball. At the next annual meeting the Ayres ball was again thrown out and this time the Wright and Ditson ball was adopted.

Until this time it had been the custom at Newport, the venue of the championships, to play a round of singles in the morning and a round of doubles in the afternoon, and as it had now been decided that all sets, both in singles and doubles, should be the best of five 'vantage sets, it was decided to play the singles, only, at Newport, and the doubles were awarded to the Orange Club in Orange, New Jersey. The date for the doubles was set for three weeks after the finish of the singles. This did not prove as satisfactory as had been hoped, for, as all the players thought so much more of the singles than the doubles, the latter event became much of an anticlimax and the play fell off considerably.

During these first seven years of the championships there was no consistent following in of the service. If a player had attempted to do this in a five-set match with any player about his equal, and his opponent had only done this occasionally, when a good opening offered, the man who continually rushed in would certainly have been obliged to win before five sets had been played as there was no rest whatever allowed in those years. It is quite true that I did follow in at times, but certainly not as a habit, and as became so often the custom in later years after the rests were allowed; and owing to this, it seems to me that our leading players had a more evenly developed all-round game than a great majority of the later ones. Of course in the doubles, most of us followed in on every point as you only have your service once in every four games. After the first year the most successful method of doubles play was the same as today, the partners keeping as much as possible alongside of each other.

Until the Bagnall-Wilde system of the draw came in, a new drawing was made after each round, whether there had been any byes in the completed round or not, so that you never knew when you would come up against any particular entrant in case you were both successful.

During the first two or three years the general trend in the shape of the rackets was to work away from the old court tennis shape and to straighten out more like the rackets of today, though nearly all of the center pieces were convex for some reason or other, while today they are mostly concave. There appeared, however, during this period, three abnormally shaped frames. One was about twelve inches long in the head by about seven inches wide, and another was almost triangular in shape, with a flat head and with the sides slightly bowed, just enough to withstand the strain of stringing. The theory for the first one I do not recall, but the idea governing the triangular shaped one was that it would facilitate making a half volley. I tried them both but I did not find either of them as satisfactory as my oval-shaped one.

The third one was the invention of Fred Taylor of Philadelphia, the doubles champion in 1881. In this racket, when you came to the center piece, it first curved backwards and then came forward again, like a table fork or coal shovel, bringing the plane of the playing surface at a slight angle forward from the handle. I do not remember that Taylor used this for any length of time but certainly no one else that I know of ever used it. I can only suppose that Mr Taylor found himself a little late in striking the ball and, instead of altering his stroke, tried to correct it in this way. I tried it once in a knock-up as a handicap and I must confess that I was surprised to do as well as I did with it.

The history of one other racket, anything but a freak, was remarkable. It was given me in 1884 by William Renshaw as I was leaving England to defend my championship at home. Much to my surprise and delight he gave this to me with best wishes for my success, saying that it was the best racket that he had ever had in his hand. It was made by Thomas J. Tate, by far the best racket maker in England at that time. Renshaw had won the Irish and English singles and doubles championships with it that year and it was still as good as when new, except for the need of restringing. The balance was perfect. When I got home I had it carefully restrung, won the singles with it, and, for precaution, used it only in the final of the doubles, winning again. I then cut out the stringing, gave the frame a slight oiling, placed it very carefully in a press and put it away. When the 1885 championship came around it was restrung, holding its shape wonderfully, and I won both the singles and doubles with it again. All told, it won eight championships!

The Fireside Book of Tennis, 1972

11 The Great Match

The Goddess and the American Girl
LARRY ENGELMANN

When we have match'd our rackets to these balls
We will, in France, by God's grace play a set,
Shall strike his father's crown into the hazard.
Tell him, he hath made a match with such a wrangler,
That all the courts of France will be disturb'd
With chases.

William Shakespeare, *Henry V*

A simple game of tennis, yet a game which made
continents stand still and was the most important
sporting event of modern times exclusively in the hands
of the fairer sex.

Ferdinand Tuohy, Cannes, 1926

On the evening of 15 February 1926, Helen Wills went to bed early.
Several days earlier she had decided to block from her mind all the
confusion and bluster surrounding her on the Riviera. To a remarkable
degree she succeeded. She was not nervous at all, she felt good, healthy,
confident. With her mother, Helen had enjoyed a dinner of steak and
potatoes and had capped the meal with her favourite dessert, cake and ice
cream. Later, after turning down an invitation to a party, Helen was
lulled to sleep by the faint strains of an orchestra somewhere near by
playing the romantic 'Valencia,' the most popular song of the day. Outside,
on the streets of Cannes, there was a carnival atmosphere as thousands
of visitors to this spot on the Côte d'Azure danced and laughed and
tipped their glasses and passed the last few hours before the beginning
of the long-awaited match with Suzanne Lenglen.

Suzanne Lenglen, on the other hand, was not so fortunate. She faced
yet another major crisis in her career on the night before the big match,

and she did not sleep at all. Later she would tell reporters that during the match she suffered from 'physical weakness through private worry.' But few people knew that on the night of 15 February 1926, Suzanne reached a turning point in her career. During the course of that evening she was compelled to make her declaration of independence from Papa.

As his illness became increasingly severe in late 1925 and early 1926, Charles Lenglen gradually lost control over Suzanne's affairs. The major commercial interests on the Riviera had vetoed an earlier match between Suzanne and Helen at the Nice Club – a match Papa Lenglen wanted very much. And then, without seeking his prior approval, the match was awarded to the Carlton Club in Cannes. For a while Papa Lenglen had gone along with the way things were arranged, but enough was enough. And on the evening of 15 February, he simply said, 'No!' Suzanne must not play at the Carlton Club. Out of touch with those handling the arrangements for the match, Papa was suspicious. It might be another Forest Hills. Who knew what they were plotting? Suzanne would again be humiliated and humbled. So Papa Lenglen intervened to protect his little one from the slings and arrows of outrageous newsmen and promoters. Suzanne must scratch from the tournament, he said. She must stay at home with Papa and not play in Cannes.

An uproarious argument followed Papa's pronouncement. Suzanne had been given an agent now, an American, Major Charles Willen. Introduced to Suzanne by F. M. B. Fisher, Willen was to take over Papa's role and look after her personal finances. Willen now insisted that a scratch or a default at this stage would be utterly disastrous for Suzanne's career. She would never recover from it: she would be branded a quitter forever; she would go down in history not as a champion but as a coward and a chump. Willen said that she could defeat that American girl easily, perhaps even in love sets. This was no set up. Suzanne was going to win. But if she scratched at this final moment nobody would ever take her seriously again. She had to play. It was just too late to back out now.

Papa remained adamant. He shouted and railed and denounced Suzanne and Willen. The cries and the pleading from the Villa Ariem were so loud that pedestrians passing by were distracted by the bitter wrangle. Mama Lenglen burst into tears and sided with Papa. Suzanne must not play. Suzanne became hysterical and pleaded for her father's blessing. She had to play, and he had to be there at courtside. But he refused. Willen intervened and told Papa that it was absolutely essential he be at courtside for the match, the most important and the most profitable in Suzanne's career.

The next morning, exhausted and emotionally enervated, Suzanne made her choice: she would play. With or without Papa's blessing, she would play. She dressed for the match, carefully caked on makeup to cover her pale, heavily lined face, and faced Papa one last time. In place of a blessing, Papa cursed her. Moments later Suzanne, Mama, and Willen stepped into the sleek black Voisin which transported them in silence along the coastal road toward the Carlton Club and the waiting American Girl.

The Carlton Club. Before the Lenglen–Wills contest was scheduled to be held there, few newsmen paid much attention to its facilities. Now, when they examined more closely the club where the highly touted tennis match was to be staged, they were, in a word, shocked. John Tunis accurately described it as 'a tawdry little excuse for a tennis club.' The Carlton Club consisted of six clay tennis courts, a small grandstand, and a hut that served as a clubhouse. It was located a short walk from the Croisette and directly adjacent to the grand Carlton Hotel, which loomed up over the palms bordering the club. The club courts had been constructed carelessly with an apparent disregard for the angle of the winter sun. Consequently, except for the hours from about 11.00 a.m. to 1.00 p.m., one player or another faced directly into the distractingly bright champagne sunshine. Adjacent to the number one court – the Burkes euphemistically referred to it as *le court d'honneur* – was the small concrete grandstand. And behind the grandstand rose the blank wall of a large garage and warehouse. Across the street on another side was a sawmill, and the buzzing and rasping sounds from the mill provided another unwelcome distraction for players and spectators alike. The clubhouse provided for the players was a small wood structure enclosing one room 17 feet by 11 feet. The room included two dozen lockers, a shower that never worked, several washstands with cold water only, and nothing else. There were no towels provided and no electric lighting.

These facilities had been adequate in the past for the winter tournaments on the Riviera, and they seemed only a cut or two below the facilities of other small clubs in the region. Once or twice during the winter tennis season the stands would be filled with several hundred spectators when Suzanne Lenglen played. But during matches between less noteworthy contestants only a sprinkling of spectators occupied the Carlton grandstand. Special accommodations for the press had not been necessary in the past, nor were they provided by the Burkes for the finals of the 1926 tournament.

Yet, despite obvious inadequacies, the Carlton Club had won the right to stage the first Lenglen–Wills match. All the necessary business and financial arrangements had been worked out carefully between the Burkes and the various interests represented by F. M. B. Fisher. The only snag in the preliminary dealings had been over the sale of the exclusive film rights. And even with the collapse of the attempt by Fisher and the Burkes to milk the media, rumors persisted that an enormous profit was to result from the wildly enthusiastic public interest in the match. John Tunis tried to follow the money to find out exactly who was making how much from this match.

Tunis calculated that 3,000 tickets were sold for the finals of the Carlton Club tournament at an average price of 200 francs each. That was, however, a low estimate. Other reporters guessed that as many as 4,000 people would pay admission to the final match, and a large number of those tickets were sold for as much as 3,000 francs. Using a low estimate, nonetheless, and disregarding funds from ticket sales for the preliminary matches, Tunis estimated that the Burkes would take in about 600,000 francs. About 100,000 of which would go to the French government in taxes; another 100,000 for expenses such as advertising and building new seats for the final. Where would the remainder go? Fisher responded to Tunis's inquiry by suggesting that the Burkes would make only 100,000 francs on the match. And where did the other funds go? Tunis simply did not know. He pointed out that the amount of 'leakage' from the admission money was substantial. How much of that leakage found its way into the coffers of the Lenglens was anyone's guess. Suzanne insisted that she profited nothing from the match. Most American newsmen believed she was lying.

Money was to be made from this match by ticket-scalping also – an illegal enterprise that boomed during the final hours before play began. There was simply no upper limit as to how much many people were willing to pay for a good seat at the confrontation between the Goddess and the American Girl. Tunis found, though, that attempting to buy a ticket at the last moment was like trying 'to buy a Pullman reservation to heaven.' And just as expensive.

And why shouldn't there be such a mad rush for tickets? The match had been played up for weeks as though 'it was a cross between the French Revolution and the Battle of Gettysburg.' This was not a game of tennis. This was an international incident. This was history. And millions of people wanted to be part of it. In America, one newsman noticed, people who had never before seen a match or were without even a passing interest in tennis now talked glibly on the street about the chances of Wills against Lenglen. Men and women who could not tell you the difference between a game and a set were now offering to risk cash on this match. Paul Gallico found it difficult to keep what was happening in Cannes in any perspective: 'we were whooping it up in those days and it was ballyhooed into the battle of the ages, with the cool peaches-and-cream-skinned, clear-eyed beautiful Helen fighting for the forces of youth and light, democracy and right, against the unattractive Suzanne, a foreigner representing the menace that is always met and defeated by our fine American manhood and womanhood.'

In northern California scores of Helen's supporters were outspoken in their conviction that the American girl would bring off the upset of the century in this match of the century. All-night parties were arranged by several organizations so that celebrants could wait together for the good news from Cannes. San Francisco radio station KPO prepared to come on the air early in the morning to broadcast the first bulletins from Cannes. The presses for the morning editions of the daily newspapers were stopped and space was reserved for the first wire-service reports.

And then there were the last-minute predictions. George Wightman, former USLTA president, said he believed it was still 'anybody's match. If Miss Wills is on her game she cannot be beaten except by a player who can hit harder than she can. When Miss Wills plays her drive with all the speed she is capable of, no woman and indeed few men players can withstand the withering pace.' Big Bill Tilden and Sam Hardy agreed. Helen's hope for victory against the more experienced and uncannily talented Suzanne lay in the awesome power of her attack. Relentless aggressiveness would, they believed, shatter Suzanne's defense, upset her control, erode her self-confidence, and bring victory. Molla Mallory insisted that Helen could win only if she went at Suzanne like a lion, using all of her strength on every shot. It would be difficult, but it could be done. In fact, it had been done, Molla pointed out. Once. At Forest Hills in 1921. And it could be done again.

Most Riviera clubs scheduled final tournament matches for the early afternoon. But the women's singles final at the Carlton Club, due to the awkward play of the sunlight on the courts in the afternoon, was sched-uled for 11.15 a.m. It was the best time. Helen found on the morning of

16 February 1926, a Tuesday, that 'the sky was blue and the air fresh and the sunshine sparkling – a perfect day for tennis. Heaven had looked after the weather,' she wrote, 'and the Burkes had looked after the arrangements, which were partly good and partly bad.' After a light breakfast with her mother, Helen dressed in her white pleated cotton dress and heavily starched middy top, and Waite shoes and stockings. She adjusted her white visor over the light net covering her hair, pulled on her red wool sweater, and carried her heavy winter coat. She carefully selected from her array of rackets four that felt right. Then, shortly before 11.00 a.m., she walked with her mother the short distance to the Carlton Club.

All around the club, since early in the morning, pandemonium prevailed. John Tunis had expected a huge crowd, so he left his hotel room two hours before the match was scheduled to start to avoid the inevitable final rush for seats. But he was completely unprepared for what he found. Hundreds of people had been standing in line all night waiting to get in. The Train Bleu had arrived from Paris packed with fans eager to see the match, and the roads leading into Cannes were jammed with cars carrying partisans. Tunis found a line of people four across stretching from the gate of the club all the way back to the Croisette, some five hundred yards away. And it was growing steadily, stretching down the street and around the corner and out of sight. Near the entrance the line was flattened out into a large seething, shouting, milling mass of people. Many seemed to have no tickets and tried frantically to thrust bundles of francs into the hands of club officials standing guard at the gate. People around the gate jostled each other and pushed and shoved as they tried to make their way into the club. Just inside the gate Tunis spotted F. M. B. Fisher and Albert Burke trying to maintain a semblance of order and to admit only paying customers.

Tunis was directed to a club entrance reserved for the press. He hurried to that gate but found it resembled the foyer of the Tower of Babel. There was another impatient mob, some with tickets and most without. Many were shouting that they were friends of the Burkes or friends of Fisher or friends of the players or reporters or photographers – a confusing mishmash of professions and a profusion of languages. It took Tunis half an hour of maneuvering and pushing before he was finally squeezed through the gate and onto the club grounds.

Al Laney had similar problems making his way. At first he found it absolutely impossible to push his way through the crowd and into the press entrance. Laney eventually teamed up with a group of photographers and reporters who formed a solid flying wedge and successfully stormed the gate. Once inside the group was directed to a special press section of the bleachers. But in the mad scramble for seats Laney missed the press section, as did most of the reporters. The entire atmosphere was one of confusion and of unrestrained individualism. It was, he observed, as they used to say at Ebbetts Field, 'everyone for theirself!'

Tunis found – with only 90 minutes remaining until the start of the match – carpenters were still busy constructing bleacher seats. As they worked away frantically, those fortunate enough to make it into the club surrounded them. And as each section of the new bleachers was completed and a board dropped down, people clambered carelessly and fearlessly around the carpenters to take their seats. Many dropped all restraint and ran for their seats. Tunis was amused by a rather pathetic situation he witnessed that seemed to sum up the utter insanity surrounding this event. He saw a man with a ticket in his hand staring up into space. The man's bleacher seat was still in the process of being built, but at the moment was just air. The man stood there, patiently, as the carpenters hammered away creating the place he would perch on to observe this historic clash of the Goddess and the American Girl.

Tunis examined the stands and the thin boards used for scaffolding and the two-by-four braces and supports for the bleachers. When he pushed against some of the boards to see how solidly constructed they were, there were instant cries of protest and frightened shouts from those already seated. When a member of the Carlton Club tennis committee came by, Tunis stopped him and asked, 'Has this been inspected by your local building inspector?' The man was annoyed by the question and replied, '*Mais, mon vieux*, do you not see that it is only just being finished?' 'Yes, but what if it falls down?' Tunis asked.

The official simply shrugged his shoulders 'with a delightful Gallic gesture' and responded, 'Ah, the club is assured — .' Then he dashed off without finishing his comment. Tunis spotted a nurse in uniform sitting in the referee's tent and had no doubt as to why she was there. Tunis consequently climbed very cautiously up to his seat as the boards wavered beneath his feet. 'And the mere fact that the Carlton Tennis Club would have to pay nothing to my heirs in case I was buried in the wreckage did not reassure me in the least,' he said. After finding a reasonably stable slot, Tunis sat down and then looked around to see what other foolhardy souls had ascended this jerry-built contraption.

Tunis saw groups of reporters sitting together in various parts of the bleachers. If there was a special press section nobody seemed to have found it. He spotted Blasco Ibañez, the Spanish novelist who was being paid 40,000 francs for his account of this match for the INS, sitting with a few 'mere journalists.' Max Eastman was there and so was Stanley Doust of the London *Daily Mail* and Powell Blackmore of the *Express* and Sparrow Robertson of the Paris *Herald* and Tom Topping of the Associated Press. A few journalists had carried in typewriters, and they tried to balance them on their knees while being squeezed into the mass of fans ever more tightly with the constant flow of new arrivals.

Al Laney seated himself behind Tom Topping, who was writing out his reports in long hand. Topping wrote quickly and then handed his completed pages back to Laney, who corrected the copy, put a paper clip on it, and then dropped it to a man standing behind the bleachers. That man in turn passed the page over the fence to a runner who rushed it off to a wire service for transmission to America.

Laney was struck by Topping's anxiousness in scribbling off descriptions of the club grounds and the crowds, but Topping explained it all to him in a few words. 'You know where this wench comes from?' Topping asked. 'Berkeley, California. You know what time it is in Berkeley, California? Three o'clock in the morning. Some of the AM's are holding for this, and the guy gets there first gets his stuff in the paper.' Looking around, Laney saw that other wire service writers were working just as frantically as Topping, racing to keep up with events.

While the newsmen settled into their cramped quarters the gate was finally crashed successfully by what Tunis called 'French flappers.' The gate was blocked again, and the crowd outside became larger and ever more threatening. Thousands of people were pushing their way forward and yelling and swarming around like enraged bees in their effort to get inside. Some of those who saw no chance at all of making it inside climbed a large eucalyptus tree just outside the gate. But when the club officials saw this group of nonpaying arboreal customers they shouted orders to a policeman to get the climbers down. Tunis observed that 'as a tree climber he was a good traffic cop.' He scaled the tree while solemnly ordering the climbers down. They, in turn, simply climbed higher. Finally, deciding that enough was enough, the policeman slid back down amid jeers and cheers from the multitude.

Across the street from the club were several small villas with red tile roofs. The owner of one of them, after seeing the crowd of people, hit upon a way of making money. He stood at the door of his house and sold places at one of his windows to fans who had given up all hope of crashing the gates. For 20 francs each tennis fan could gather around a small second-story window and look down on the courts. The window spots were sold out six or seven times over. The entrepreneur's wife rushed downstairs and shouted that the rooms were full and that people were complaining they could not see. Yet there remained room for an additional profit. The roof of the house, like that of many Riviera villas, was constructed of clay tiles placed across beams. The tiles could easily be removed from within. The owner of the villa began dismantling his roof. Men and women paid at the door and carted chairs to the attic, stood on them, removed tiles, and then poked their heads out. The villa quickly took on a surrealistic look as human heads suddenly filled holes in the roof. This profitable venture gave residents of other nearby villas ideas, and heads began protruding from other rooftops across from the club.

Then, much like a group of smartly attired marines making an alpine assault, there appeared a crowd of men and women climbing carefully up over the wide sloping roof of the garage behind the Carlton Club. They found comfortable places to stand or sit and perched rather precariously in their makeshift open-air balcony. Still other enthusiasts, who concluded wisely that they could never fight their way inside, rented ladders and leaned them against the fence at the end of the section of the club near the street. Next a large bus pulled up to the fence and parked. The people inside who had hired it for the afternoon scrambled out and up onto the hood and roof so they could peek over the fence and watch the match. Long before match time the roofs of most buildings within sight of the club were thick with spectators, and the balconies and windows of the Carlton Hotel were filled with onlookers. There were in fact many more spectators for this match outside the club grounds than there were inside. And no wonder. Ticket prices during the morning had skyrocketed. Scalpers on the street were getting as much as 1,200 francs – 44 American dollars – for each ticket. And that was for an impossibly narrow seat in an unstable bleachers. That was about twenty-two times what one might expect to pay at Forest Hills to see a final match between Bill Tilden and Bill Johnston, the most popular American male players. For 1,200 francs one could buy a good suit, a pair of shoes, a train ticket from Paris to Cannes, and room and board in a grand hotel on the Riviera for one day. Or, for that same 1,200 francs one might buy

– if one were very lucky – one ticket to a tennis match in Cannes at 11.15 a.m., 16 February 1926.

During the long wait for the appearance of the featured players on this morning, newsmen seated in the newly constructed bleachers watched the better-known members of European high society stroll to their reserved seats in the permanent gallery. Among the most easily recognizable figures of that elite group were Grand Duke Cyril of Russia, King Gustav of Sweden, Manuel, ex-king of Portugal, the Duke of Sutherland, the Count de Bourbel (president of the Tennis Committee of the Riviera), Baron de Graffenried, and the Rajah and Ranee of Pudukota. The American diplomat and author Brand Whitlock was also there along with what John Tunis guessed was 'half the Russian and English nobility.' When the army of newsmen weren't scribbling notes on the background for the big match or scrutinizing the stands across the way for somebody who was somebody, they joked and jostled each other. Many of them were a little giddy and somewhat embarrassed by the necessity of assaulting the gates in order to get into the club two hours before match time. They were disappointed at the lack of facilities available for their creative efforts, and what remaining pretence of sophistication they possessed once they battered their way to their seats was squeezed out of them by the crush of the crowd. They laughed hysterically at every trivial incident. They howled with delight when fashionably attired young women stepped across rooftops and the sun behind them made their clothing suddenly transparent or when the gendarmes undertook their tree-top pursuits and tried to coax fans down from the palms. The entrance of each new celebrity into the club was hailed by newsmen as on a Broadway opening night and then followed by jokes and wisecracks. All of this went on while carpenters continued their feverish hammering and sawing while propping up more bleachers.

Shortly after eleven o'clock the officials for the match walked to their stations round the court. Commander George Hillyard had been selected as umpire, and the linesmen included Lord Charles Hope, Cyril Tolley, Roman Najouch, the residential professional of the Cannes Club, Victor Cazalet, Sir Francis Towle, and R. Dunkerely. These officials, ostensibly, had been approved previously by both players. Some newsmen noticed what they guessed was an oversight in the selection of the match officials. There was no foot-fault judge. Yet, considering the difficulties Suzanne Lenglen had experienced with foot faults called against her in the semi-final, it seems not unlikely that the Goddess or one of her concerned partisans among the officials had suggested just such an omission. The French champion would not suffer from distracting accusations of rule violations in this critical contest.

The three-ring circus atmosphere in the Carlton Club – the shouting and the loudly expressed partisanship of the fans – shocked traditionalists. Tennis had never before been played in such an explosively exciting setting. Troubled by the reported behaviour of the crowds at courtside in Cannes, an editor for the *New York Times* reminded his readers that 'tennis is nothing if not a game for gentlemen and gentlewomen. To degrade it by outbursts of rowdyism is to put at hazard something too fine to be carelessly thrown away.' Overlooking the pivotal role of the press in drumming up the extraordinary excitement for this match in the first place, the editor concluded that 'things seem to have been carried to an intolerable excess at Cannes. If this sort of boorishness is allowed to continue, the game of tennis will soon be in urgent need of being saved from its patrons and professed friends.'

Meanwhile, in Cannes, the patrons and professed friends of tennis were much more interested in seeing than in saving tennis. In the last few hectic moments before the big match was scheduled to start, it seemed that the swirling crowd would burst right through the fences and flood out onto the courts and make any confrontation between contestants impossible. The Carlton Club had become a besieged sports Bastille under assault by an army of energetic and determined fans. There were regular charges at the gates by organized wedges of impatient people, and the constant roar of the crowd outside rose and fell almost ominously, like the deep reverberations of ocean waves beating against a beach. Then, just after 11.00 a.m., the noise outside suddenly stopped. There was an odd – even a frightening – moment of quiet. Why? A few of those inside instinctively stood to peer out over the fence to see what was happening. But before they could relay back any information the quiet was shattered by an ear-splitting eruption of shouting and screaming and ecstatic howling. And above that mad din, one single word could be heard again and again – 'Suzanne!' The Goddess had arrived! The Goddess was here! 'Suzanne!' the people shouted and sang. 'Suzanne! Vive la Suzanne! Vive la belle Suzanne!'

The French champion was quickly escorted through the sea of cheering partisans that parted with almost religious obeisance before her. She proceeded triumphantly through that human corridor into the Carlton

Club. Just inside the gate she saw the American girl waiting for her in silence.

Helen and Catherine Wills had walked the short distance from their hotel to the Carlton Club. When they arrived at the gate they found an impenetrable crowd blocking the way. Fortunately, a club official spotted the pair and made his way through the crowd. He then led the Wills women through the confusion to another entrance where there was yet another impatient mob fighting to get inside. At first those around the entrance refused to budge and make way despite the threats and the pleading from the club official. But then, gradually, many of them recognized Helen and began to move back to make room for her to pass. They stared in silent wonder as she glided past them like a phantom. If she was excited or appalled, she showed no sign. She seemed very shy and perhaps a bit embarrassed as she was swallowed up in the crowd whose actions seemed more like an enthusiastic outbreak in a madhouse than a celebration of tennis. Helen was not accustomed to such behaviour, to such demonstrative enthusiasm. Tennis, in the course of only a few weeks, had become show business and big business. And Helen Wills was now a star. Just inside the gate she was welcomed by club officials and by a small army of photographers. Only seconds later Suzanne made her perfectly timed arrival.

Helen Wills wore her red sweater and her customary costume. But Suzanne! Ah, Suzanne Lenglen was fully attired for this festive occasion. She wore a rose bandeau and a matching wide-knit rose sweater over a short white pleated silk dress. And over all of this she wore her white ermine coat.

After the two women exchanged a perfunctory salutation they turned to face the familiar phalanx of photographers. The cameramen, lined up in a triple row, shouted commands and requests to the two women. Suzanne smiled a lot and placed her hand smartly on her hip. Helen, on the other hand, remained quiet and unemotional, as unemotional, one man described her, as 'a Methodist minister at a funeral.' Helen looked around at the sea of faces turned towards her, strange and foreign faces, she thought. And she believed that many of them reflected a dislike of her. Suzanne seemed comfortable with the crowd. She executed some bravura gestures and blew kisses to friends in the crowd. When she moved in front of the cameras, she was like a feather dancing in the wind, turning and prancing here and there to the absolute delight of the cameramen. When the picture-taking session had almost ended there was a squawking commotion just outside the gate and everyone turned to see a policeman trying to drag someone down from a tree. The photographers laughed. The two women laughed. But Helen noticed now that Suzanne's laugh was unusual. It was dry throated and forced – almost a nervous cackle.

At a signal from a club official, the picture-taking session ended, and the two women were escorted towards the court. Suzanne virtually danced her way onto the clay. Close behind her and to one side came Helen, walking with a flatfooted padding cat-like walk and a demeanor that seemed to whisper to those watching, 'I really am quite a modest little girl, much too modest for all of this.'

As the two women walked out onto the court they were preceded by several reporters and photographers walking backwards, hoping to get the very last word or picture before the match was under way.

There was continuous shouting and applause inside the club now. It was already a magnificent and thrilling and wonderful show. In the bleacher seats there was a sudden speeded up rapid machine-gun chatter of typewriters as correspondents tried frantically, frenetically, to capture all of this on paper in order to relay it to runners who would convey it to the wire services who would send it to cities around the world where it would again be printed on paper and read by tens of millions eager to envision this spectacle. But those readers could never experience the rush of excitement felt by the correspondents and the spectators that sunny morning next to this clay court beside the beautiful azure sea in a sparkling city in the south of France where the two greatest women tennis players in the world were about to test each other.

The correspondents strained for the right words to express pride and awe. The phrases and adjectives poured out steadily again – Our Girl of the Golden West, the American Girl, Helen of America, Our Helen, Our Hope. Even Little Helen – Americans could easily envision that. Little Helen out to slay the Gallic Goliath. There was only one thing wrong with that description. Helen was obviously taller and heavier than Suzanne. Yet her serenity and quietude seemed to make her somehow look smaller than the bouncing, bubbling Suzanne. The Little American. And so in their mind's eye, newspaper readers could envision a racket-swinging diminutive Mary Pickford off to do great things for her country. To bring down the hard-hearted villain. And make no doubt about it, Suzanne was the villain. And what a story it was. Helen stood there like, well, like a little Calvin Coolidge about to deliver a humble homily. The images and the descriptions were important not for their accuracy but to convey contrast. Surely, few athletes engaged against each other in the same sport ever contrasted more than this pair, this Goddess and this American Girl.

Helen Wills had already noticed something unusual in Suzanne Lenglen's behavior. Something was not right. The Goddess appeared to be trembling slightly. Helen felt it first when she grasped Suzanne's extended hand after the French woman's grand entrance into the club grounds. And when Suzanne smiled, her lips quivered as though that bright smile might in a moment reassemble itself into a miserable frown. Suzanne was clearly struggling to seem happy. She was wavering even before the contest began. She was, perhaps, even a bit frightened. Helen wondered at this since it was obviously the challenger who should be more anxious. The thought of Suzanne's emotional vulnerability gave Helen a little more confidence. She became even more relaxed and emotionally placid as she walked out onto the clay court to play.

From his seat Al Laney could see Lenglen's face clearly. Laney was a bit surprised by her appearance. There were dark lines on her face, and her eyes seemed drawn. She looked like she had not slept. 'She did not look well,' he observed. And although the sun was nearly directly overhead and it was getting warm, Suzanne kept her sweater on. As she proceeded out onto the court, the dark French woman further betrayed her uneasiness. Her smile disappeared. She snapped her fingers impatiently at the ball boy and was quick and jerky in her motions. She did not like the noise of the crowd, and she did not like the carpenters. She was tired, and she had a nervous tic in her right arm. In her preliminary rally with Helen she struggled inwardly to relax, to arouse her confidence. She practiced her strokes carefully, not rushing after any ball, staying right in the middle of the baseline and taking only the forehand and backhand shots that came directly to her. At the same time she studied Helen's movement, analyzing the mechanics of the motion, measuring the pace of the shots. Did Helen hesitate on any shots? Where was her weakness today? And why did she remain so flatfooted?

As the two women warmed up, the final arrangements for the match were made. The carpenters were escorted from the club. The officials settled into their places around the court. Commander Hillyard climbed up into the umpire's chair. The cheering and the noise continued. Suzanne seemed particularly annoyed by the chanting of a group of spectators outside the fence standing on the top of a bus. She gave them an impatient look, a pleading look, but a look that made no difference at all in their behavior. Despite her obvious wishes to the contrary, the crowd outside continued its enthusiastic demonstration.

During the warm-up Helen was trying hard to think of nothing but the game, of the drives and the angles and the spin and rebound of the ball. The position of the sun and the effect of the dry clay were taken into consideration and analyzed. She betrayed no emotion. She seemed to have shut out the noise of the crowd completely from her mind. Al Laney noted that she was 'placidly unemotional' and stolid, still the Coolidge of the courts. He also noticed for the first time what large capable-looking hands she had, and he wondered to himself if she was actually as talented a painter as she was supposed to be. Hard to believe. At the moment she looked more and more the dedicated and superbly coordinated athlete.

As Helen Wills focused her concentration, everything – the crowd, the cameras, the background commotion – faded into silence. There must be nothing but the game. Nothing but the game. And, as always, she began to repeat her secret mantra to herself over and over again: 'Every shot. Every shot. Every shot.' She studied the ball and thought of every shot.

Suzanne won the spin of the racket and elected to serve the first game. As Helen moved back to receive service several reporters noticed a stiffness in her knee. There was still a bandage dressing covering the wound incurred in the semi-final match. But Helen had made no mention of it, not on this day or after. No apologies. She had come to play tennis, come to win. And she believed she could win. Despite that knee.

Suzanne Lenglen blew softly into her right palm and then carefully wiped both palms on her skirt. Then she turned to the ball boy who tossed out three balls in quick succession – she liked to hold all three at once in order to speed up the game. She did not bounce the balls. She merely turned to signal that she was ready to begin. Hillyard signaled for the match to commence. Suzanne tiptoed up to the baseline, paused for just a fraction of a second, and then gracefully lifted the white ball high into the air above her left shoulder. With a familiar incomparably fluid motion she arched backward to watch the ball and then leaned forward while bringing her racket up and over her head to strike the ball and send it gliding straight and flat and without spin deep into the corner of Wills's service court. The American girl skipped from the base-line to make a solid forehand return. The crowd of 4,000 spectators inside and the equally large multitude outside became silent. The match of the century had just begun.

The Goddess and the American Girl, 1988

Lenglen–Wills Match at Cannes
JAMES THURBER

A rush of people struggling around a livid woman in pink-colored silk, a sudden rioting of flowers from somewhere, a bright glittering of silver in the sun. The crowd that watched from the stands was a little stupefied. It had all been too swift and too dazzling.

And then a girl in white walked silently away from the colorful, frenzied throne they were building around the woman in pink silk. The crowd that watched from the stands could comprehend it now. The silent girl in white detaching herself from the mad maelstrom was a note of familiar sanity. Helen Wills had been defeated and was going home.

She went home quietly, directly, without looking around, as she always does when a match is ended. The only color that relieved the whiteness of her face and of her dress, a whiteness so pathetically odd against that silver and red and pink-colored scene, was a bright flush on her cheeks. No one knew what she thought exactly. She didn't say anything – even when she was spoken to. But it wasn't a flush that comes from being ashamed or being crushed. It might well have been a flush of pride. At any rate, to the crowd that watched from the stands it was a sort of red badge of courage with as much significance as the glory that broke about the victorious head of Suzanne Lenglen.

Helen Wills was defeated yesterday on the Carlton court in Cannes by Suzanne Lenglen, 6–3, 8–6. Those were the statistics. But it was a match that transcended statistics... They had said Helen Wills might not get a game. They had bet she wouldn't get six. She got nine. But those again are merely figures.

The heart of the game was that 'Little Poker Face' from California met for the first time in the singles the greatest woman tennis player in the world since the time when Helen was fondling dolls, fought her with everything she had, smashed with her, drove with her, volleyed with her, until she had the French champion so greatly on the run that at times it seemed like the baseline on Mlle Lenglen's side of the court was the dropping off place.

That was the heart of the game. The body of it was made up of a variety of things, very complicated things. But a component part that can not be overlooked was the fact that Suzanne Lenglen won a hard and brilliantly fought match, proved herself every inch the queen of the courts. If she was on the run at times, she almost broke Helen Wills' heart in a certain part of that tremendous second set when she sent her speeding from one alley-line to the other in a magnificent series of those sharp, accurate, hard-shot placements in which, at her best, she is the best there is.

She had to be the best to win in two sets yesterday. She may perhaps have to be a little better than the best to do it again. Helen Wills met a baptism of fire which was strange and new to her: she encountered a variety and a brilliance of technique that she has never encountered before. And having come through it so superbly, the unfinished sentence on everybody's lips yesterday was: 'The next time . . . ?'

Helen Wills, with the eyes of Lenglen on her across a net, all alone, for the first time, as the game began, was nervous. She showed it in her first quick wide-of-the-baseline returns of Suzanne's service. The Frenchwoman took an easy love game quickly. The next game was a little different, but neither player was yet warmed up. Wills saw the game go to 15–40 against her. Then abruptly it was deuce, her advantage, her game. And almost before the stands knew it she took the next game, by the same route exactly, on her opponent's service. 2–1 Wills.

Lenglen made up for it rapidly and irresistibly. She took two love games in succession and fairly toyed with the American in the second one. Then she made it ten straight points by going to 30–love in the sixth game. Wills held, to 30–40; then Lenglen took her third straight game to make the score 4–2, her favor. The seventh game was Wills' best in this set. She took it to 40–love on Lenglen's service, lost a point, and then shot over a nice winning placement.

With the score thus 4–3 in her favor, Lenglen asserted herself and beat Wills' service in the eighth game, four points to one. She went into the last game of the set with a nice high lob to begin with, shot over a placement to make it 30–love, lost a point, and took the next two – game and set.

Neither player had yet attained the form she was to show in the second set. Wills' early nervousness resulted in several wide outs and even more netted shots. They had been fairly even at the net, to which, however, they were yet to commit themselves for a real test. In her two straight love games the Frenchwoman's easy placements, that left Helen's racket wide of the ball in several cases, were abetted by Miss Wills' failure to take advantage of her opportunities.

The second set got off in a blaze of Wills. She took her first and only love game against the total of four that Suzanne scored in the two sets. After outshooting the French start to reach 30–love, Wills was helped to 40 when her opponent outed widely, and the California girl broke into her top-form stride in the next exchange, winning her love game by a pretty placement.

They were both now at it in earnest, and from this point on the game took on a thrilling aspect that kept spectators on the edge of their chairs, made hearts beat thickly in throats, and brought out involuntary shouts from the watchers.

With Lenglen serving the second game, Helen stepped into her first serve and began one of the most beautifully played point-battles of the match. She outplayed her opponent at this point in every phase of play, and the variety was becoming fast and furious. Wills took the next point also, only to yield the next two; then she made it 40–30, whereupon Suzanne forged to the front, deuced the game, and despite some of the most splendid brilliance of the afternoon, gained the advantage and the game.

Helen Wills was now in the match hammer and tongs, with fire in her eye and every trace of the nervousness which had visibly restrained her early play entirely vanished. She was playing not the greatest woman tennis player in the world but just a woman who happened to be finalist in the same match. With this attitude showing in every stroke, she served to 40–15 in the third game and then won it, four points to two. Score: 2–1, Wills.

At this point Helen Wills had Suzanne Lenglen on the run. She outplayed her at every turn in the fourth game, smashing through the Frenchwoman's service with the loss of only one point. Score: 3–1, Wills. But Suzanne Lenglen was not swept aside, partly due to a little overanxiety on the part of the American girl. Suzanne broke through Wills' service in return by the identical point score of the preceding game. Score: 3–2, Wills.

The Frenchwoman tied the count in the next game, winning it four points to one. But that was just the beginning of the struggle. The seventh game was one of the most thrilling and terrifically fought of the afternoon, and the Berkeley youngster won it in the end after it had gone four times to deuce. Moreover, she won it in spite of the fact that Lenglen had it in her grasp, 15–40, before the American, making good her reputation for hard, cool playing in a crisis, carried it to deuce, her ad, deuce again, Suzanne's ad, deuce again, Wills' ad, deuce again, Wills' ad and game. Score: 4–3, Wills.

On her serve, Lenglen took the next game, four points to two. It was in this hot sector of the match that Wills suffered one of her worst blows, a blow bad enough to break stuff less stern than the heart of the American fighter. With the score at 30–all, Lenglen outed, but the line judge failed to see or to call it. It practically presented this crucial game to the Frenchwoman. The stands yelled 'out' in a chorus, but the heartbreaking 'boner' was a *fait accompli*. Score: 4–4. The other blow that hit the American girl in the middle of this set was not a bad break but Lenglen's terrifically swift battery of placements all around the edges of the court that left the American panting.

Wills took the ninth game, however, in one of the most splendidly fought encounters of the set, replete with hard playing on both sides of the net. She served to deuce, her advantage, and game. The tenth game became Lenglen's fourth love game. Score: 5–5.

Both players were fagged, but Wills seemed suddenly a little ill in the bargain, for at one point in this terrific dueling, with Lenglen in place ready to serve, the youngster bent over and leaned pathetically on her racket. With her racket in the air and ball in hand, Lenglen had to call to the girl to get her to look up and receive the serve.

Later, however, the American rallied, while Lenglen was visibly fatigued – a fatigue that showed in every line of her face. The light was a little drained from her eyes and the lines around her mouth showed sheer misery. It seemed that at several points she was on the verge of stampede, and she evidenced it in one notable case by failing to play a stroke near the baseline and looking rather abjectly at the line judge. It was good and Wills won the point. Wills won the applause of the crowd in the terrific eleventh game when, with the points at love – 40 against her on her service, she moved to 30–40 before yielding. Score: 6–5, Lenglen.

The next game was sheer tribute to Wills' 'stuff.' And incidentally it will go down as one of the most grotesque and thrilling and momentous games on record. Lenglen needed the game to win the set and match and the virtual championship of the world. It was her serve. It seemed to her that she could rest soon. And she had to rest soon. So did Wills.

Lenglen won the first two points. Wills fought with everything she had and won the next point. Lenglen went to 40–15. And here came the incident that brought the stands to their feet, cheering Lenglen, the 'winner' of the great confrontation. She shot the ball perilously near the line. The line judge was silent. Silence means the shot is good. Lenglen upped her racket and prepared to quit the court. Wills started for the net, her hand out to congratulate the winner. The stands rose. And suddenly there was a conference of officials, and a loud voice announced, '40–30.' Wills had been saved. The game went on. Wills took it to deuce, her advantage, game. Score: 6–6.

The next game was almost as nerve-wracking and it was again a great tribute to the American girl's remarkable grit in the face of defeat. On Helen's service, Suzanne rushed to 0–40. Then Wills rallied and fought back to deuce, then to her advantage. Lenglen deuced it, went to ad, and then took the game.

The next and last game, similarly, went to deuce twice. After Lenglen had stood at 30–15, Wills climbed to 30–40, Lenglen brought it to deuce, then to her advantage. Here the French star faltered and double-faulted. Deuce. But she came back, won the advantage again, and then the game, set, and match. There was the meeting at the net, and the 'battle of the century' was over.

Wills, tired, game, defeated, but carrying a radiance all her own, left the court of honor with its cups and its flowers and its 'bravos' to Suzanne Lenglen. Suzanne Lenglen was tired. Tired, pale and drawn.

'She knew she was in a match,' someone breathed, a little awestruck. It was like seeing a goddess in pain. Even in her moment of glory she was, first of all, tired and worn. The youngster from America had had her on the run.

Both stars revived remarkably after a few hours' rest and took to the courts in a women's doubles final that was, in its way, almost as thrilling as the great match itself. Mlle Lenglen and Mlle Vlasto won it, 6–4, 7–5, from Miss Wills and Mlle Contostavlos. All four played splendidly. Miss Wills was the weakest of all, perhaps, in the first set, but she made up for every fault by taking, almost single-handedly, the fifth, sixth and seventh games of the second set, all at love, in the most remarkably sustained brilliance of the whole day of playing. She won just about every point, and there might as well have been no one on the other side of the net.

The Fireside Book of Tennis, 1972

My Match against Mlle Lenglen
HELEN WILLS

I was happy when I persuaded my father and mother to let me go to the South of France. Both had thought that there wasn't really any reason for traveling such a long distance for tennis, because I could play all that I wanted to at home in California. Finally, my mother consented to go with me. The United States Lawn Tennis Association advised me not to go there for the tournaments and said that I could not be considered as their representative. But it seemed to me, at twenty, that the Riviera tournaments were the most alluring things in all the world.

So we started out, leaving California sunshine and tennis, shortly after Christmas, to journey six thousand miles to the South of France, where there would be more sunshine and more tennis. I found, when we arrived, that the sunshine was not nearly so warm as that in California, but that the tennis was worth having made the trip for. All the best players were gathered there for the tournaments that year – Mlle Lenglen, who lived in Nice; Eileen Bennett; Betty Nuthall; Didi Vlasto, the pretty Greek champion; Lili Alvarez, the colorful Spanish player; and Helene Contostavlos, another excellent Greek player, who is a cousin of Didi . . .

I was so eager to begin playing at once that I entered a tournament in Cannes the next day after arriving. The pink clay courts felt very different under foot from the asphalt courts to which I had been accustomed in California. The balls bounced differently too. There had been rain and the clay was damp, so that the bound was low. It was several days before my drives reached their usual form. And I found it difficult to be steady and accurate . . .

In the South of France Mlle Lenglen was queen. The whole of the Riviera was Mlle Lenglen's home town. She lived in Nice, in a villa opposite the Nice Tennis Club, but so closely situated were all the towns that from a tennis point of view they were one. The first time that I saw Mlle Lenglen in Nice was from the terrace on the top of the Nice Tennis Club. She leaned out of an upper window of her villa and waved at us. She was wearing a white tennis dress and a yellow sweater. Soon she was over on the terrace with us, welcoming us pleasantly to her home club.

Mlle Lenglen knew every inch of every court on the coast, and it was not surprising that she chose the very excellent courts of the Carlton

Club at Cannes for the scene of her appearance in the singles. The courts were owned and run by her good friends, the Burkes, who are well-known professionals. There are several Burke brothers. One of them used to practice with Mlle Lenglen continually.

In California I had vaguely thought that if I were fortunate enough to win my preliminary matches, I would have the opportunity of meeting Mlle Lenglen in a number of tournaments, and thereby learn a great deal about tennis. I was disappointed when I realized that these imagined meetings were to be boiled down into one, and that my whole visit to the South of France would have in it just one match with Mlle Lenglen . . .

The buzzing which had surrounded the tournament became concentrated on the final bracket. It had seemed to me that the week preceding and the week of the tournament had been entirely too hectic. No tennis match deserved the attention which this one received . . . Our match was bounced upon by the newspaper correspondents, who waited on the courts or else in the bar at the corner. I know that I, and probably Mlle Lenglen, too, was inclined to think that the outcome of the match meant more than it really did. It is not always easy to maintain a sense of proportion at a time like this . . .

The court was a marvel of smoothness. The roller had done double duty. The seating facilities were very cramped, as there were not enough places for people who wished to see the match. The tickets had got into the hands of speculators and were being sold for four and five times what they had originally cost. The gates were so narrow and the ticket takers so stubborn – as they always are abroad – that there was much congestion around the one entrance. It was with difficulty that my mother and I got into the court at all.

The linesmen had been carefully chosen – men who had played tennis themselves, who were supposed to have an eye for a moving tennis ball. Among the linesmen was a titled Englishman of distinguished mien. On one line was an English golfer who had been a champion.

The match started with the usual spin of racket, the choosing of side and the preliminary rally. From the first I knew that Mlle Lenglen was determined to extract the most out of her own game. She intended to bring forth the concentrated knowledge that had accumulated with her years of tournament play. She meant, also, to make the most of her understanding of strategy. She always did do these two things, for, curiously enough, she was one of the most consistent of players in her matches, contrary to general belief. But on this occasion she seemed to fix her mind on these two ideas with more determination than ever – or so I thought, because it was myself who was experiencing the full power of her concentration.

I also felt that she was saving her strength as much as possible – making her mind do the running instead of her feet. Indeed, it was I who was the stronger player physically, and the one who had the greater powers of endurance. But she was the superior in experience and in the understanding of the tactics of the game, as, in fact, she should have been, because she was seven years my senior.

Her favorite bit of strategy in our match was to keep me running back and forth, and then, at an opportune moment, to angle a shorter ball, so that I would have to run the longest distance for it – that is, on the diagonal, instead of sideways. Unless I made a very satisfactory return from this short ball, then she would be able to send a passing shot down the line.

Now, there is nothing particularly new about tactics of this variety in tennis; they have been often used. But probably never with the accurate touch which Mlle Lenglen gave to them. In other words, she accomplished and carried to their ideal completion strategic plans which other players try but cannot always consistently finish.

As I remember, I had no definite plan of strategy or attack, because it was so difficult to find any way of attacking Mlle Lenglen's game. And my three years of big tournament play were not sufficient to warrant my being called a general of strategy. I felt that I could run as far on the court and for as long a time as Mlle Lenglen. This was a consoling thought. I felt that I could meet enough of her balls so that the rallies would be prolonged. But as to the actual placing of the balls, I could not figure out a way beforehand. However, I hoped that the match itself might indicate what my strategic moves should be. As it turned out, my idea had been right about actual physical strength. As the match wore on, Mlle Lenglen showed signs of weariness, and it was because of this that the second set went to the score of eight games to six. But clearly, throughout the match, Mlle Lenglen was my superior as regards tactics and placing, and it was this which enabled her to win; coupled, of course, with her usual steadiness.

A thing that surprised me was that I found her balls not unusually difficult to hit, nor did they carry as much speed as the balls of several other of the leading women players whom I had met in matches. But her balls kept coming back, coming back, and each time to a spot on the court which was a little more difficult to get to.

It may seem that I am overdoing my description of my experiences when playing against Mlle Lenglen. A match seven years ago – why, that is older than old news! But the interesting thing about it – at least to me – is that I believe that that match, for me, will be the unique experience of all my tennis-playing days. The reason being that Mlle Lenglen was a unique player. No woman player that I have met since at Wimbledon or Forest Hills can compare with her in playing ability. Since Mlle Lenglen showed how tennis can be played, there has been a marked rise in the standard of women's tennis, but no one has yet equaled her mastery and skill.

Unconsciously, I compare other matches that I play with the Lenglen one, and use it as a yardstick of measurement. To me, of course, at the time, with my game at the point where it might improve or cease to improve, the lesson was a most opportune one, and I feel that I learned things in that one match, as I said before, which have stuck with me ever since.

The match – the actual playing part of it – may be called uneventful, with the exception of one incident – at least from the point of view of the onlooker. The reason being that the white ball went back and forth, back and forth. Neither player did anything out of the ordinary, such as scolding ball boys or arguing with the linesmen. The comedy of the match was supplied by a eucalyptus tree that grew at the end of the court just behind the backstop. It was partly trimmed off, so that its shadows would not fall on the court, but in the leaves that were left were hidden more small boys than you would have believed possible. At intervals they fell out, or were dragged down by red-faced gendarmes who disturbed the peace more than the boys.

Several roofs of surrounding houses might have given way because of the unaccustomed weight of people, but did not. Americans, who were present in large numbers, clapped for their player, and the French for theirs. Patriotism holds true to form at a tennis match. I do not know which player the English onlookers wanted to have win. Perhaps they clapped for the ball itself, in the interests of pure sport.

From the eucalyptus-tree end of the court there were distractions, but both players were equally handicapped – perhaps Mlle Lenglen more than I, because of her highly strung nature. A crowd of people from the town, unwilling to buy tickets, pressed against the backstop at one time and threatened to knock it over. Mlle Lenglen, who was nearest, with a few sharp words, stilled the commotion. There was only one unusual incident in the play itself. Toward the end of the second set, Mlle Lenglen needed only one more point to win the match. I sent over a ball down the line on her backhand that she thought was outside. She moved forward to the net and held out her hand for the final handshake. I thought, seeing her do this, that the match was over, so I went forward to the net too. Linesmen rose from their chairs and moved over to the court. Suddenly the voice of the Englishman on the line – Lord Hope – was heard at the end of the court. He said, 'The ball was good! I did not call "out." ' Then a number of people became excited. Some thought that Mlle Lenglen would become upset and play badly, after the surprise of finding that she had not yet won the match, after all. But Mlle Lenglen remained calm. This incident, better than any, shows that she was a truly splendid match player.

After our second handshake – for she won the second set a few games after this unusual incident – Mlle Lenglen was immediately surrounded, where she sat on a chair by the umpire's stand, with crowds of linesmen and officials. She was weeping, now that the match was over. Above the heads of the circle about her was passed a great bouquet of American beauty roses.

So interested was I in the hubbub and general mass of gesticulating people who surrounded Mlle Lenglen that I did not become aware, until some moments later, that I was standing entirely alone on the court. Turning my thoughts upon myself, I found that I did not feel so sad as I really should have, but at the same time I began to feel rather overcome at being in the middle of the court by myself. Then suddenly a young man whom I had met a few days before vaulted over the balustrade from the grandstand at the side of the court and came over to me. He said, 'You played awfully well.' It was Mr Moody.

Saturday Evening Post, 1933

Two Queens
FERDINAND TUOHY

Some spectacles will remain forever, even in a newspaperman's mind. Such a one was that of Suzanne Lenglen, lying on a bed on the sixth floor of the Carlton Hotel here at noon today, directly after her grueling victory over Helen Wills, 6–3, 8–6, in a simple game of tennis, yet a game which made continents stand still and was the most important sporting event of modern times exclusively in the hands of the fair sex.

A few minutes before, I had left her enthroned in a flowery bower in the middle of the tennis court, like a Broadway favorite after a successful first night. From a balcony high above the Mediterranean, I next glimpsed her being swept along a side street by a frantically cheering mob. Then she lay before me in complete whiteness of coat and skirt, capped by her vivid crimson face.

Only Mme Lenglen moved about the room, arranging gifts of dolls and flowers above the furor still arising from the street, as I asked Suzanne how she had won, and waited while she gasped back to breath and then broke into a torrent of French, openly, perhaps challengingly, as if to say, 'Now, for God's sake, will you English and Americans leave me alone for a moment and accept my supremacy, however much it may be getting boresome!'

In fact, I believe she said something very like that, though her first frantic thoughts were for her stricken father at Nice, while I fought with time to capture every notion, opinion, thought and reaction from the victor of Europe. Nor was Suzanne silent. She rebelled against being forced to play; maintained the champion's right to do what she pleases; explained away her indifferent display by her private worry and the public din during the match; developed praise for her rival, though somewhat grudgingly; and concluded on the defiant note that she, Suzanne, intended to remain enthroned for many years more.

With difficulty I dragged from the prostrate girl such grim little verbal bouquets as 'Helen showed more intelligence than I imagined. She has style and production of strokes. She will improve.'

Yet none of this – not even Helen's splendid drives and placings – worried Suzanne, according to Suzanne. A little more magnanimity might have issued from that white couch and its palpitating burden, and with little damage to the truth of the day, as most of those present saw it.

'*Elle se defende, la petite*,' said a French spectator of our amazing court-side champion.

'What a game Helen is putting up,' echoed the serried Anglo-Saxon brigade. 'She'll have her yet.'

Suzanne, too, played like a champion. For many games in the memorable second set she fell steadily behind, yet she overhauled the challenger, to win fresher than Helen, and this afternoon the French girl gave one of the luckiest performances ever seen on a tennis court when she was carried, in collapsing state, to victory with Didi Vlasto in the women's doubles over Miss Wills and Helene Contostavlos. She is absolutely all in and is cancelling tonight's celebration held here in her honor.

Since eight in the morning the entire social register of the Riviera, linked by a goodly slice of the Almanac de Gotha and Debrett, had been fighting their way to the Carlton courts in one long procession of automobiles stretching out along the Nice and Monte Carlo road. And for three hours we sat there in the bleachers, 4,000 strong, just as when we were waiting for Dempsey and Carpentier, laughing hysterically at each trivial incident – as when chic women trod the skyline transparently on the rooftops or when the gendarmes engaged in arboreal pursuits in trying to compel the young locals to descend from the branches of trees.

Then each celebrity would be hailed on his entry as at a first night, and perilous jokes would be cracked anent the building of stands, which went on beneath us until Suzanne sent her first service over. At that moment one surely never beheld such a vivid rainbow effect beneath a blazing sun as was afforded by hundreds of the smartest women of Europe all assembled in their Helen and Suzanne frocks especially ordered for the occasion.

Once the game began we ceased to behave. Within we applauded each stroke while the rally still proceeded, cheering frantically when Helen excelled, while without, a thousand-strong company of locals rooted through the uplifted draping of Suzanne and France. From hotel windows and roofs hundreds of yards away little figures signaled their participation in the contest by waving handkerchiefs and flags at each point.

Repeatedly, poor susceptible Suzanne implored for calm, only for the turmoil to break out anew, sending her almost down in defeat before the outwardly unperturbed but inwardly quivering little poker face.

Then when the battle was at the tensest moment came the errors of linesmen, giving three outs against Miss Wills, all of which were in, and ending in letting Suzanne think she had won the match before she actually had. As events turned out, Helen proceeded to win two more games before the end. Upon this, of course, the dukes and movie men invaded the court one and all, and the limp and gasping Suzanne was held up in the midst of masses of floral offerings.

The Fireside Book of Tennis, 1972

III The Old Guard

Tilden: The American Mountain
TED TINLING

For Big Bill the spring of 1921 represented the sunrise of a glorious era. He was champion of Wimbledon and the US, but had not previously competed in the so-called World championships on hard courts, which were still played at Saint-Cloud on the outskirts of Paris.

On 12 May Tilden, with his friends, Jed and Arnold Jones, sailed from New York to Cherbourg on the then fashionable SS *Mauretania*. Molla Mallory and her friend, the ninth-ranking American, Edith Sigourney, travelled separately, and they all met for a romantic spring amid the flowering chestnut trees of Paris.

At last Tilden enjoyed the rewards of his long years of hard work. The highest authorities of the French Tennis Federation treated him like some sort of god. Soon after their arrival Tilden introduced the Jones's to Suzanne at the Racing Club, and thereafter there were ceremonial lunches each day at which the crowned heads of tennis, Lenglen and Tilden, placed side by side at the top table on every occasion, were the subject of formal eulogies.

After five days at sea and two weeks in Paris the Americans were still complaining of not having found their land legs. Their practice matches were so much below form that the whole party decided to drown their sorrows in a visit to the Folies Bergères. History records that Tilden was 'reluctant' to go. Nevertheless, everyone was in much better form the next day.

On 27 May, Suzanne was again Tilden's lunchtime neighbour and, with all the speeches and the hilarity, she allowed herself to be drawn into a one-set challenge in singles with Tilden.

The French were so impressed by Tilden's presence they would only let him practise on their centre court, a unique honour at Saint-Cloud. Suzanne and Tilden played their challenge set there, 'amid a great furor'.

Not one to be upstaged, even by an Empress in her own country, Tilden inflicted an ignominious 6–0 defeat on Suzanne. On being asked the result afterwards in the dressing room, Suzanne, always the star of stars, replied elusively, 'Someone won 6–0, but I don't recall who it was.'

In revenge, Suzanne immediately challenged Tilden to play the next day with his protégé, Arnold Jones, against her and Max Decugis, eight times French champion. She realized it would be degrading for two men to lose to a mixed-doubles team. The rivalry between Suzanne and Tilden, which was to become so deeply antagonistic very soon afterwards, had already been set in motion, and Suzanne assured her vindication by beating Tilden and Jones with a one-set, 6–4 victory.

Suzanne's vindication turned out to be all the more impressive because Tilden and young Arnold fought their way through several internationally known doubles teams to reach the semi-finals of the World championships, against the top French team of André Gobert and William Laurentz.

Tilden beat the Belgian champion, Jean Washer, in the singles final. But, with the social rounds and the strain of completing his triple victories of Wimbledon, Forest Hills, and Paris, he developed a serious attack of boils and spent two weeks recovering in hospital.

While the English were falling in love with Tilden, and Americans were at last forced to show him the respect he thought he deserved, Tilden was becoming infatuated with yet another protégé. This time it was an amusing twenty-one-year-old from South Africa. Brian Norton, or 'Babe', as Tilden nicknamed him, with fair hair and an impish face, was originally just a raw South African boy. But he was a fine natural player and a born show-off. In these respects he was a miniature of Tilden himself.

Norton revelled in the fame and attention his tennis brought him, but his apparently romantic association with Tilden was the spark that really lit up his talent. For a few short years Tilden made him an international celebrity. This relationship produced one of the most controversial matches ever seen at Wimbledon, when Tilden defended his title against Norton in the 1921 challenge round.

In accordance with the system operating before 1922, Tilden, as current champion, had to sit around for two weeks waiting for a challenger to emerge from the 'all-comers' event, and this could not have helped his condition. Incidentally, he declared from the outset his challenger would be Norton.

Because of his physical condition, Tilden did not enter the men's doubles with either of his protégés, Norton or Jones, and only survived two rounds of mixed doubles with Molla Mallory. Thus, before the challenge round, Tilden played only three matches in four weeks, and Wallis Merrihew recounts that he had still not 'regained his wind' when the time came for the eventual confrontation with Norton.

The Wimbledon referee, F. R. Burrow, who had attended every Wimbledon championship since 1886, told me the public's behaviour at that match was the most disgraceful he ever saw. Norton won the first two sets and in desperation Tilden started to drop-shot. At one moment he played three untouchable drop shots in four points. A section of the crowd began to voice its disapproval of Tilden's tactics and the situation reached boiling point when a spectator rose in his seat, shouting, 'Play the game, Tilden!' Arguments broke out among spectators until they were strongly admonished by the umpire.

At one stage, parts of the crowd were so anti-Tilden, Big Bill told the umpire that if the spectators could not be controlled, he would leave the court. Norton, jumping to the defence of his mentor, said that if anyone was going to retire from the match, it would be he. Clearly Norton had a deep infatuation for Tilden, and it is widely accepted that 'Babe' deliberately threw the next two sets. The throwing of whole sets amazed and disgusted the Wimbledon spectators, who had never seen anything like this before in their gentlemanly game. Norton obviously felt his idol was being disgraced and their relationship could be destroyed as a result.

It has been suggested that Norton could never bring himself to defeat Tilden. This theory is probably correct, but in the fifth set Norton nevertheless returned to the attack and led 4–2 and 5–4, reaching double match-point.

The first match-point produced one of the strangest incidents of all. Tilden chanced a daring drive to Norton's sideline. The ball looked to be sailing out, but fell dead on the line. Tilden followed his shot to the net, but not, as Norton supposed, to volley. In reality, Tilden had resigned himself to the fact that his shot missed the line and was running forward to congratulate Babe. He had even transferred his racquet to his left hand.

Did Norton realize? At all events, he tried a difficult passing shot and missed. Thus reprieved, Tilden made short work of the second match-point with an ace and went on, in two quick games, to retain his title. The final scores were 4–6, 1–6, 6–1, 6–0, 7–5.

Sixty-two years have now elapsed since this unfathomed mystery but, by many accounts, the match held an unusual and strange quality throughout. I have known several connoisseurs who were present and all accepted the fact that a psychological, probably homosexual, relationship affected the result. Merrihew described this last Wimbledon challenge round, which took place on 2 July 1921, saying, 'It will always remain one of the great enigmas of tennis.'

The year 1921 saw the last of many old traditions on which lawn tennis had been raised: the last Wimbledon championships at Worple Road; the last challenge round; the end of the vicarage-garden-party atmosphere. In 1919 the advent of Suzanne had outdated Worple Road overnight, and the ovations for Tilden the following year confirmed its legitimate demise. Suzanne's startling debut caused five thousand applications for the five hundred bookable seats and the Wimbledon Committee decided forthwith to commission an architect to design a 'grand new stadium' on a larger site. By 1921 the excitement of Lenglen plus Tilden overtaxed to bursting point the Worple Road seating capacity of seven thousand. The committee must have been relieved that the following year the new stadium would provide for seventeen thousand spectators on the Centre Court alone.

Another feature of 1921 was the deep rivalry that developed between Suzanne and Bill. Lenglen and Tilden both had the same strong drive for success, the same extraordinary instinct for showmanship, and the same reading of public taste. Both also had boundless technical knowledge of the game, induced by determination to excel and an unbelievable capacity for practice. Tilden actually invented strokes never previously conceived. To this day, his book *Match Play and the Spin of the Ball* remains the outstanding masterpiece of technical tennis analysis.

Meanwhile Suzanne became such a dominating figure that the world was automatically her stage. Everything she did was scrutinized in detail by the world press. She did not need to seek adulation. Tilden, however, had to draw attention to himself, and did. I remember Tilden once becoming infuriated and stopping an entire match because he noticed a woman spectator in the second row repairing her make-up from her compact. This upset Big Bill mostly because she was not concentrating on him. The excuse for his anger was that the reflection from her mirror was distracting him.

Suzanne's pride of performance also stood in direct contrast to Tilden's in that she regarded it as the ultimate sin to miss a shot. Bill, in his prime, would throw a whole set for the sole purpose of showing spectators how he could then demean his opponent at will.

When I played Tilden on the Riviera in 1930 I took one game in the first set and three in the second. There is not the slightest doubt that if he had wished to beat me 6–0, 6–0, he could have. I remember praying that his flat first serve would come in because there was a chance of blocking this back. His second serve kicked from outside my right foot to well over my left ear, and even on soft clay courts many good players found this impossible to handle.

It was inevitable there should be clashes between Lenglen and Tilden. I do not believe Suzanne ever felt the same degree of antagonism toward Big Bill as he toward her. Possibly Tilden felt the enormous publicity given to Lenglen's bandeau upstaged the almost equal publicity his 'woolly bear' sweaters were attracting. Tennis clothing has always caused out-of-proportion emotions with the British press and the spectators, and Bill seemed to dress for maximum effect.

From 1921 on Tilden never passed up an opportunity to denigrate Suzanne in public or in conversation. At the same time he never missed the chance of backing Molla Mallory in her feud with Suzanne, culminating in his famous brainwashing session before her historic match against Suzanne at Forest Hills in 1921.

One aspect that Suzanne and Tilden had in common was a special magnetism that caused other great personalities to want to watch them. Just as Suzanne's audiences invariably included kings, rajahs, and international tycoons, Tilden always attracted the queens of Broadway and Hollywood. Tallulah Bankhead was a great Tilden devotee. I remember during his Wimbledon semi-final against René Lacoste in 1928, Tallulah chewed a pink rose down to the thorns in sheer nervous excitement as Tilden lost in five sets.

In 1921, after winning Wimbledon for the second time, Tilden returned to the States and conducted his activities out of Philadelphia, confining all his tennis to America. At last he had established unanswerable proof that he had brought the US to the summit of men's tennis, and made himself champion of the world. From Philadelphia he looked down and declared that if there were any aspiring Mohammeds around they would have to come to the American Mountain.

The American Mountain remained impregnable for six years, during which Tilden led the US Davis Cup team to victory every year, and won no fewer than forty-two consecutive matches in the US national singles.

He was the absolute monarch in what is now called the Golden Age of Sports. On the courts he was the complete autocrat, and away from them he indulged a luxurious life-style that he considered appropriate to his status. From tournament organizers he demanded only the best in travel, hotel accommodation, and food, but they knew Tilden's name kept the turnstiles clicking merrily and most often obliged. Tilden did what pleased him and did it when he wanted to, trampling on tournament committees and officials in general. Above all, he incurred the wrath of the Establishment, which continually tried to make him toe its line.

But in America of the 1920s 'Tilden and Tennis', in that order, was the catchphrase always associated with the game. Whether or not he was homosexual, whether or not he antagonized people with his abrasive manner, I have still to meet anyone of Tilden's era who would not rather watch him on court than any other player of his time.

The dawning of professionalism in tennis after World War I brought an unprecedented set of problems because the majority of the leading administrators of the game were volunteers. The very essence of the words volunteer and professional implies contradictions in schools of thought. Long before the revolutionary period in tennis in the late 1960s, Tilden on the one hand and Lenglen on the other indulged in almost day-to-day confrontations with the USTA and the French Federation. The professional postures already adopted by Tilden and Lenglen in the 1920s, when both were theoretically amateurs, put the American and French Establishments in a state of shock.

Money, of course, was considered the villain of the piece by the adminis-trators, but considered the just reward for their efforts by the stars. Tilden is said to have spurned outwardly the 'taint' of monetary reward for playing tennis. However, he thoroughly enjoyed writing for the press as an ego trip and it seems that he did not refuse the considerable sums the newspapers offered to stars in those days. Lenglen naturally had her share, though she never considered it a fair share. The administrators, as volunteer protectors of the amateur code, considered both Tilden and Lenglen as something close to criminals for earning anything whatever from their tennis.

In My Story, written by Tilden five years before his death, he says, 'I must own to a special dislike of amateur sports officials.' One way and another the mutual recriminations between all concerned never let up until Suzanne and Big Bill decided to become 'legitimate' professionals; Suzanne in 1926; and Tilden in 1930.

So Bill, arrogant and single-minded, fought the Establishment continually through his amateur days in the 1920s. Throughout this period he had a running feud with the 'strong man' of the USTA, Julian (Mike) Myrick, who had been trying unsuccessfully to gag him for years. Myrick and Tilden were so polarized in their thinking that they were constantly at each other's throats. The US authorities were also scared that the original effete image of American men's tennis that they had been at such pains to obliterate since its pioneer days, could be revived by the world's No. 1 player projecting a homosexual aura.

The bitter feud came to boiling point in 1928. While I was watching Tallulah Bankhead nibble her pink rose down to the stem at Wimbledon, Tilden was reporting regularly for the American press on the championships. On learning of Tilden's defiance of the rule that precluded players from writing about events in which they were still competing, the US authorities finally suspended him on the eve of the 1928 Davis Cup semifinal against Italy, scheduled to take place in Paris. Beating Italy was considered a formality for the Americans, so that the controversy really centred about the final round against France. France, with its Four Musketeers – Brugnon, Borotra, Cochet, and Lacoste – ready to defend the Cup for the first time since toppling Tilden in Philadelphia the previous year, were shocked and amazed when Tilden's suspension was announced.

First, the French had just completed their new Roland Garros Stadium in Paris and were relying on Tilden's box-office power to help pay for it. Second, they could not believe anyone in his right senses could be so uncommercial as to suspend his top star performer. The French, on receiving absolute refusal to cooperate from the USTA, appealed in the first place to their own Department of Foreign Affairs, the Quai d'Orsay. This meant, in effect, the controversy would soon reach the Secretary of State in Washington.

In the days following, the cables between Washington and the Quai d'Orsay resembled a ping-pong game. Eventually, the US Ambassador in Paris, Myron T. Herrick, fortunately a sportsman himself, realized that though time was short, no real progress was being made. Through his personal efforts the case finally came to the President of the United States. This was no storm in a teacup.

Herrick clearly advised that in the circumstances, Tilden's absence from the American team would seriously damage American/French diplomatic relations. This was not the first time a President of the United States felt obliged to intervene in Tilden's squabbles with the USTA, who were incapable of considering the country's international relations. Tilden was unpopular at home and the American tennis Establishment was never willing to admit that abroad Tilden was a fine ambassador of goodwill for his country. In 1921 USTA president and tough guy, Mike Myrick, had refused Tilden's conditions for going to Europe, but President Harding intervened personally and overruled Myrick.

In 1928, again on behalf of international relations, President Coolidge put pressure on the USTA, at the same time giving Ambassador Herrick an unofficial nod from the White House. Eventually it was the Ambassador himself who renominated Tilden to the team. Herrick did an on-the-spot deal with Tilden to go ahead if he would take the consequences later.

Big Bill won the only match of the challenge round for the United States. Roland Garros was packed to overflowing and the USTA derived considerably more money from the box office than if Tilden had not appeared.

Meanwhile, within the minds of the tennis Establishment, rules were rules, discipline was discipline, and Tilden was suspended for the rest of the year.

By a curious twist of fate Lenglen and Tilden simultaneously created a new concept of tennis, their stardom attracting thousands of young players from areas never previously exposed to the game. Just as curiously, the lights of both were dimmed within months of each other in 1926; Lenglen's by her tragic exit from Wimbledon; and Tilden's in New York, where he experienced his first-ever loss to Jean Borotra. On that day Borotra became the first European to dent the glory that was American tennis and Tilden.

Tilden was then thirty-four, and before the year's end two of the other Musketeers, René Lacoste and Henri Cochet, were to beat him in major American events. Lacoste beat him in a Davis Cup match for the first time and Cochet dethroned him in his own kingdom of the American singles championship.

In 1926 three of the four Musketeers dominated the semi-finals at Forest Hills and the final was all-French. The coming of the Frenchmen was an ominous danger sign for Big Bill.

But it was to spark a new challenge.

Tinling: Sixty Years in Tennis, 1983

Lacoste Defeats Tilden in US Final
ALLISON DANZIG

For the first time in the forty-six years' history of the tournament, the national tennis championship was won by a foreign player a second time yesterday when Jean René Lacoste of France retained the title which he succeeded to last year after the six-year reign of William T. Tilden 2d of Philadelphia had been brought to an end by Henri Cochet, another Frenchman.

In one of the greatest struggles that ever brought the championship to a conclusion, the twenty-three-year-old Parisian triumphed over Tilden in three sets, frustrating the hopes of the American of equaling the record of seven victories established by Richard D. Sears and marking the first time that Tilden has failed to win a set from Lacoste in their many meetings on turf courts. The score was 11–9, 6–3, 11–9.

Close to two hours, an hour and fifty-three minutes to be exact, was required for a decision in this titanic struggle between the player who formerly stood as the invincible monarch of the courts and the youth who had succeeded to his position. Many a five-set match has been finished in far less time than that, but no five-set struggle that Tilden has lost or saved with one of his dramatic climbs to unassailable heights under stress has surpassed yesterday's harrowing battle between age and youth in the desperateness of the conflict and its appeal to the emotions, or in the magnificent quality of the play.

A gallery of 14,000 spectators, a gallery that packed the Forest Hills stadium to the last seat and that stood at the top of the last tier and in every other available space, looked down upon this terrific struggle, and at the end it knew that it had been privileged to see one of the most ennobling fights a former champion ever made to regain his crown.

Tilden, in the years of his most ruthless sway, was never a more majestic figure, never played more upon the heart-strings of a gallery than he did yesterday as he gave the last ounce of his superb physique to break through a defense that was as enduring as rock, and failed; failed in spite of the fact that he was three times at set point in the first chapter, in spite of the fact that he led at 3–1 in the second set, and once again in spite of the fact that he held the commanding lead of 5–2 in the third set and was twice within a stroke of taking this chapter.

He failed because youth stood in the balance against him – youth in the person of an untiring sphinx that was as deadly as fate in the uncanny perfection of his control, who assimilated the giant Tilden's most murderous swipes and cannonball serves as though they were mere pat balls and who made such incredible saves as to have broken the spirit of nine men out of ten.

But the spirit of Tilden was one thing that never broke. Long before the end of the match, yes, by the end of that agonizing first set which had the gallery cheering Tilden madly and beseeching him to put over the one vital stroke that was lacking, those marvelous legs of the Philadelphian were slowing up.

By the second set the fires of his wrathful forehanders were slumbering, and the third set found him a drooping figure, his head slunk forward, so utterly exhausted that not even the pitchers of ice water that he doused over himself could stimulate his frayed nerves, which must have ached painfully.

It was a spectacle to have won the heart of the most partisan French protagonist, the sight of this giant of the courts, once the mightiest of the mighty, flogging on his tired body in the unequal battle between youth and age. If there were any French partisans present, they did not make themselves known. One and all those 14,000 spectators were heart and soul for Tilden as he made his heroic fight to prevent the last of the world's biggest tennis crowns go the way of all crowns.

If they cheered him in the first set, if they raised the roof when he gained his lead of 3–1 in the second chapter and again when he slashed his way ahead at 5–2 in the third, the din was nothing compared to the ovation Tilden received when, later on in the final chapter, the Philadelphian came back like a man from the grave to save himself from defeat twice by a single point in the fourteenth game. That game was one of the most agonizing a tennis gallery ever sat through as a shell of a man staved off the inevitable by a classic exhibition of fighting entirely on nerve.

The gallery, hopelessly in the despond as the machine-like Lacoste pulled up from 2–5 to 5–all and then to 7–6, took one despairing look at the drooping figure of Tilden as Lacoste began to serve, and resigned itself to seeing the end. In spite of the fact that the American steeled himself and sent the ball back like rifle fire, he could make no impression against a youth who dug his chops out of the ground and made the most heartbreaking gets of his cannonball drives.

So Lacoste reached 40–30, one point away from victory. The suspense was terrific as the next rally began, and when Tilden pulled up to deuce on Lacoste's out, a sigh of relief went up. But the next moment Lacoste was again at match point as Tilden failed to return safely.

Again the French youth netted at the crucial point and the game went on and on until finally, after deuce had been called the fifth time, Lacoste drove out and Tilden whipped home a lightning drive down the line for the game.

How they cheered Tilden! And when he went on to win the fifteenth game at 4–1, with his cannonball service, to lead at 8–7, the crowd was fairly wild with delight. Visions arose again of victory for him, at least in this set, but they speedily vanished when Lacoste won the next two games, breaking through in the seventeenth as Tilden lost all control.

Once more the American aroused the gallery to a wild pitch when he broke through for a love game with two placements, but that was the end. Dead on his feet, Tilden fought Lacoste tooth and nail in the nineteenth, which finally went to the younger player at 8–6, as he scored on three placements in a row, and then, utterly at the end of his rope, he yielded quickly in the twentieth through his errors, to bring the match to an end.

It was a match, the like of which will not be seen again soon. As an exposition of the utmost daring and brilliancy of shot-making and equally of the perfect stage to which the defense can be developed, it has had few equals in the history of tennis.

On the one side of the net stood the perfect tactician and most ruthless attacker the game probably has ever seen, master of every shot and skilled in the necromancy of spin. On the other side was the player who has reduced the defense to a mathematical science; who has done more than that, who has developed his defense to the state when it becomes an offense, subconscious in its working but none the less effective in the pressure it brings to bear as the ball is sent back deeper and deeper and into more and more remote territory.

Both exponents of the attack and the defense were at their best yesterday, and the reaction of the gallery at the end was that it had seen the best that tennis can offer. As one of the spectators remarked, everything else will seem stale after this match. He had seen the zenith.

The defensive player won, but in no small measure it was because youth was on his side. As perfect as was Lacoste's defense, Tilden still might well have prevailed through the sheer magnificence of his stroking had not fatigue set in and robbed him of the strength to control his shots.

In the first set, when Tilden led at 7–6 and 40–love on his own service, it was his errors that robbed him of his big chance. His cannonball service failed him at this critical point, though it was only by a hair that he failed to put over an ace for the set, and when Tilden cannot put over an ace in a pinch he is usually tired.

Had the American put over that one point for which the gallery begged there is no telling who would have won the match. With the first set in the bag he could have loafed through the second and saved himself entirely for the third. Instead he had to keep going in the second, and while he switched from a driving to a chopping game that did not take so much out of him, still the strain was too much for him.

The day has passed when Tilden can maintain a burning pace for two full sets. He knows that as well as the next man, and so he plans his campaign to go 'all out' in the first, coast in the second and come back strong in the third, relying upon the rest period to regenerate the dynamo for the fourth.

Had he won the first and relaxed in the second, it is hardly conceivable that he could have failed to make good his 5–2 lead in the third, which would have given him a 2–1 lead to work on after the intermission, with the psychological advantage on his side.

However, even had Tilden won the first set, it may be presuming too much to concede that he would have gone on to victory in the third. After all, this twenty-three-year-old Lacoste is a wonder, a miracle-worker, and he might have stopped even a rampant Tilden at 5–2.

There are moments when Lacoste has had bad spells, when he is human, if to err is human, but those moments are rarer than an American victory over France. When he is in the hole and sets himself to the task, such moments are practically non-existent. You can drive away at him all the day long, mix chops, slices, drives and volleys in a mad melange, run him to the corners until he is dizzy, and always you get nothing for your pains but the chance to hit the ball again. It always comes back like no champion ever does.

The gallery, as partisan as it was, as whole-heartedly as it favored Tilden, could not help but be carried away by the incredible feats of Lacoste. Unmindful of the cheers for his opponent, playing a lone hand, the youthful invader concentrated upon his work and kept the ball in play – kept it in play when Tilden was sending his terrific service straight at him, kept it in play when he had to scramble to the far corners of the court for a blistering drive to his backhand, and kept it in play when the American was loading his shots with such heavy spin that a spoon would have been needed by any other player to dig it out of the turf.

A defense so impregnable as that, a defense which confounded all of Tilden's ingenuity as he brought all of his artifices to bear, along with his devastating speed and power, should have undermined the morale of any opponent. That Tilden stuck to his guns and fought on as he has seldom fought before, in spite of the fact that he was on his last legs, while his adversary was flitting nimbly about the court on his toes, is to the American's glory.

In victory Tilden was never more magnificent a figure than he was yesterday in defeat, and Lacoste, in his years of triumph, was never greater than he was in the victory at Forest Hills.

Jean Borotra, Lacoste's team-mate, who seldom before has been heard to extol the merits of his compatriots, could only shake his head at the end. 'If René keeps on playing tennis like that,' he said, 'how is any one ever going to beat him?'

With the French and American championships both in his possession and victories to his credit over both Tilden and Johnston in the Davis Cup challenge round, the twenty-three-year-old Parisian stands as the unchallenged monarch of the courts, the pride of France and her hope for a continuation of her sweeping success in the future.

All the honors belong to her. She has the Davis Cup, Cochet has the Wimbledon championship and Lacoste has the French and the American indoor and outdoor championships. What else is there to say, except that the season is over, and the French will all be back in the United States again after the Davis Cup challenge round matches in Paris in July?

The Fireside Book of Tennis, 1972

My Matches against Helen Wills Moody
HELEN JACOBS

My first national championship singles encounter with Helen Wills occurred in the 1927 tournament at Forest Hills. I think it may be said that she had reached the top of her form in that year. Driving with the same fury that marked her game in the Wimbledon final in July, when she won her first world's championship from Lili d'Alvarez (without the loss of a set), she seemed content to remain in the backcourt, hammering the ball relentlessly to the corners, alternating line drives with fast-dropping crosscourt shots. Seldom did she go to the net, depending largely upon lobs to offset the advantage of the net player against her. Although a recapitulation of the match showed that I earned more points than she, her errors were negligible in comparison with mine as I overhit the lines in an effort to match her length.

I had watched Helen often in practice against men in Berkeley. Most of them were able to defeat her without much trouble when they took to the net against her, played the drop shot [and] drew her to the net, where she was not naturally agile, very imaginative, or subtle with the volley. That, I knew, was the only game that could win from her; all the women players with skillful volleys and overhead knew this to be true. The difficulty was in making the opening to get to the net, for, aware of her limitations in that position, Helen had perfected a defense against the volleyer that required on the part of her opponent a baseline game as sound as the net game.

To play Helen Wills was to play a machine. There was little if any conversation, no joviality, and to this the gallery obviously reacted, becoming almost grim in its partisanship. The press had long since confused incompatibility with the elements of a 'feud' in our matches, which became less agreeable to both of us as they inevitably occurred. I remember no laughter from the crowded stands, though admiring applause was often thunderous. Thus, one had a feeling, would one watch the Derby at Churchill Downs, some hoping for the favorite to win, others hoping that the challenger would come through. Helen Wills fought on the court much as Gene Tunney fought in the ring – with implacable concentration and undeniable skill but without the color or imagination of a Dempsey or a Lenglen.

Matches against her were fun only in the sense of the satisfaction that one derives from pitting one's skill against the champion's. Most of Helen's opponents whom I knew well and played often had the same impression. Yet all had the greatest admiration for her game, and if the indomitable quality of her match play could only be sustained by concentration that must exclude every possibility of diversion, that was her business, for it is the undeniable purpose of champions to win.

Helen defeated me in my first American championship final, 6–2, 6–1, in 1928. My only consolation was that I won half as many points in the first set as she did and a little better than half as many in the second, and that I had been beaten by a player who had not lost a set in her triumphant march to the English and United States singles titles. To say that Helen Wills was pre-eminent, actually unchallenged, in the world of women's tennis would be redundant. She stood head and shoulders above the field. Though the challenger might fight to the last ditch, she was invariably exhausted by rallies that might be prolonged to prodigious lengths if necessary or, at the least evidence of her faltering, concluded in merciless style.

In the spring of 1929, the United States Lawn Tennis Association announced that a team would be sent to Europe for a series of international matches. The team was to consist of Helen Wills and a partner of her choosing. In this year I was ranked second in the American lists and fully expected to be invited to join the team for the tour that would have seasoned my game tremendously. Instead, however, Helen selected Edith Cross, thereby creating almost as much controversial discussion as that which was to follow our match in 1933. I could see no justification for the decision, nor could I understand the Tennis Association's acquiescence in it, considering the fact that it customarily chose its own teams.

Though I missed out on that trip, a group of San Francisco and East Bay tennis enthusiasts, who felt as I did on the subject, sent me to England for the Wimbledon championships, where Helen and I met in the final. Our match was a repetition of the final at Forest Hills in 1928. Everything written about one would apply to the other; the same can be said of my 1930 final against her in the French championships. I had not acquired the finesse to defeat Helen Wills at Wimbledon. Neither of us played in the American championships in 1930, and I did not have the chance to play her at Forest Hills in 1932, for she did not compete that year . . .

The 1933 season saw Helen extended to defend her title successfully in the Wimbledon final against Dorothy Round. She was forced to three sets for the first time since her initial victory in 1927. I played her that year in the final of the American championship. No tennis match within memory except the Lenglen–Mallory second-round match at Forest Hills in 1921 had quite such unpleasant repercussions as this one; none, I am sure, was more trying to both contestants.

There had been some doubts as to the value of my winning my first national championship in 1932, when, as I have written, Helen did not defend her title though she had won Wimbledon for the fifth time in July. With the opening of the 1933 season, it was considered almost certain that my reign as singles champion of my country would be short-lived; this, of course, in view of Helen's almost certain entry in the championships. A final match between us at Forest Hills was anticipated with much speculation – our supporters aligned vehemently against each other . . .

Helen was trying for her eighth championship, having, by this summer of 1933, held the title in 1923, 1924, 1925, 1927, 1928, 1929, and 1931. I was defending a title won only one year before, and perhaps the more precious for that reason.

The gallery was not a particularly large one the day we played – a midweek match, and uncertain weather, in addition to my tournament record against Helen Wills, were undoubtedly responsible. The day brought perfect tennis weather – no wind, not too hot – a day for exploiting all the shots Suzanne Lenglen had advocated: shots requiring accurate touch and little deflection by wind. It was also the ideal day for the volleyer who disliked more than anything else the drive that cannot be truly gauged or the lob that is pulled down toward the player by a sudden gust of wind.

I had determined that in this match I would go to the net at every opportunity. There was little sense standing in the backcourt swapping drives with anyone as superlative as Helen in that department. Of course, a net game was not enough of itself, but I had more confidence in my forehand than I had felt in years and was certain that it would stand up against the pounding I could anticipate from her, and also help to make the desired openings that would pave the way to the net. My backhand drive had seldom let me down.

It appeared, from the opening of the first set, that Helen was going to play me as she had done in every one of our meetings – playing chiefly to my forehand and, at the first evidence of my being off balance, using the short crosscourt drive to the opposite side. It was, at its best, a devastating placement, which I was determined to prevent. To do this I put everything I could into the force and placement of my service with the intention of drawing Helen out of court for the drive to the opposite side, then going to the net.

The first three games went with service. In the fourth I broke Helen's service, for a 3–1 lead. This lead seemed to inspire her to a stonewall driving defense in which she employed her familiar accuracy of corner placements, coupled with speed and pace. Games went to 3–3 as she broke my service. Then again service held to 6–6. For a while, during this stage of the first set, Helen also was playing for the net position, and it became a question of who would get there first. My backhand drive, particularly down the line, and my volley and overhead were serving me well enough to come within one point of the set at 5–4, but the fine variety of Helen's shots and her punishing steadiness saved the game for her. She was forcing me to hit lobs of difficult depth. Anticipating them, I had practiced smashing on an outside court for some time before the match began, and the practice was certainly justified. Helen Wills' lob can be a formidable weapon.

Breaking her service at 7–6 by the use of sliced drives to the corners and the volley, I ran out the set, 8–6. I had created a record for myself, winning my first set against Helen. It startled the press into wild activity. Typewriters and telegraphic instruments clacked furiously from the marquee. The set encouraged me, proving the wisdom of the net attack, which was certainly my chief weapon, and increasing my confidence in my forehand drive and slice as either aggressive or defensive shots on this day.

But one set was not the match. I had no illusions about the roughness of the road ahead of me. Helen was a fighter; she was a master of the drive and the lob. Her service required constant alertness and careful timing for the return. If I was to win, I must maintain my game at the same level for two more sets, if necessary, and hope that fatigue would impair neither my coordination nor my timing. I did not agree with those who claimed that a woman player could not attack at the net for three sets. In fact, I found it less tiring to go to the net, volley and smash, than to remain in the backcourt covering twice the ground in pursuit of Helen's magnificent drives.

But I had to continue to go to the net, and as the second set opened, it was apparent how difficult the task might become. Winning my service in the opening game, Helen lashed out with blistering drives, varied by deftly placed soft shots that gave her a quick 3–0 lead. With desperate risk, I went to the net on anything close to her backline and was lucky to smash lobs for winners until I drew level at 3–3. Two obviously erroneous decisions against each of us in the next game caused an uproar from the gallery. Right or wrong, they were so patently miscalled at such an important stage in the match that neither of us could resist throwing a point in an attempt to even matters.

A series of drives overreaching the baseline, forced by Helen's deep and paceful drives and her sudden short crosscourt shots, gave her three games running and the set at 6–3.

I was glad of the respite that came at the end of the second set, as I am sure Helen must have been. But she remained on the court, sitting on a chair at the umpire's stand, while I went to the dressing room to refresh myself. When I returned to the court after the ten-minute intermission, Helen opened the third set with service, going to 30–15 in spite of a double fault before I won the game. On my service two unretrievable drives by Helen forced errors from me and she led 0–30. Then, in turn, she overdrove twice, evening the score. A winning volley took me to 40–30, and a netted drive by Helen brought me to 2–0. Helen won the first point of the third game on a forcing service, but forehand and backhand passing shots, successful for me, and a forehand drive beyond the line by Helen gave me the lead at 3–0.

I turned to the ball-boy for the balls, speaking to him once and then again, before I realized that his eyes were fixed on the opposite court. I repeated my request before I turned to see that Helen had walked to the umpire's stand and was reaching for her sweater. It was a confusing moment. I hurried to the stand as Ben Dwight, the venerable umpire, announced that I had won by default. As Helen put on her sweater I went to her.

'My leg is bothering me. I can't go on,' she said.

'Would you like to rest for a while?' I asked.

'No, I can't go on,' she answered.

Officials, press, photographers rushed onto the court. It seemed unnecessary to subject her to this post-match ordeal. 'If you're in pain there's no sense in continuing,' I told her. 'Why don't you leave before the photographers descend on us,' I suggested. Helen left then, escorted from the court by one of the tournament officials.

I went back to the dressing room, where Molla Mallory was waiting for me. A radio commentator had asked her immediately after the match to broadcast a statement on the default in view of her experience with Suzanne Lenglen. She did, in biting terms, and was still full of it when we met.

There is no doubt that Helen, for her own sake, would have been wiser if she had remained on the court for the twelve points necessary for me to end the match in the third set. But what one does under the stress of emotion and pain cannot be calculated in the cold-blooded terms of the spectator. Helen's temperament had always been her most valuable asset. On this day it was her greatest liability.

Before I had finished dressing, Elizabeth Ryan came into the locker room in a state of wild excitement. Helen, her partner in the ladies' doubles, had announced that she would play the doubles final. Knowing the probable reaction of the gallery if she did, Elizabeth was determined to default. Fortunately, one of the officials, who had long been a friend of Helen's, persuaded her that she simply couldn't return to the court after the default.

As far as I was concerned, Forest Hills was real bedlam that day. A stream of reporters was in and out of my apartment until late in the evening; the phone never seemed to stop ringing. 'Would I make a statement?' was a question that fell on my ears like a phonograph record stuck in a groove. There was nothing I could say. Of course, I was disappointed that the match had ended as it did – who wouldn't have been? But that was water over the dam. I had retained my championship and was happy about that. But how could I, how could anyone for that matter, dispute with Helen her statement that she felt on the verge of fainting when she defaulted. The fact that she walked back to her apartment in the Forest Hills Inn and later wanted to play the doubles final did not make her lot any easier with the reporters who knew of it, but I still did not feel that anything except the winning of my match concerned me.

There were repercussions of the match for months to come. The story of its ending was greatly distorted by many reporters, in most instances by those who obviously had not seen it. What I said to Helen was garbled by journalists whose hearing couldn't have extended to the umpire's chair. Some had it that I begged her to go on, the last request it would have occurred to me to make. Some wrote that she refused to shake hands and others that we shook hands, were photographed, and that she was then helped from the court. The truth of the matter is that, although we did not shake hands, Helen did not refuse to do so, nor was she assisted from the court. She left it, as soon as she had donned her sweater, under her own power.

She appeared next in major championship tennis in 1935 at Wimbledon. Beaten by Kay Stammers at the Beckenham tournament while she was again getting her 'tournament legs,' Helen had, with one exception (a three-set match against Fräulein Cepkova in the fourth round), a fairly easy time to the final of the Wimbledon meeting.

We met again, this time on an intensely hot afternoon with a slight breeze blowing. Both of us were playing well, but Helen went to a 3–0 lead in the first set before I could make much of an impression on the match. I believe she has always liked the fast Center Court turf, and she was hitting with wonderful length and great speed. The next three games to me evened the score, then Helen took the set, 6–3. The second set began with a determined net attack by Helen, surprising to anyone who had played her so often. It was only the functioning of my passing shots that enabled me to win this set, 6–3.

Up to this stage the match had not been as scintillating as our Forest Hills final of 1933. To defeat Helen once was to draw forth from her a more wary game; and having defeated her was to emphasize to the opponent the importance of taking chances at every opportunity, of playing boldly from backcourt and net, and yet of maintaining a sound defense and steadiness to match hers – a considerable challenge.

I think there was, in the beginning of the third set (which started without the ten-minute intermission that is customary in this country), some restraint in our hitting. But with the advantage of service, I was able to go to 4–2 and then, as Helen missed an easy smash, to 5–2. Helen won my service for 5–3. It was in that game that I held match point. At 30–15 in my favor, on Helen's service, a questionable sideline decision caused some delay before we could resume play. I hit a drive along Helen's forehand sideline that appeared to be in. Evidently the umpire thought it was in, but the linesman called it out. The umpire questioned the linesman, who repeated his call, and the game went on. With the score at 30–30, I won the next point to move to within one point of the match. After one of the longest rallies I can remember ever having survived, Helen, out of court on her backhand side, put up a shallow lob. The lob appeared to be headed for mid-court. I moved in to hit it, but a gust of wind caught it, pulling it in toward the net. By the time I was able to judge where it could best be hit, it was a short lob, very close to the net. I was almost on my knees for the smash, the ball hit the edge of my racket frame and rolled along the net cord before it fell onto my court.

That was really the end of the match. Though we were at 30–30 and deuce in the eleventh and twelfth games, Helen won the set at 7–5. She had made a magnificent comeback to win her seventh Wimbledon championship. Unfortunately, some widely read members of the press reported what had been an exciting sporting test in such a manner that the so-called feud between us was the highlight of the reports. I, the loser, was represented as accepting defeat with tears in my eyes; Helen was represented as a far more jubilant victor than good taste would have dictated. These reports were so contrary to the facts as to make one wonder if it is not better not to report at all than to report inaccurately. Far from having tears in my eyes after this match with Helen Moody, I had enjoyed the match, for it had been a real test of skill and staying power, of tactics and strategy and nerve. Naturally, one regrets losing any big championship final, but it seems to me an unfair commentary on the behavior of women in competitive sport that it should be necessary, in order to create reader interest, to report the loser in tears and the winner gloating.

It has been my experience during eighteen years of tournament tennis that women are no more given to tears in defeat than men, nor is their enthusiasm in victory more excessive. To claim, even facetiously, that it is, is to lessen public regard for the important place that women have achieved, against immeasurable disadvantages, in all the games that Americans, Europeans and Asiatics love to play.

Gallery of Champions, 1949

The Finest Athlete I Ever Saw
GEORGE LOTT

During the second week of July in the year 1934, I was sitting in the players' section of the Wimbledon Center Court pulling for my friend, Jack Crawford, to beat the daylights out of a cocky Englishman named Fred Perry. An hour and one half later I was still sitting in the players' section, contemplating the drama that had taken place. On that particular day, in that particular match, I had seen the perfectly conditioned athlete play the perfect match.

Perry had the swashbuckling good looks and the air of supreme confidence of a Walter Hagen; the grace and ease of a Joe DiMaggio gathering in a fly ball; the cleverness and agility of a Billy Conn; the brute strength of a Man Mountain Dean; and the skill and know-how of a Tilden. Here was a man who not only possessed but also exhibited the qualities so necessary in a champion, namely, confidence, concentration, condition, co-ordination, courage and fortitude, determination, stamina, quickness and speed.

It was an awe-inspiring exhibition. Perry played many important matches before this one and many after, but I know (and I am sure that Fred also knows) that on this day he reached the peak of his effectiveness. I see Perry from time to time and we always wind up talking about

Fred's 1934 Wimbledon. Ordinarily this would bore me considerably, but it gives me almost as much pleasure to go over the details as it does Fred. I appreciate a champion and on that day I saw one. Then again, during the reminiscences with Fred, while he recounts his victorious march through the field, I occasionally get a word in to the effect that Stoefen and I won the doubles that year, and I receive a 'Righto' from Fred which increases the enjoyment of the memory.

I first came across Perry in 1928 or 1929 when the English Association sent a team to play at Newport, Longwood and Forest Hills. He had a match with John Van Ryn on a side court at Newport. It was a close one and I was quite impressed with this Englishman who didn't seem quite like an Englishman. I thought he was an American with an English accent and a pipe. The accent came naturally but not the pipe. He carried it around unlit because he thought it would make him seem more British – and British was what he wanted to be. In those days English society peered down its nose at anyone who didn't wear the old school tie. Fred's parents were in 'trade' and, consequently, Fred's education did not include Eton or Harrow, which left him outside the inner circle. This class consciousness always annoyed Fred but it acted in his favor; it made him more determined than ever to reach the top. His compatriot and teammate, Bunny Austin, did wear the old school tie and, consequently, was the darling of the English officials and tennis fans. Fred was a new breed of Englishman and, in the end, he won them all with his ability.

In 1931 the United States had a Davis Cup team that looked, on paper, a certain bet to bring back the Cup from France. Our singles players were Ellsworth Vines and Wilmer Allison; John Van Ryn and I were the doubles team. We spent considerable time figuring out how we would defeat the French in the Challenge Round and very little thought was given to the Inter-Zone Final against Great Britain. Our chickens were never hatched and, in a tie that featured Vines' famous lunch of cream of tomato soup, cucumbers, pork chops, vanilla ice cream with chocolate sauce and grapefruit juice, Mr Perry and company took care of us to the tune of 4–1. We were able to salvage only the doubles. Perry won over Vines when Elly collapsed in the heat, but at this point in his career Fred was beginning to 'arrive.' I believe he could have eaten Elly's lunch that day and still won.

After the tie, Fred commented to me that 'your boys seemed very overconfident and they are really not that good, you know.' This observation, while not grammatically perfect, was factually correct. Perry was on the way up and we did not realize it at the time. He had been World Champion at Table Tennis and he knew what it was to be a winner.

Perry finally arrived at or very near the top in the year 1933. He always had a really great forehand, but it was his backhand that had been keeping him back. I used to tell him that he looked like he was swatting a fly when he hit a backhand. He undercut it and even then he did not have much control. Under severe pressure it would give way, but by 1933 he had firmed it up and, while it never reached the efficiency and dispatch of his forehand, it was equal to most occasions. This year he led the British team to a Challenge Round victory over the French, who had held the Cup for six years. To win this tie it was absolutely necessary for Perry to beat Henri Cochet, and in those days it was no easy matter. Cochet was the idol of 15,000 fans and had an equally high standing with all French linesmen (see Wilmer Allison for confirmation). Six games to one in the fifth set was the margin by which Perry won, and a great accomplishment it was. At Forest Hills that year I asked Fred how he did it. Censorship forbids an exact quote, but the gist was that he ran Cochet into the ground until the Frenchman ran out of gas.

For the next three years Fred won two singles in each Challenge Round and firmly established himself as an English hero as well as World Champion. His final Challenge Round record was nine won against one lost. The only loss occurred in 1931 when, after having beaten Vines and Allison in the Inter-Zone Final, he was beaten by Cochet.

Tennis fans occasionally ask me about an all-time world ranking, and when I place Perry in the First Three they are amazed. What is not generally realized is that during a four year span (1933–36) Perry won eight Challenge Round singles matches, three successive Wimbledons (1934–35–36), one French Singles, three US singles (1933, '34 and '36) and, for good measure, one Australian Singles (1934). I know of no player who so dominated the tennis scene over an equal period of time.

When Perry lost in the semi-finals to Allison at Forest Hills, it only confirmed my opinion that I had been watching a champion. Allison beat him handily, and there were rumors galore about Fred's condition. He certainly wasn't the Perry I had seen on so many other occasions. I, being of a curious nature, went to the locker room after the match and waited until the reporters had left. I asked him what happened. No alibis were forthcoming. He simply commented that 'I got the bloody hell beat out of me.' However, I knew for a fact he was lucky to be able to lift his arm high enough to serve.

Fred Perry was a real champion, in spite of the pipe.

The Fireside Book of Tennis, 1972

A Little Bit of Luck
FRED PERRY

I must admit I never thought I'd live to see the day when a statue was put up to the son of a Labour MP inside the manicured grounds of Wimbledon. There will be a few former members of the All England Club and the LTA revolving in their graves at the thought of such a tribute paid to the man they regarded as a rebel from the wrong side of the tennis tramlines.

I am, of course, bowled over by the All England Club's decision to commemorate the fiftieth anniversary of my first Wimbledon win in 1934 by renaming the Somerset Road entrance to the ground the Fred Perry Gates, and honouring me still further by erecting the statue, commissioned from the famous sculptor David Wynne. I can only compare it to the Football Association putting one up for Stanley Matthews at Wembley Stadium, and I'm thrilled to bits.

It shows how we have all mellowed over those fifty years from the days when some elements in the All England Club and the LTA looked down on me as a hot-headed, outspoken, tearaway rebel, not quite the class of chap they *really* wanted to see winning Wimbledon, even if he *was* English. I've mellowed, too. I think I'm very much a leopard who has changed his spots. Looking back fifty years later, I have to concede that I was sometimes a little brash and aggressive about what I regarded as the class-ridden set-up there. But at the time, a young man with my background was bound to feel that snobbery very keenly, and I still get angry about the shabby way I was treated when I won Wimbledon in 1934 – the first Englishman to do it for twenty-five years.

In those days there was no formal presentation of the championship trophy on court. You simply shook hands with your opponent, picked up your gear and walked back to the dressing room. I had beaten the Australian Jack Crawford, and I went for a long soak in the bath to ease my muscles and let the significance of it all sink in with the bathwater. I was the proudest bloke in a bathtub anywhere in England.

Suddenly, out in the dressing room, I overheard the distinctive voice of Brame Hillyard, Club committee man, talking to Crawford. 'Congratulations,' said Hillyard. 'This was one day when the best man didn't win.' I couldn't believe my ears. What about the two previous times I'd beaten him, in the finals of the US and Australian Championships?

Hillyard had brought a bottle of champagne into the dressing room and given it to Jack, whom I so clearly remember having beaten in straight sets not half an hour before. I leapt from the tub, rushed out and, sure enough, found Crawford holding the bottle. True, I hadn't been quite forgotten: there, draped over the back of my seat, was the official acknowledgement of my championship, an honorary All England Club member's tie.

Nobody said, 'Here's your tie, Fred. Welcome to the Club.' Nobody even said, 'Congratulations.' The tie was just dropped there for me to find when I came out of the bath. Instead of Fred J. Perry the champ, I felt like Fred J. Muggs the chimp. The Perry balloon was certainly deflated.

An Autobiography, 1984

iv Money and Tennis

The Show on the Road

FRED PERRY

Whenever I think back about my decision to turn professional I recall the lecture I received on the subject one day from Harpo Marx at the Beverly Hills Tennis Club. Although he was supposed to be the silent one of the famous brothers, Harpo did plenty of talking that day. According to Milton Holmes, who wrote about the incident in *Liberty* magazine, the conversation went like this:

Harpo to Perry: 'You can't buy groceries with glory. Why don't you turn professional now and cash in? There's your opponent [pointing out of the window at Ellsworth Vines, who was giving a lesson]. You and Vines could clean up. It's your greatest chance. Why not grab it?'

Perry: 'I can't let England down.'

Well, that was back in 1934. Now it was 1936 and my stance had shifted. Pops Summers put it in perspective after I beat Von Cramm in the 1936 Wimbledon final. 'What now?' he asked me. 'You've won three in a row and you could perhaps win four. But can you win six? It's got to be three or six.'

Despite those three Wimbledons and the four Davis Cup years, I deeply resented not having been accepted by the officialdom at home. I was from the North Country rather than old-school-tie country, and I didn't get on with Sir Samuel Hoare, the president of the Lawn Tennis Association. Most of my confrontations were with him and certain other members of the LTA hierarchy, or with a couple of committee members at the All England LTC. It was a question of a lack of understanding with 'the Establishment' and I always had the feeling that I was tolerated but not really wanted – I had forced my way in. Maybe I was wrong, but I never bothered with people who didn't want to bother with me. I was simply never part of the Establishment end of British tennis.

I knew exactly what I wanted to do in the sport and how I wanted to do it. Maybe the way I went about it wasn't very flexible, to say the least. I was uncompromising because I was all for getting straight to the point, rather than beating about the bush. It wasn't my style to deal in platitudes and get around two weeks later to something I could have accomplished in five minutes.

Basically, I suppose, I never took the time to understand the people at the LTA and the All England Club, and they never took the time to understand me. So there was always a bit of a confrontation, a rough edge, when we were in contact.

What they failed to understand most of all was the intense pressure that had been on me throughout the previous two years, and in the end I got the feeling that they actually wanted to thwart me rather than help me, although this probably wasn't so.

It was perhaps just their defensive reaction to the threat of losing their top player and three-time Wimbledon champion. It was also, I must admit, a new problem to lose an Englishman to the professional game. The American authorities had been through it, of course, and so had the French with Cochet, but Henri was almost at the end of his career by the time he turned pro, whereas I wasn't.

I think a lot of the antagonism towards me stemmed from the feeling, 'How could an Englishman even be contemplating such a step?' As far as I was concerned, how could an Englishman not contemplate it? In any case, I was married to an American by then and wanted to make my home in California, and perhaps make films. As I've said before, I liked the American way of life. It was freer and easier and the tempo was a bit faster. But what I particularly liked (and still like) about America is that people accept you for what you are, as a friend or as an acquaintance, until you do something to prove you're not worthy of that acceptance – then God help you. But you click right off the bat, and that's it. In England, by contrast, I was never exactly made welcome, or made to feel that I belonged, and that didn't sit very well with me.

While I waited around in California for the deal to be worked out by my lawyer, I listened to other offers. Racket companies wanted me to do deals which would have been very advantageous, but I was already committed to Slazengers. There were also approaches from motorcar and cigarette people, but it wasn't on anything like the scale you get today. There were no endorsements around in those days, nor agents. The movie stars had them, of course, but not sportsmen. You stood to make a good income from touring and teaching, but nothing more, and with

the whole of the amateur tennis world against us we were very much
lone pioneers.

Later on, others got away with what I had been prevented from doing.
Their associations turned a blind eye to subtle financial arrangements in
order to keep them from turning pro. I always hated being told by the
authorities that something wasn't possible 'because it wasn't done',
although in fact it *was* possible, provided they didn't know about it
officially. I'm quite sure, since I was the first Englishman involved, that
I got clobbered because I was openly embarking on something that 'wasn't
done'.

Of course, none of this deterred me at the time I was going to do it
because I thought it would mean I could take care of everybody in my
family. I couldn't have foreseen the rocks that lay ahead: my marital
difficulties or the divorce which would follow.

I turned pro. Britain lost the Davis Cup the next year, and we have
never won it since. Nor has an Englishman won Wimbledon.

The day when, in the words of the *Philadelphia Inquirer*, 'Fred Perry
swapped glory for gold,' was 6 November 1936. The signing ceremony
was in New York, at the Wall Street offices of my law firm, Donovan,
Leisure, Newton & Lombard. The plan that had been drawn up was for
me to embark on a four-month tour of North America, starting the
following January, in a head-to-head series against Ellsworth Vines, with
Bill Tilden joining the troupe at some of the bigger venues. I was
guaranteed $100,000 for five and a half months' tennis, but I ended up
earning more than that. I never actually realized what '$100,000 or more'
meant until we went to lunch with the lawyers that day. I hesitated
before crossing the street and George Leisure asked me what I was
waiting for. 'For the lights to turn green,' I said. 'Oh, to hell with that,'
replied George. 'You're amply insured with Lloyd's of London anyway,
so everybody's taken care of. What do you care? Go ahead!'

Some of the syndicate putting up the money for the tour weren't sure
if it was a good business move. I treasure the story about one of them
who told another of the partners, 'If we make any money out of this I'll
give you a horse's ass in diamonds.' Well, they *did* make money, a hell
of a lot — we all did — and the man who had lost the bet presented his
partner with a gold cigarette case with a horse's rear end in diamonds
and a ruby set right in the middle of it!

The format for the pro tour was that the incoming professional (usually the Wimbledon champion) played the reigning professional champion, with the newcomer getting the major percentage in the first year.

Naturally, this arrangement was fine by me, but first we needed Vines's agreement. It turned out that he was in Tokyo with Tilden, but nobody knew exactly where. Within an hour, however, after contacting the shipping line which had taken them to Japan, we had Vines on the end of the phone, which I considered pretty nifty going at that time, even for Americans.

'What the hell's going on?' Vines demanded, when I spoke to him. 'Do you know it's six o'clock in the morning here?' So I told him, 'Listen, Ellie, would you like to make some money?' 'That's different,' he said. He was immediately wide awake and didn't take very long to agree to the offer.

For Vines and myself that was the start of a great partnership. We were in business together for the next twenty years, touring various parts of the world. We bought the Beverly Hills Tennis Club, operated it together and sold it together. Yet in all that time the extraordinary thing was that we never had a contract.

By the second year of our pro tour we were sharing the operating end of it, too, and we had complete trust in each other. On the mainland USA, Vines was in charge of finances. Anywhere else, it was my job. I would say, 'Well, Ellie, we took so much money, our expenses were so much, you've already had so much, and you've got so much to come,' and he'd just say, 'Fine.'

We were friends then and we're still friends. We respected each other's ability, yet we didn't pull any punches. I must have played Vines in something like 350 matches, yet there was never any fixing, as most people thought.

There were always people willing to believe that our pro matches weren't strictly on the level, that they were just 'exhibitions'. But as far as we were concerned, we always gave everything we had. If you've got any pride, every match you are involved in counts. You have to go on court with this attitude, otherwise you have no pride in your performance nor any respect for the game you play.

One of the first messages I received after signing my contract was from Sir Samuel Hoare. I wasn't exactly expecting him to tell me, 'Congratulations, I hope you earn a million,' but I was still a bit offended to be asked, 'Why did you do it?' I was a little hurt, too – but not surprised – to be told that I would be relieved forthwith of my honorary membership of Wimbledon and the tie that went with it. And after all the trouble they'd gone to presenting it to me.

As a member of British teams that had toured the world I had also been automatically made an honorary member of whatever club I played at. I was thrown out of every one of those, too. I wasn't reinstated at Wimbledon until 1949, twelve years later.

An Autobiography, 1984

The Lowdown on Amateur Tennis
PANCHO GONZALEZ

Let's journey down memory lane . . .

Remember the case of Wes Santee, former Kansas University track star and America's premier miler, who was banned for receiving overpayment of allowable expenses?

Remember the University of California at Los Angeles football recruiters accused of winking at various conference rules, resulting in a $93,000 fine and being placed on probation for three years?

Remember disciplinary measures taken against the University of Kentucky basketball team?

Remember relieving Jim Thorpe of his Olympic Games medals after discovering he had played some semi-professional baseball?

These alleged violations of the concepts of amateurism would pale into insignificance today if Dan Ferris, Avery Brundage or Pincus Sober, the Kefauvers of the Amateur Athletic Union, investigated the amateur tennis situation.

They could obtain an injunction to prevent participation in all major tournaments by any of the first twenty ranking amateurs.

In tennis the difference between an amateur and a professional player is related to a phantom table. The amateur receives money under it, the professional over it. Today, a sought-after amateur can make from $8,000 to $10,000 yearly; yet in the eyes of the public he is pure as a virgin snow drift.

The United States Lawn Tennis Association, governing body of the sport, is blameless. The USLTA is composed of successful men of unassailable integrity. Rumours of the taints of amateurism have reached their ears. Some believe it. Others don't. Merely hearsay. Furthermore, it isn't their job to employ secret police or a spy system to track down such rumours. They merely impart the spirit and letter of the amateur code.

The code is antiquated. It provides ten dollars daily expense money.

Throw it out, I say; or make sweeping revisions.

Being that I'm in the playing end of the tennis business and not a member of its brain trust, I won't be presumptuous enough to name any cure-alls. However, unqualified as I may be, I'm bold enough to offer a few suggestions.

First, let me present, minus distortion, a clear-cut photo of amateur tennis today.

Put yourself in the role of the amateur. You're out of school and in the 20- to 30-year-old bracket. Perhaps you have a wife and a child or two. You may even have a grandmother who wants to take lessons from Mercer Beasley.

Maintaining a high ranking is synonymous with playing the Eastern tournament circuit. Europe too. Tennis becomes a grind.

Missing is the exuberance once derived from hitting a perfect crosscourt placement. The game becomes a chore. Believe me, a tennis player can suffer the same daily boredom as a CPA poring over columns of figures. Day after day he runs countless miles swinging at a wool-covered ball with strings made from a lamb's intestines. Physically, the game exacts its toll. He's dehydrated as a squeezed sponge. His feet take a terrific pounding on cement, clay, and the slightly kinder surface – grass. His sacroiliac is endangered. His disposition can sour after defeats. His heart and body are taxed to the limits of physical endurance.

While he may not realize it – he's in business. And he's putting as much into it as the business man carrying the brief case under his arm. Sometimes much more. Players are not the sons of the rich who burst upon a fashionable gathering wearing expensively tailored clothes and call: 'Anyone for tennis?' More often, clad in a cheap T-shirt and part woolen socks, they're the sons of the poor whose parents keep repeating: 'What are you getting out of all this with your education when you could have been a banker?'

Undiluted amateurism implies that you cannot take one penny above the allotted expense money. On the ten-dollar-a-day allowance you're supposed to travel. Why, it almost means desertion and non-support to the wife left at home. So what recourse can you take? Tournament sponsors are bidding for your services. You become receptive to the highest bid offered.

You have ready excuses to make for yourself. Chiefly, you need the money. Sponsors can afford to pay; and after all, it's your name luring the customers.

The first time you take this money a few qualms of honesty prick you like dull needles. The second time you hurdle mental barriers much faster. It's becoming easier. The third time you merely extend your hand and wait for it to be filled.

The next step involves negotiations. You're getting real smart; and you finally realize that due to your high ranking you've got bargaining power. So you take the initiative. Instead of sticking a gun into some promoter's back and holding him up for more, you shove a tennis racket into his ribs and make your demands. Usually, the victim ups the ante.

True, that all this finagling might provide a modicum of business training, but think of the moral effect. You're not getting your money legally, coupled with the fact it's fraught with hypocrisy. A player seldom discusses his banditry with another player. One reason is a guilt complex. Don't bring it out into the open and it won't prick your conscience as strongly. Another is that some sponsors make you feel you got a better deal than the other players and it shouldn't be bandied about. This reminds me of a family hotel I knew about where each guest had a confidential rate which he or she thought particularly favored them. Had the matter been freely discussed, they would have unearthed the fact that everyone was being robbed.

Personally, I don't care to see an investigation of amateur tennis ending in a complete whitewashing of the sport. Unpleasant repercussions could kill off the game. From the amateur ranks spring the pros and, I hope, suitable opponents to challenge me. It's awful to run out of opponents. I know.

I don't believe an open tournament would solve anything either. Everybody who won prize money would end up a pro. The same pros would repeatedly take the cash prizes.

Amateur tennis can be a year-round activity if players want to follow the sun and are skilled enough to be in demand. You can chase the footsteps of Hugh Stewart or Tony Vincent and others – play America, Mexico, Europe, and even South America and Australia. But for the most part our amateurs compete only in the United States, with a stab at Wimbledon, the French Championships, and occasionally the Australian Championships.

It wouldn't be feasible to be in a business – even for themselves – and take that much time off. Frank Stranahan, as an amateur, could do it in golf, but no tennis player has the financial assets of this fine golfer. Dick Savitt and Ted Schroeder abandoned tennis careers for the world of business, and neither is employed by the type of organization where it's necessary to focus on their tennis reputations to boom sales.

Monetarily speaking, an athlete attending college is provided for through scholarships and jobs for just about his four school years. Couldn't the same be done for a tennis player? There must be some way he can receive monies while he isn't playing if he's expected to drop everything when the season opens.

In the last few decades the tennis scene has changed completely. Once the game belonged to the white flannel, polo-coated set. Not only did a player have to learn the book of social etiquette backwards, and grip a racket properly, he had to be able to lift a cup of tea without spilling a drop. Tennis and the Long Island horsey set were loving cousins. There was no so-called 'wrong side of the tracks players.' This group owned the tracks.

Came the evolution. Tennis became the people's game. Public park courts mushroomed. Expensive clothes for players were unnecessary. All a man needed was a drugstore T-shirt, a pair of cheap shorts, dime-store socks and shoes that could be adhesive-patched if your toes broke through, or vulcanized on the soles when your feet showed.

Audiences became plebeian, more demonstrative. Where formerly ripples of applause rewarded shotmakers, there were now roars of appreciation from shirtsleeved masses, and even choruses of boos directed at bad calls.

Tennis became of age and widespread in popularity. Then the attendant evil followed – bidding for the services of the players. I don't know who was first guilty. That is of small concern. Once the cash payments gained momentum, they fanned out in all directions.

True enough, tennis players get a lot of free things in life – food, rackets, balls, strings, shirts, shoes, sweaters, lodging, and lots of advice, none of which helps them later in life. In the life of each tennis player there's the point of no return. Here, you either drop the sport and concentrate on making a livelihood or stick with it, trying to live off its sometimes frugal returns.

At the frayed edge of an amateur career, when a player touches the age of thirty, it's later than he thinks. To regress to the business world and try to carve a niche for himself is a mammoth undertaking. He's already lost ten productive years. He's too old to start at the bottom, too inexperienced to hold down a top position. All he's got to show for his efforts is a scrapbook, blistered feet, and tarnished trophies.

Please bear in mind I'm not turning copper and blowing the whistle on amateur tennis. It's still the purist of the popular spectator sports. Only a handful of amateurs in tennis really make any money. Total these against the earnings of football, basketball, and track athletes. The difference is monumental.

What's to be done about it?

Let's face up to the situation. No circumvention. Shouldn't we make a choice between honesty and hypocrisy? But not a compromise. Otherwise, the evil side can undermine the strong side until the roots decay and collapse the entire structure.

The line of demarcation between pros and amateurs is wavy and vacillating. A rigid line with no overstepping is necessary.

To make a sincere start, let's compile an amateur tennis code that makes sense.

Man with a Racket, 1959

Pancho and the Challenge
LEW HOAD

I arrived in New York confident and chirpy, pleased to be free at last of the petty restrictions and rule books which prevent amateur tennis stars from taking a share of the money they attract through the turnstiles of six continents. I had that wonderful feeling which only the knowledge that you are worth $125,000 can provide.

I was proud of my achievements, and I carried the rare, purring, inner pleasure of having just won Wimbledon for the second successive year. And yet within a few days the grinding realities of professionalism transformed me into a worried, hurt, moody figure, entirely lacking in confidence, apprehensive that my easy-going make-up might prevent me from becoming a successful professional.

The harassing differences in my new status started to show before I went along to the courts at Forest Hills for the first tournament in which I would not have to hide what I got paid. At the Forest Hills Inn, where Jack Kramer and Ted Schroeder installed us after our flight from London, I was immediately overwhelmed by business offers. Fast-talking men wanted me to endorse hair oils, soaps, shirts, shorts, shoes, racket gut, socks, pullovers, underwear and an incredible list of other goods. Sportswriters wanted me to sell them my life story, articles on how to play tennis and exposures of amateur tennis rackets, if any. To boost attendances, I had to appear on radio or TV as often as Kramer and his staff could arrange it. Contracts I was urged to sign arrived in every mail; the telephone never stopped buzzing.

I had always thought life as a top amateur was busy and disorganized – this was sheer turmoil. I took the advice of my fellow professionals as often as I could get it, but most of the time I had to make my own decisions and hope they were sensible. I had no experience to fit me for this bartering, no way of knowing whether $2,000 a year was a good or bad price for endorsing, say, a hair tonic. I just had to take a stab at it. Overnight I had become a one-man band, a combination of salesman, press relations expert, huckster, newsprint celebrity, sporting hero for pay. The bustling activity of suddenly being able to make dollars without worrying if amateur officials would catch me unsettled my poise and my tennis.

Kramer and I agreed on the details of my employment very quickly, but we did not get down to signing contracts. He expected me to beat every member of his highly-talented troupe with the possible exception of Pancho Gonzales. Kramer believed that of all the players in the world, amateur or professional, I was the one most likely to deprive Gonzales of his standing as the best player of our time. His faith in me seemed sound for exactly two days after the tennis had started.

I began so well that everyone was mesmerized into believing I would beat the lot. I was lucky to meet Frank Sedgman in the first round of Kramer's $10,000 Round-Robin tournament. He'd just flown in from Australia with hardly time left to tune up. I won in straight sets, and the next day I had another lucky break which helped me defeat Pancho Segura without dropping a set. Segura was badly tired from three tough matches in four days.

That night the experts raved about my tennis and compared me with the all-time greats, but already I had sensed that every match I would play as a professional would be like a Wimbledon final or a Davis Cup Challenge Round match. As an amateur, I had been able to set myself for one or two big efforts every year, building up gradually through minor events, coasting through the easy early rounds of the tournaments.

Now there was no respite, and to slip any day even slightly below my best would be suicide.

'Hoad really looked sensational in his first two pro matches,' Australian star Dinny Pails told pressmen. 'I watched every move he made, and he looked just about the greatest player I'd ever seen. He hit the ball with terrific power, served with tremendous pace, put away his volleys the first time and looked the fastest man you'd ever seen chase a tennis ball. At that stage I think all the players in Kramer's troupe must have thought they were in for a hiding. I know I did. And then – phhht! Lew lost it.'

The player who first showed me what a drastic adjustment lay ahead of me if I was to justify the sum Kramer guaranteed me was a little fella with flash-bulb quickness named – you've guessed it – Kenneth Robert Rosewall, beloved of many tennis fans and in the opinion of many critics, my personal hoodoo, hex, and Nemesis. The lesson he gave hurt and disillusioned me, for I suppose subconsciously I had rated him the one pro I should be able to beat. I had overcome his early lead over me as an amateur, I had improved since beating him in the 1956 Wimbledon final, and meanwhile he had taken a morale-busting drubbing from Gonzales.

None of this appeared to occur to Rosewall, who showed how much he had learned as a professional. Instead of the sporadic brilliance of his amateur days, he played now with steady, unrelenting pressure. He did not miss easy shots any more, and I found his soft service curiously tricky to handle after the booming services of Sedgman and Segura on the two previous days. Rosewall got down to business quickly, broke my service in the first game and went on to win in four sets, 6–3, 9–7, 4–6, 6–3. I left the court still convinced I was the better player.

For this standard of tennis, I fluffed too many easy shots, chipping and poking at the ball with a lackadaisical nonchalance, especially when I went to the net. I would get near the net and behave as if hitting a winner was inevitable, and instead the ball would plop into the bottom of the rigging. By comparison, Rosewall's return of service was superb, and he had more decisiveness and punch at the net than I had ever seen before from him. I saw then that I had to learn his art of reducing errors.

I suppose I still thought I could go on to the final of that tournament and defeat Gonzales, despite my loss to Rosewall, but in the next round I lost again to Tony Trabert, my old rival from our Davis Cup days – Trabert whom I have always considered slow-footed and whose service looked to me too weak for this caliber of tennis. In the grandstand, Jenny patted her eyes, near to tears as Tony hammered away the winning point.

I tried hard all the way for I was desperate to beat Trabert. But this time he served beautifully with that characteristic pause before he flipped the ball up. If he made a mistake, it was never on an important point. I just could not get the feel of the ball, and I played dumb tennis. I had to fight for the sets I won. Tony skated through those he won and finally took the match 6–4, 10–12, 6–2, 3–6, 6–3. He knew I was too loose for professional tennis and exploited this by putting up several floaters which I bashed into the net, cursing deep inside me like a gambler who has risked the rent and lost.

These defeats chastened me because they showed me Gonzales would not be my sole problem as a professional. They were all anxious to take a cut at my prestige. From what seemed to me a sound stroke repertoire full of strong points my game had suddenly been shot full of weaknesses. I took stock again and noted that my volleying was slack and my returns of service miserable because I used too much backswing and stood too far inside the baseline to handle the swinging, speedy deliveries these players whacked down at me. My second service was so shallow they could walk around it as I aimed it at their backhand and thump it with a forehand drive for exasperating winners.

My collapsing morale did not receive any support when I had my first match against Gonzales, though the critics said I made a curiously favourable impression. I was like a boxer who tries to fight every minute of fifteen rounds without resting, holding or stalling. I sought to play every point at a fearsome, crowding pace, and every time I saw the ball loom near, I larruped it. With his awesome control, Gonzales took advantage of the slightest lapse.

My first impression of him as I looked up over the net at his handsome, fleet-footed frame was that he was the most consistent player I had ever met, a man with vast physical toughness and unwavering mental strength who had reduced his percentage of errors lower than any man has ever done. He had the best physical equipment nature can give a tennis player – height, reach, and a hard body which could endure sweaty exertion for hours at a time.

The pressure Gonzales applied to my laboriously-molded strokes was so tight that I had the eerie feeling of a man trying to force apart the jaws of a vice which is crushing him. But I had a few, fleeting moments of ascendancy which encouraged me to think I would eventually beat him. Most surprisingly of all, I did not find his famous service as difficult to return as I had anticipated; there was hope that I could break it often enough later on to worry him. And I saw, too, that my stamina and strength were equal to his and that I would not succumb through physical weariness as Rosewall had done at times in the long hauls from city to city in a one-hundred-match series.

In each set we played in this match, a single service break decided the issue. Gonzales' weakness was his return of service, which convinced me I would give him a severe thrashing at least now and then. It was slam-bang tennis, which critics described as far more dramatic than the duels between Rosewall and Gonzales, and we both enjoyed matching our hitting powers against a similarly strong hitter. There were few rallies, points were over quickly and Gonzales won 9–7, 6–4, 3–6, 6–3. He had earlier clinched the first prize of $2,700 by whipping Sedgman over five sets.

Gonzales had the reputation of being temperamental and rude to his opponents, but on the court none of it showed – he was making an appraisal. He is a talented hot-rodder, snooker player and bowling alley gambler who thrives on big-stake poker games, and in a match his calm is astounding. The breaks can go against him for point after point and his opponents come near to a crucial advantage, but big Pancho does not lose his quiet, sullen confidence. All this comes from an intense, searing belief in the pre-eminence of his own game. I would have to defeat *him;* *he* would not defeat himself.

Gonzales is six years older than I, and he has had seven more years' experience behind him as a pro. We have a lot in common. We were both bad scholars in school, and we were both crazy about any type of sport. We came from families which had to struggle to feed us and keep us clothed, and in our tennis careers we have had long periods of decline when our future stake in the game seemed jeopardized.

In practice the ideas Harry Hopman and I worked out to beat Gonzales when we sat together a few months earlier in the stand at Kooyong, Melbourne, failed because of my errors. I found I could not pound the ball back at Gonzales' feet as he came to the net in the way Hopman thought would unsettle him. His backhand was not as inferior as it sometimes appears from up in the crowd.

I could have used Hopman's advice in my second professional tournament at Los Angeles, although Jack Kramer did a lot to help eliminate my faults. I have often amused myself by idling with the thought of what a jarring clash of tennis wisdom would result if Kramer and Hopman managed rival teams. Yes, that would really be a struggle! Unhappily, Kramer's connection with the pay-for-play set prevents his being nominated to lead an American Davis Cup team.

The lessons of Forest Hills were sharply underlined on the concrete courts of Los Angeles. I knew I would have to learn to like concrete surfaces, just as I would have to get to like indoor board courts – dancehalls covered with canvas. I would have to get to like a lot of things I automatically recoiled from, but the constant cracks that professional tennis is fixed would be the hardest to bear. All money sports are accustomed to snide attacks on their integrity, but it's hard to take when you come off a court tired and dripping perspiration after playing your heart out.

I got $300 in Los Angeles for running last, more than I ever got there as an amateur for finishing near the top of the pile. Ken Rosewall beat me again in straight sets, as I double-faulted away any chance I had of winning. Then Frank Sedgman revenged his defeat at Forest Hills by defeating me 7–5, 6–1. My morale slumped even lower, however, when Dinny Pails whipped me 6–3, 3–6, 6–4 in the third round because at thirty-six Dinny himself would be the first to admit he is no longer a threat to a good player.

I hit the ball well for a few games at a stretch and then lapsed into that riling casualness nobody can account for. The only solace I got from this debacle was that I seemed to have attracted some people to the courts for my boss, Kramer. I had not played enough to be tired, and yet I felt utterly weary, torn by mental anguish, gloomy because I could not get away from tennis altogether but had to go on non-stop for at least two years.

Rosewall brilliantly defeated Pancho Gonzales on the same day I lost to Pails, winning 22–20, 1–6, 6–2. I began to understand what Kramer meant when he said Rosewall would have broken even in his series against Gonzales if he had been able to count on winning a single point at the moment he chose in ten of their grim marathon matches.

Next day Pancho Segura handed me my seventh successive professional defeat with the loss of only three games. He was fourteen years my senior, and on that day it was no contest. I just could not play at all. I had hit rock-bottom, and it was not that I was unable to hit my volleys or ground shots which depressed and soured me – I just could not locate them at all. They didn't exist. I was like a novice trying to learn these strokes as Segura won 6–3, 6–0. Actually my trouble was more deep-seated. I had been busy with publicity shows and television and was not used to playing at night under lights. But what was the answer? What strange quirk of my mind had converted me into a listless, sluggish dolt? I didn't know, and trying to discover the answer rattled me all the more.

I decided that all I could do to fight my way out of this slump was to struggle for every point, to try to turn my concentration away from the off-court deals once I walked out under the lights. Kramer took the indulgent view that these early professional appearances were merely a change-over period for me, a chance to make adjustments before my big clash with Gonzales the following January. He kept coaching me to eliminate my technical flaws, painstakingly trying to build for me a tactical pattern which would survive in the professional set-up.

I lost again to Gonzales, 6–3, 6–2, and then went down for the ninth successive time as a professional when Tony Trabert defeated me 9–7, 7–5. I had not won a match in the Los Angeles tournament, but against Gonzales and Trabert I had improved on my disastrous performances against Pails and Segura. Gonzales won the decisive match against Sedgman to take the tournament first prize of $2,000. I was very upset when we left this tournament. I hate to lose, and losing had become a habit.

We went on to Memphis and broke my losing sequence by defeating Rosewall. Then we climbed in and out of airplanes for a couple of days until we arrived at Vittel, France, where I won and lost a couple of matches. Next came Paris and a win over Kramer, who coached me as we played. Jenny had left me in America and flown back to Australia so that she could be with our daughter. Suddenly the off-court deals started to thin out, and I had time to relax when I was not junketing through France or playing against Rosewall, Kramer and Segura. My form improved, and when we went on to Geneva, I beat Kramer again. The next day in Zurich I whipped Segura.

While we were flying to Dhahran in Saudi Arabia and back, another dispute broke out that was headlined on page one across Australia. It started over an article I had written for the *Saturday Evening Post*, 'I Was a Tennis Slave.' It was written in collaboration with a respected American sportswriter, Will Grimsley, and the material it contained caused Kramer's press relations man, Myron McNamarra, to write a letter to the Lawn Tennis Association of Australia stressing that the views I expressed were not those of the Kramer organization. The title of the article and its appearance at a time when he was about to complete the dates with Australian associations for his troupe's Australian trip that year could have seriously embarrassed Kramer.

He had cleaned up the previous year on an Australian tour, and there was as much money there for his troupe as in any country in the world. He sent Ted Schroeder to Australia by plane to see that his troupe's tour was not threatened. Meanwhile Australian tennis chiefs made statements saying I was ungrateful to them. I had not meant to attack amateur tennis, which made me, but merely to point out its deficiencies. I understood then the wisdom of Hopman's press gag.

In Dhahran I beat Rosewall in a fantastic three-and-a-half-hour battle. I instinctively rebel against playing in very hot weather, but on this day I outlasted him despite a temperature of 110 degrees. We lost eight pounds in weight between us, and when we left the court, the beer tasted better than any I ever quaffed.

The cities in which we played flickered by in a dizzy kaleidoscope – La Baule, La Hague, Paris, London – and we barely had time for anything but eating, sleeping, traveling and playing tennis. I won a few matches, lost a few, and the tough life of professional tennis was daily driven home to me. I heard how Kramer had had a few curt, pointedly-worded phrases to address to Rosewall when his form slumped on a South American tour, and I half-expected a similar reprimand about my inconsistency. But all the time Kramer nurtured and coaxed and persevered with me, hoping I would 'come good' under my own steam.

We flew back to London for the Wembley indoor tournament, run on amateur lines, and I had the humiliation of losing in the first round to Kramer and thus taking no further part in the singles. Kramer wanted me to play well far more than he wanted to win that match, but he did not try to throw me an unearned success. Throughout the match he shouted advice to me from the other end, but he did not slacken the speed or accuracy of his shotmaking. He was determined I should deserve any victories I had over him.

The people who hint that professional tennis is fixed should have seen that match. No corrupt promoter would have allowed a player in whom he had so heavily invested to be downed so consistently as I was in my first few months as a professional. But most of all, I believe the struggles between Segura and Gonzales emphasize the honesty of Kramer's promotions. They are close pals who have been in a lot of fun and a lot of trouble together in a lot of countries. Their rich friendship has bloomed in their own vernacular Spanish. And yet, as I have seen, when they go out on the court, they try to belt the heck out of each other.

It's an intriguing duel between characters, who, like the rest of the best pros, were born on the wrong side of the tracks. Little Segura is thirty-six, pigeon-toed, slightly-built, subtle, full of tricks, and talks to 'key himself up' after years of non-stop competition. His histrionics are never irksome to the crowds, who quickly recognize his warm humanity. And big Gonzales, six feet, three inches tall, scar-faced, and the father of three sons, swats at the ball with a fierce, almost mean air, fighting his friend like a tiger, ever ready to invite hecklers down onto the court to try to do better than he can.

This time at Wembley, on a surface covering the pool where the 1948 Olympic Games races were swum, little Segura beat the big fellow. I don't think anyone can win all the time in this league, as Rosewall showed when he defeated Segura in a brilliant five-setter, continuously cheered by 9,000 spectators, to win the tournament. It was Rosewall's biggest success as a professional up to that time, and it encouraged me because I had beaten Rosewall often enough to know how slight the margin was between my failure and success.

Already, I have tasted blood in my duel with Richard Gonzales. Playing at an admitted advantage – in my home country and on turf courts more to my liking than to Gonzales' – I was able to get off to a nice start in our hundred-match series by winning eight of the thirteen contests played before our departure for the United States. Everyone predicted that the balance would begin to swing when we found ourselves on the canvas-covered courts of the indoor American arenas, but I think I surprised a few people, including some of my favorite friends and foes alike. In any event, time and potential are on my side.

As I see it, my future as a professional tennis player will depend on how successfully I can change my lazy mental make-up and how I take to the constant traveling, throw off the inevitable defeats and come back unperturbed the next night. I hope I can maintain my position in Kramer's troupe until these adjustments are permanent. Sedgman, Rosewall, Segura and Trabert, will not surrender their prestige without a fight, and all of them will be keen to prevent me from achieving a standing as the best pro behind Gonzales.

But that is the smallest of the struggles which confront me. Ahead of everything else lies the great challenge of my encounters with Richard Gonzales. I may not be able to oust him from the number one spot

immediately, but I believe that within two years the game I first learned barefoot while I still attended kindergarten will have reached its ultimate achievement and made me the greatest player in the world. It's an honorable ambition, the desire to be the best at your chosen vocation; and in my heart I sincerely believe it is within my grasp. It is already so very close.

The Lew Hoad Story, 1959

Grooming Monica
NICK BOLLETTIERI

The first time I heard of Monica Seles, she was eleven years old and she was going to Disney World. Not to see Mickey. To play tennis. In a tournament named after Goofy.

At the time, we had a twelve-year-old at the academy named Kim Kessaris, who was, we felt, the best player her age in the United States. She played Monica in Goofy's tournament, and when my pros told me that Kim had lost, 6–1, 6–0, to an eleven-year-old from Yugoslavia, I said, 'I've got to see that girl.'

A couple of months later, in December 1985, I went to the Orange Bowl tournament in Miami with a man named Tony Cacic, a former soccer player from Zagreb in Yugoslavia, who had just moved to Bradenton so that his twelve-year-old daughter, Sandra, could attend the academy.

Cacic had heard of Monica Seles from friends back home, and when he saw her play, he turned to me and said, 'I will buy plane tickets for her. You give her room and board.' I told Tony that sounded good to me.

Cacic introduced himself to the Seles family and offered to pay for Monica to fly to the States. He explained that Nick Bollettieri, the owner of the NBTA, would provide Monica with room and board and training facilities. The Seles family accepted. Tony bought two tickets, one for Monica and one for her teenage brother, Zoltan. The parents would come over later.

The youngsters moved into the dormitory at the academy, and Monica enrolled in Bradenton Academy. After several months, Monica's parents were ready to join them. Tony Cacic said he would pay for their tickets. By then, I knew how talented Monica was. I paid for the parents' tickets and gave Tony back the money he had spent on the children's tickets.

Incidentally, Tony's wife, Anna, came to work for me at the academy. She still works in the snack bar. Their daughter Sandra won the first tournament on the women's tour in 1996, a tune-up for the Australian Open, and moved into the top hundred in the world.

Early in her stay at the academy, Monica practiced out in the open on our showpiece front court, and she hit against Rafaella Reggi, Carling Bassett, and Lisa Bonder, young women six to eight years older than she, veterans of the professional tour. Monica wore them all out. She was the toughest twelve-year-old I'd ever seen. She had only one thing on her mind, and that was to be No. 1.

From the beginning, Monica did not believe in keeping the ball in play. She did not believe in rallying. She believed in hitting winners. She tried to put every shot away. This helped her become a great tennis player and a terrible hitting partner.

Soon, Monica stopped hitting against girls. She hit against Agassi and Blackman, and wore them out, too. She beat up everybody. Even my pros hid when they knew I was looking for someone to hit with Monica. José Lambert, Raul Ordonez, and René Gomez, three of my elite pros, all served time as Monica's hitting partners. She aimed at the corners and ran them ragged. She not only wore them out, she wore out their shoes. A pair of tennis shoes didn't last a week against Monica. Yet Karolj Seles, Monica's father, was always scornful of the efforts of the pros.

Poppa Seles was not a tolerant man. He was tough on all my pros. I once saw José Lambert crying like a baby; he said he had never been treated like such shit. Poppa Seles was extremely paranoid about Monica's training. Once, he demanded that I fire René Gomez because he said Gomez was stealing Monica's drills, using the same drills with his own students. The truth is, he was. We had been using the same drills for years with all of our students. I didn't fire René.

What made Monica so special was not the drills, it was the effort she put into them. She was tireless, persistent, dogged. She worked hard from the moment she stepped on the court. From the first ball till the last, she was always focused. She would hit the same shot over and over and over till she had it down. Not for an hour. Not for a day. For weeks. She would hit nothing but two-handed backhands for two or three weeks, then nothing but two-handed forehands for two or three weeks, followed by nothing but overheads for two or three weeks. She practiced for three or four hours at a stretch. She wouldn't leave the court until she had hit the perfect shot. She once went more than a year without playing a single match. Monica spoke almost as rarely, but she listened. To her father and to me. And she hit. And hit. And hit. I couldn't have asked for a more dedicated student.

Once, when Monica was practicing on the front court, not yet into her teens, my friend Jerry Glauser, the Mercedes dealer, watched her and offered to put up $500,000 for an interest in her career. Another time, my friend Dick Vitale, the basketball announcer, watched me coaching Monica hour after hour and screamed at me, 'When are you going to spend some time with my daughters?' Dick tends to scream when he says, 'Hello.'

Poppa Seles insisted that we move to a back court so that people would not steal his secrets and Monica's. He insisted that we put a fence and a canvas curtain around the court. A thick canvas curtain that no one could see through. We left openings in the corners of the canvas for the wind to blow through. Poppa Seles insisted that we close the openings to protect his privacy, and after we did, a howling wind blew the canvas and the fence down three different times. On windy and rainy days, we moved to the indoor center, and Poppa Seles demanded we put a curtain around the indoor court, too. He also wanted the music turned off at the nearby fitness center, and he told us to bar students from walking past Monica, detour them around her court; he would tolerate no distractions.

Poppa Seles insisted that we buy a thirty-five-foot-long rope and hang it from the ceiling of the indoor center. He wanted Monica to exercise on the rope. He explained she could develop upper-body strength holding herself out parallel to the ground, like an aerialist in the circus. The special sturdy rope cost more than $2,000, and when Greg Breunich couldn't get it installed quickly enough, Poppa Seles wanted me to fire Greg. Monica never used the rope. Nor did anyone else. It still hangs from the ceiling of the indoor center.

Often Monica hit with her brother, Zoltan, who was a good tennis player, willing to work endless hours without complaint. When Zoltan couldn't catch up to her shots, Poppa Seles was as tough on him as he was on my pros. Zoltan grew confused and depressed. His moods and personality fluctuated wildly. So did his appearance. One day, he had a goatee; the next, he shaved his head. One Christmas Day, he was so angry to find the pro shop closed when he wanted to pick up some restrung racquets he kicked the door down. 'Each day you are an entirely different person,' I told Zoltan, 'and yet no matter who you are, everyone else is always wrong.'

The Seleses were, by far, the most demanding family I ever worked with. Whatever we gave them – food, shelter, equipment, transportation, thousands of dollars worth of orthodontia for Monica, an operation for her mother – they wanted more. What they didn't eat in our dining room, they would throw into a big bag and take back to their condo, which we had already stocked with food. They were always demanding new tennis balls, and we hardly ever got used balls back. I still can't figure out where all the balls went.

One early letter from the Seleses said that they would stay and train at the academy *if* we provided an apartment, meals, schooling for Monica, preferably from 10 a.m. to 1 p.m. each day, medical care, jobs for her father and brother as coaches and trainers at the academy, working only mornings because in the 'afternoon, Karolj and Zoltan want to work, together with you, with Monica on a tennis court.' They also wanted a job for Poppa as a cartoonist and training for Momma to work on computers plus a fistful of round-trip airline tickets between Yugoslavia and the States, and all of the aforementioned had to be guaranteed in writing. 'Mr Bollettieri,' the letter stated, 'we want from you to answer our every request, and if you have some better solutions, please contact with us. Please, Mr Bollettieri, all these our requests you don't understand as our blackmailing, because these requests are the minimal conditions for a life and working in the US.'

Over the years, their demands intensified and multiplied, and in 1988, when Monica was fourteen, I wrote to the Seleses:

I have done and am prepared to continue to do more for Monica Seles than I have ever done for any student I have ever coached, including Andre Agassi. But I *cannot* place one student in a position above that of the NBTA itself. This would be unfair to our parent company, to my staff, and, even more important, to my family and to myself.

I have already told you that Andre and Monica will always be my top priority, but I cannot refuse to supervise the training of anyone else. What about my traveling team students, Jim Courier, David Wheaton, and countless other kids whose parents pay the tuition bills that ultimately allow me to feed, clothe, and house my family?

I will devote to you as much time as I possibly can. But cannot guarantee that all your practices can be completely closed to the public. There will be times when we are so busy that this will be impossible!

I cannot kick everyone out of everywhere you are practicing, and it is not right of you calling them names. They are people and must be treated as people.

I put in hundreds of hours working with Monica, maybe thousands, as much work as I've ever put into a student. (Carling Bassett used to say, 'Nick, you've given more time to Monica than you gave to me and Kathleen Horvath and Jimmy Arias put together.') I changed her backswing; she was using too much wrist, risking tendinitis. I changed her serve — the motion and the toss. I urged her to use a punch volley. I marveled at the two-handed forehand and backhand Poppa Seles had drilled into her. I encouraged her, applauded her, praised her. Once, while I was on the court with Monica, I was called to the telephone. Someone representing Jennifer Capriati was calling, asking me if I would be interested in working with Jennifer. I thanked him for the compliment, but I told him I had committed myself to Monica Seles and that I could truly focus on only one young woman at a time. I was as loyal as I could be to Monica, hardly suspecting that she and her family would abandon me as soon as they started making money on the pro tour, that they would state publicly that I had had nothing to do with shaping her talents or launching her career.

Monica's career skyrocketed. In 1988, after she turned fifteen, in only her second tournament as a professional, Monica beat Chris Evert in the final at Houston and won her first pro title. By the end of the year, she ranked sixth in the world. I kept offering her advice. Here is part of a letter I wrote to Zoltan early in 1989:

Backhand
The slice must become a weapon, not just getting the ball back.

Serve
The basic construction of her serve is letter-perfect. Ordinary development of the body will make it better, *but*

A We must now work on the kicker.

B She is now adjusting her grip just a little to hit the flat serve.

C She must develop the breaking slice as well as the jammer to the body.

Overhead

Must practice every day. Tends to get into position too quickly and then has difficulty when she has to make a last-second adjustment.

Angles

Letter-perfect.

Monica's Greatest Strengths

A Return of serve!!!

B Always forcing the opponent and moving forward.

C Variety of strokes.

D Serve technique.

E Anticipation and movement.

F Serve technique.

Comment

We all must never let her change the return of serve, which is the very best in women's tennis today.

When Monica was seventeen, she was No. 1 and already owned four Grand Slam titles. She won seven of the eight Grand Slam tournaments she entered before the stabbing in Hamburg, losing only at Wimbledon in the final. Before she turned twenty, she had already earned $7 million in prize money and millions more in endorsements. She could have given the academy a small token gift. Or at least said thank you. 'It was a marriage of convenience,' Karolj Seles told *Tennis* magazine when he was asked about his years at the academy. 'We benefited from the facilities, and he benefited from the publicity.' Chris Evert said on NBC television that she thought the Seleses were not giving Nick Bollettieri enough credit.

In 1989 and 1990, I don't know how many letters I wrote to the Seleses, offering to coach, to counsel, to be a friend and a second parent to Monica. I was willing to commit myself to her; all I wanted was a small sign of commitment from her family. I never got it.

Early in 1990, soon after she turned sixteen, Monica and her father and brother decided she would play tournaments in Chicago and Washington before she competed in the Lipton Championships. Monica did not play particularly well in those two events, and her family was dispirited.

I suggested that we cheer up, take a low-key approach to Lipton, remember that Monica was only sixteen. For the week before Lipton, I had Raul Ordonez working with her and with Andre Agassi, trying to get them both sharp.

A few days before we left for Key Biscayne, Poppa Seles and Zoltan came into my office and said they wanted to have lunch with me. They said they had very important matters to discuss. We went to Steak & Shake, and as we were eating, Mr Seles took out a yellow pad that had several pages of notes written in both black and red ink. He said he had a few questions for me, seventeen or eighteen of them, as I recall, including:

- How much time will you give to Monica?
- Will you take any other students besides Monica and Andre?
- Would you take care of Monica if anything happened to Poppa?
- How would you market Monica?

Mr Seles also talked about how I would be compensated for the years Monica had spent at the academy, for my work and my staff's. He said he would like me to reply immediately because he wanted to finalize an agreement before the start of the Lipton.

I paid for the lunch. Zoltan had forgotten to bring money.

That night, I sat down and answered all the questions in detail, reaffirmed that I would coach only Monica and Andre, that I would divide my time and my efforts between them. I delivered my reply to the Seles family the next day and waited to hear from them. Not a word.

We all went off to Key Biscayne, and when I saw the draw and saw the way they were playing, I had a suspicion that both Andre and Monica would win. I was right. Andre beat Stefan Edberg in the men's final, and Monica beat Judith Wiesner in the women's.

Two champions! I couldn't have been happier. I raced back to Bradenton, and the next day Poppa Seles came into my office and told me to get Raul ready to go to the next tournament. I asked Mr Seles if he had read my answers to his questions. He said we would talk about it some other time. I pointed out that he was the one who had demanded my answers immediately, who had wanted to formalize our relationship so that there would be no misunderstanding. Mr Seles said nothing.

'Until you tell me where I stand,' I said, 'I'm not going to be helping Monica anymore. Nor is the academy.'

The Seleses moved out the next day.

Monica said she wanted someplace quieter to practice. She said it was a great move for her career, for her game, for her health, and for herself. Funny, but I didn't notice that her career, her game, her health, or herself had suffered during her four years at the academy.

Scouting Report: MONICA SELES

Born: 2 December, 1973
Height: 5 feet, 10½ inches
Weight: 145 pounds

Forehand and Backhand

She is a two-handed player who hits her forehand and her backhand with her hands in exactly the same position. Her swing is very compact, a smooth, circular motion, and she can adjust it to any shot coming at her, no matter the speed, no matter the degree of difficulty, in a fraction of a second.

She prepares early and, on contact, transfers her weight perfectly. Her follow-through is long and aggressive, helping her not only hit harder, but recover quickly.

She almost always makes contact inside the baseline and uses the opponent's power to magnify her own power.

Even though her ground strokes are hit with topspin, she still hits through the ball instead of excessively brushing up the ball. Her spin gives her control, but at the same time her ball is almost flat and runs away from her opponent.

No other player, male or female, has so many formidable weapons at his or her command.

Serve

Her serve has improved greatly. She is no Brenda Schultz, with a big booming serve, but she gets excellent depth, and as a lefty, which is an advantage in tennis, she has learned to deliver a low breaking slice which is very difficult to attack.

Return of Serve

No matter how hard a serve is hit to her, no matter where it is hit, no matter how it kicks, it will come back. Her return makes you think that you need lessons on your serve.

Volley

Monica can be quite effective with a full-stroke volley similar to Agassi's. But often, because of her devastating ground strokes, which force a weak return, and because she takes the ball early, moving forward, it is easy for her to take another couple of steps to the net and win the point with a simple block volley or, at times, a swinging volley.

Movement

No matter what her foot speed may be, she anticipates the return and gets a very quick jump on the ball. Most often, she is coming forward, hitting the ball on the rise and catching her opponent out of position.

Mentality

Her will to win is unmatched. No one is more determined than Monica. No one is more difficult to distract.

How To Beat Her

There is only one way to beat Monica:

Our Father, Who art in heaven . . . (use a variety of serves and come to the net on a few of them) . . . hallowed be Thy name . . . (try every shot you can think of, including at least a few drop shots) . . . Thy Kingdom come . . . (be aggressive, gamble, go for the low-percentage shot because she's going to beat you a high percentage of the time) . . . Thy will be done . . . (If this doesn't work, try Hebrew, Islamic, and Buddhist prayers.)

My Aces, My Faults, 1996

v Race and Nationality

Cernik and I Choose Exile

JAROSLAV DROBNY

Now I must come to the story of how I broke with my country.

It all began with our preparations for the defence of our title as European Davis Cup Champions. We began our training in Egypt.

No objections had been raised, either by our Association, now included in the Communist Sports Organization, or the Government to Cernik and me going there. Indeed, Kopecky gave us a special sum of money to buy tennis racket gut for the leading players at home. At the time it was unobtainable in Czechoslovakia.

The Gezira is one of the most famous, and probably the best appointed, sporting clubs in the world. Every sport is played or takes place there from horse racing to football, golf, squash and lawn tennis. Those two great squash players, Amr Bey (formerly the Egyptian Ambassador in Britain) and the professional Mahmoud Karim, learned their game at the club.

The Egyptian Championships are played at Gezira every year and on this particular occasion I met Budge Patty in the semi-final. It was our second meeting. Early in the first set – I was down by the odd game – I stretched for a shot at the net and fell down. I could not get up for a pain in my back. Lumbago, I thought; I had had it before, and even now get it if I sit in a draught for any length of time. I put it down to the changing rooms at the Gezira Sporting Club, which, with their open windows, are very draughty. Since then I wear a sleeveless sweater most of the time.

I had to default, but neither the committee nor the public believed my reasons. They thought I had done it on purpose as Cernik and I were due to meet Jack Harper, an Australian, and von Cramm in the men's doubles final. Talk was that we had been forbidden by our Government to play because von Cramm was a German. There was a good deal of enmity between the Czech Communists and the Germans.

All this talk was sheer nonsense, of course, but being a sensitive person the aspersion that I had thrown a match cut me deeply. I left for home without saying goodbye to anyone. Cernik went on to Alexandria, where Cramm was also playing, but despite this there are still people in Cairo who do not believe I had lumbago.

I got rid of it at home by taking frequent hot baths and wrapping myself up in a large towel. A week or so later I was on my way to Bucharest as captain for the first time of a Czech lawn tennis team to play Rumania. They could always find non-playing captains for trips to the west but no one was forthcoming to go east!

In Bucharest I met the Prime Minister, Dr Petru Groza, a big strong fellow who is mad about lawn tennis and was a regular player, even though over sixty.

I could not make out whether Dr Groza was a mental fool or a very clever leg puller. Certainly he seemed rather unbalanced, since he told me he was the best player in Rumania, had beaten such players as Asboth of Hungary and Bernard of France but had not the time to spare to play in Davis Cup matches.

Every player who visits Bucharest has to play against him at six in the morning, when he feels at his best. Naturally I was invited and when I arrived at the club at this ungodly hour I found him already there with his entourage of ten men and women who follow him everywhere.

It was a strange gathering. Being very fond of music and dancing, as well as lawn tennis, he had an opera singer, guitarist and dancing girls with him. Suddenly in the middle of a conversation he would point his finger at the singer who would respond immediately with an aria. Then the finger wagged at the guitar and off they went with a tune. Then the dancing girls. It was like the crazy gang, but what an hour!

We began our game. There was an umpire, while Dr Groza's chauffeur and valet were the ball-boys. Every ball I hit was given out; all his shots were in court. When picking up the balls the chauffeur and valet would wink at me humorously. I managed to keep the score level with him and at 5–all Dr Groza's doctor called halt, saying it was enough for the old man.

It was the first and only time I have ever played a drawn tennis match and, according to my opponent, I was the only player he had never beaten.

When, later, I had dinner with him he whispered to me quite seriously in German, 'I am the only plutocrat left in Rumania.' Today he is chairman of the Communist Praesidium of Rumania; one of the oddest characters I have ever met.

We opened our Davis Cup campaign – the champion nation of Europe – that summer with wins over Monaco and then Britain on Wimbledon's No. 1 court. Before going to London I was called to the Information Ministry to see Kopecky, who had heard about my quarrel with Karel Kozeluh during our American tour the previous year.

Kopecky asked me who I would like as captain of the team against Britain. This sounded curious to me as there were still certain old members of our Association in the Sokol Organization.

I immediately named Dr Bertl, who had captained us so many times and whose sister had married Kubelik, the famous Czech conductor then in exile. Kopecky said 'impossible', probably thinking that Dr Bertl would take the chance to flee the country and live with his brother-in-law.

Next I named Labsky, an engineer and keen member of our Association. To this Kopecky said, 'Out of the question.' Labsky had recently married a woman who worked for the Japanese Legation.

Pressed for names I mentioned another old and faithful member, Pridal. This time Kopecky without any reference to notes or files reeled off Pridal's background. He said, 'Ah, Pridal has a little shop in Prerov (Moravia) which we have just nationalized. We allow him to work there with his wife. We pay him "so much" a month and he speaks no English.' There I disagreed with Kopecky, for I had heard Pridal speak English.

Kopecky agreed to let Pridal take us to London providing I made myself responsible for his return to Czechoslovakia. This was ironic and I wanted to laugh since I was already planning my own escape.

Some years later I heard that Colonel Duncan Macauley, secretary of the All-England Club, Wimbledon, loved to tell with some amusement of an odd character who appeared to speak no English but shadowed Cernik and me. The Colonel recounts how he asked us to lunch one day at the Dog and Fox and as we got into the taxi a third party jumped in with us. Colonel Macauley had no idea who he was but accepted him as a 'guest'. It was Pridal, of course.

After beating Britain and before playing France in the next round we held our National Championships in Prague. I won the title for the tenth successive year. It was the last time, too, as a year later I was in exile.

For the past two years we had been the top nation in Europe and during that time I had lost very few matches indeed either in singles or doubles. The burden upon me was especially heavy since, against the better nations, if I lost a match then our chances of victory were lessened considerably. Cernik was a useful player and had his good wins, but he was not quite in the forefront of European players.

So it was that my luck turned and I lost to Bernard. This gave France a 3–2 win and the blame was put entirely on me. So much so that I was almost ashamed to walk in the streets. Our newspapers in Prague said I had not practised enough, that I was drinking champagne in the night clubs the day before I played Bernard and that I had been out with girls. They must have recalled that mythical girl friend I had in Palermo.

It was the worst and least true criticism of me ever written. By coincidence on the same day Zatopek broke the world record for 10,000 metres. In contrast to me he was written up as a hero and an example of real sportsmanship. That shows all too clearly how sport is regarded in Communist countries and how fickle are the people who hail you one moment and throw you down the next.

Only last year Puskas, that great Hungarian footballer, was criticized and denigrated in exactly the same way. But he had to make a public confession that his failure to train and love of good food were true criticisms of his inability to measure up to the standards set for him.

Until this moment I had been a hero, the man who carried the Czech Davis Cup team on his shoulders. One defeat and I was a scapegoat. No one bothered about Cernik, and the fact that he had, as was not uncommon, lost two singles matches against France, or that to play before a French crowd at the Stade Roland Garros is a very different thing to playing in Prague.

This strengthened my resolve to leave my country when the time was ripe; and the sooner the better. It brought home to me fully that a loser is useless in a Communist society where sport is the best and cheapest form of propaganda. Once I began to lose matches I realized that sooner or later I would be stopped from going abroad and then my chance of escape would be no more.

Every time I returned to Prague after one of these tours my friends wondered why I had come back. They were mostly convinced because of the foreign broadcasts that war between East and West was inevitable. For people in Czechoslovakia and other Communist-controlled countries war was – and still is – their only hope of liberation. I knew that this was untrue and that war was then, and again still is, far from inevitable.

But it would have been useless and even dangerous for me to say so and explain that no one west of the Iron Curtain wanted war.

The rumour soon went round that I was a Communist because I could travel more or less where I liked. But Cernik and I were very rare exceptions. We were useful to the country and the Government as international sportsmen. People forgot that we both had families in Prague.

As to the Communists, they knew we were neither members of the Party nor of their faith, yet never once did they attempt to convert or even lecture us before going abroad, as was the usual custom. They must have regarded us as a couple of prize birds to show off to the rest of the country and to the world outside, to prove that Communism in Czechoslovakia was not so bad as it was made out to be.

Being in low spirits after our Davis Cup defeat I went straight from Paris to Wimbledon, where I was determined to do well. If I failed I had already decided not to return home but ask for asylum in England.

This Wimbledon, regarded as one of the most brilliant and exciting ever played, afterwards became known as Schroeder's Year. Here was a man, Ted Schroeder from the United States and the same age as myself, who had never played at Wimbledon before.

He arrived in England in a hurry and with all the advance publicity he received and because of his dynamic personality, straightaway captured the imagination of the public. Schroeder was like a big lovable bear. He would talk to anyone. He smoked an old corncob pipe, drank lots of beer, played cards and was completely at ease with everyone.

Among his own players Schroeder was not popular because of his independence and his refusal to play along the circuit, as we call the tournament game, when players go from one place to another week after week. Schroeder had a good job and fitted in his tennis when he could. He was usually included in the US Davis Cup teams and people said it was because of his great friend, Jack Kramer.

I had met Schroeder in Los Angeles two years previously. Even then he did not look too good, just like Budge Patty. But he always seemed to win when it mattered. He paid no attention to results in the smaller tournaments. The big ones were the prizes he went for. Personally I found Schroeder a very pleasant fellow, one of the best fighters on the court and match players in the game.

In this Wimbledon Schroeder and the current US champion, Richard Gonzales, were the top two seeded players although the holder, Bob

Falkenburg, was defending. Falkenburg's pre-Wimbledon form had been unimpressive. So for that matter had Gonzales's.

Parker, the French champion, John Bromwich, runner-up the previous year, Eric Sturgess, young Frank Sedgman, making his first appearance at Wimbledon, and I were the other five seeded players. There were some world-class players not in that list and therefore, as you might say, let loose in the draw. They included Budge Patty and Geoff Brown, the finalist in 1946.

Schroeder and I were in opposite halves and for both of us, should we reach the final, the draw was tough. Schroeder, for all his luck in the playing of matches, had Gardnar Mulloy in the first round and in what I suppose was one of the greatest opening matches ever played won after being two sets down. If Mulloy had not got cramp in that last set who knows what might have happened. Even so it went 7–5 before Schroeder won.

For myself I came through a couple of fairly easy rounds before meeting my shadow, Budge Patty, for the third time including the match in which I defaulted in Cairo. Having lost to Patty in the 1947 Wimbledon and having seen him many times since I was not going to fall into any trap again.

This time I made him work really hard in the first three sets. He won two of them but they were advantage sets, and the cost to his energy and stamina was considerable. By the time the fourth set began he was really and honestly tired and I won this and the fifth set by 6–0, 6–2.

Meantime, Gonzales, who enjoyed too much the good things of life, had been beaten by Geoff Brown and when the last eight lined up it was as follows: Brown v. myself, Falkenburg v. Bromwich (a repeat of the previous year's final), Sturgess v. Parker, Schroeder v. Sedgman. Observers said this was the best last eight ever seen at Wimbledon and the matches appeared to confirm this for each of them went to five sets with the results hanging on a single shot or two.

My match with Brown, the double-handed Australian with a tremendous serve and very fast two-handed backhand, was a repeat of our meeting in the 1946 semi-final only this time I managed to win. Whereas last time I had still been tired from my match with Kramer this time I was pretty fit, having had no hard match other than the one with Patty.

I had to fight like anything to stop Brown overwhelming me with his pace. That backhand of his was the fastest shot in the game, but knowing it was not easy for him to play it off wide shots I gave him angles as much as possible, making him run from side to side. Brown led me two sets to one but I was the fitter in the last set.

Bromwich got his revenge on Falkenburg in an extraordinary match. Falkenburg having won the first two sets, threw the third and fourth 6–0, 6–0. Then Sturgess got the better of Parker in a classic baseline duel that contrasted with the other matches since neither player had much of a service or was a net rusher. Both possessed the best passing shots in the game at that time (I suppose Rosewall does nowadays) and were very fast about the court.

Finally there was that mighty match between Schroeder and Sedgman. I did not see it for it preceded my game against Brown on No. 1 court but I heard a lot about it. How, for instance, Schroeder had been footfaulted on a first service when facing match point again. How he had served his second service, and come in to the net to make a winning volley off the wood. Sedgman twice came within a shot of beating Schroeder on that hot afternoon. What a match it must have been.

My own thoughts went back to my match with Kramer when I heard about Schroeder being footfaulted. You may recall I was footfaulted too in the last game of all.

Bromwich was below his best form when he met me in the semi-final whereas I could not miss a thing. Schroeder however got tangled up in yet another five-set match with Sturgess. He won, but I would have preferred Sturgess as an opponent in the final.

By this time Schroeder had lived up to his nickname 'Lucky Schroeder' because of his facility in getting out of trouble and winning five-set matches when he looked like being beaten. I was not confident of beating him in the final. I was still relying heavily on my service while my backhand was not steady enough to withstand such a net-rushing attack as Schroeder's.

I thought I did well to take him to a fifth set and hoped for a little luck and some change of fortune for my opponent. I began the set on my service and that was an obvious advantage but could feel Schroeder putting on the pressure immediately. It became a case of when he would break my service rather than my taking his.

Being a great match player Schroeder had only to make a couple of really good shots to turn the match his way. They came all right at 3–all, when I was serving. He hit a couple of backhand returns of service that had me completely beaten. They were sufficient to give him the break through for the match. As I walked to the dressing room Princess Margaret spoke to me saying, 'Bad luck. I hope you win another time.'

Schroeder's was a popular win, and I felt that he thoroughly deserved the title after all the struggles he had had. I had then, and still have a great admiration for him. When a month or two later I played him again in California the same thing happened. That time I nearly had him beaten and somehow he escaped.

Though I had lost the final my popularity seemed to be almost as great as Schroeder's. More important to me was the fact that I had got through to the final and proved to myself that my defeat in Paris in the Davis Cup was just one of those things that happen in sport.

At home they forgot all about defeat in the Davis Cup and once more hailed me as a hero who could do no wrong. This gave me my cue. I could return to Prague, gather my things together and prepare my final escape. I knew now that, for the time being at any rate, no one would stop me coming and going. Moreover, if I returned after all the criticisms that had been made of me after the Paris defeat then they would certainly not think I had any intention of leaving.

There was, at this memorable Wimbledon, one other match that is worth recalling, a men's double in which Brown and Bill Sidwell of Australia beat Falkenburg and myself by 8–6 in the fifth set. With the score 6–all in the last set we had Brown down love–40 on his service. I remarked to Falkenburg that here was our chance. We were mistaken, since Brown served four of the fastest and most dramatic aces ever seen at Wimbledon. We got our rackets to none of them and they put the Australians ahead 7–6 where they were so confident that they took the next game for the match.

Schroeder arranged for me to be invited to the United States for their season at the expense of Perry T. Jones, of the Southern Californian LTC Association, a trip which would also enable me to play in the US Championships at Forest Hills.

As I was now *persona grata* at home I could return to Prague certain that I could get out again and go to America.

During the closing days of Wimbledon my club cabled me to invite Schroeder to come to Prague for an exhibition match on the Sunday following the last day of Wimbledon. I explained to Schroeder that this would help me a lot and ensure me being able to make my own trip to America, where I intended to stay. Moreover by then my girl friend,

Tatjana, having previously parted from me had made it up. She, too, was now in New York.

Schroeder agreed to come to Prague and asked for no money, only unlimited quantities of beer. I regard this as the hallmark of a true amateur. I assured him that we had the best beer in the world, Pilsener. I had his air ticket, and every seat at the club was booked when a cable arrived, on Saturday night, saying the show had been cancelled. Later I discovered that our Communist Government were fearful lest the public show their appreciation of a capitalist player and in so doing, exhibit their pro-west feelings.

When I arrived home the newspapers began to write about me turning professional, saying that I had been offered 100,000 dollars by Jack Kramer. People seemed to know far more about it than I did. I received no such offer then, nor have I since.

These stories, however, caused the Minister of Information, our old friend Kopecky, to call for me a couple of days later. I went along with Kozeluh who was his friend. This, I thought, was the right moment to complain about the criticism I had received after the Davis Cup defeat in France. Kopecky was very upset about one particular article and threatened to have the writer put into prison. He even picked up the telephone but then had second thoughts. The journalist concerned was in Moscow with a swimming team at the time which was, perhaps, lucky for him.

Realizing I might turn professional Kopecky offered me all sorts of inducements, including a bigger flat and a larger salary from my firm. Though I had been offered expenses from the Southern Californian LTA Kopecky would hear none of it. He said, 'You will go to America at our expense' – a most generous offer from a Communist.

Soon, said Kopecky, I would be made a Master of Sport. A law was then being prepared to create such titles and positions on the Russian system. A Master of Sport carries with it a pension large enough to live on for the rest of one's life. In return I was to promise not to turn professional and that was no trouble at all since I had had no offer.

Despite all this my mind was now made up. I had my ticket to the US and a reservation on an aeroplane. I had discussed my escape with no one, and I had not even mentioned it to my family. I felt a clean, sudden break the best way out.

With the idea of making some extra money to give my family I bought a new car. There were two ways of getting a car under the Communists, either on the free market, which was expensive, or through a permit which reduced the price by two-thirds.

I had no difficulty in acquiring a permit and was promised a further one to allow me to sell the car before the specified period of a year was up. Unfortunately the man who promised me the selling permit went on holiday and having got my car I could not dispose of it.

I began surreptitiously to clear my belongings and prizes out of my flat. I had to do this under the cover of night since one never knew who was watching. Furthermore, I had a lot of friends who came to visit me and if everything large disappeared at once they might begin to ask questions. I had therefore to leave my furniture and larger stuff knowing full well that when the news broke that I had fled the Communists would confiscate the lot.

As there were three weeks before I was due to go to America Cernik and I decided to go to Gstaad for the Swiss International Championships. We had no trouble over the permits but just before we left I had an anonymous telephone call from a man who said, 'Never mind my name. I'm a friend of yours working at the Ministry of Interior. I have seen your card and would advise you to leave Czechoslovakia as soon as you can.' With that he hung up.

This shook me for I knew, as did everyone, that there was an index at the Ministry of the Interior on which was recorded everything one said and did. When the secret police pulled someone in there was the grim record as evidence. I realized now that more than ever it was a race between them and me with even my American trip in jeopardy.

On 11 July I joined Cernik at Prague Airport for the air journey to Switzerland. It was supposed to be a one-week trip, yet there was Cernik with a couple of large suitcases. I became suspicious as I had only a weekend bag and fifty dollars. Then I thought that perhaps Cernik was carrying out suitcases for a friend who had already fled, as I had done on numerous occasions in the past.

I was not such a friend of Cernik's that I could discuss intentions with him freely, so on the plane to Switzerland neither of us spoke much, and then only about other things.

We were well received at Gstaad and put into the best hotel. Two days later we were recalled by our Government and forbidden to take any further part in the tournament because two Germans, Goepfert and Beutner, and one Spaniard, Masip, were competing. Germany was still regarded as an enemy country while there had been no diplomatic relations with Spain for many years.

This put us in a delicate position, since the Swiss had invited us and depended on our participation. So we replied that we could not leave and continued to play.

Next day two Czech officials from the Berne Legation, named Zelenka and Nemes, approached us and said they had received orders to send us home. We tried to explain the situation in a friendly way but Zelenka, younger than either of us, behaved in a most brusque and ill-mannered way. Roughly he shouted at us, 'Go, pack your bags. I will take you to Berne and put you on a plane to Prague.' This made us so furious that I nearly hit him.

Eventually we agreed not to play any more but as we were guests of Mr Scherz at the Palace Hotel we said we would remain there a couple of days before returning home. This satisfied the two officials and they left us.

That night Cernik and I talked the whole thing over. He told me for the first time that he had no intention of returning home and that the suitcases he had brought contained all his clothes and belongings. This put me on the spot, for all I had was a couple of shirts, the proverbial toothbrush and fifty dollars. All the money and clothes I had planned to take out with me were still in Prague where I had hoped to pick them up the following week before going to America.

We decided to make a definite decision in the morning. I had very little sleep that night. Turning round in my mind were all sorts of possibilities. For instance, suppose I went back to Prague as if nothing had happened while Cernik went on to other tournaments, what would the reaction be? I could pass off Cernik's absence by saying he had further invitations which I could not accept because of the American trip.

But suppose they persisted in recalling Cernik and when they got no reply or response they would suspect something and turn round on me. Then Cernik might publicly announce his flight and the Government would immediately ban all further trips. There was very little I could do other than make the break now.

Next morning Cernik and I took the funicular up the mountain where we could talk freely and in peace. He said his mind was made up absolutely. There was no return for him. He was certain they would never allow him to leave Czechoslovakia again and he did not like the life there. There was virtually nothing I could do but follow his example, and having made my decision I had no regrets.

We went to the tournament committee and told them of our decision not to return to our country. They were most helpful and sympathetic and three of the committee, Mr Scherz, Mr Siebenthal and Mr Cadonau, began to plan our next steps.

We arranged to withdraw officially from the tournament for one day. That would appear as if we were respecting the Czech Government's wishes and allay any immediate suspicions in our local Legations. It would also give us time to take certain pre-arranged steps with contacts at home. The details of these I cannot mention even now, as some of my friends concerned are still in Czechoslovakia.

In the tournament I was already in the semi-final whereas Cernik was due to play Puncec in the last eight but had withdrawn with the committee's consent.

Having got everything organized with the committee we turned up the following day as if nothing had happened and made the official announcement that we were not returning to Czechoslovakia. That was on 15 July and pinned to the club notice board was the following statement signed by both of us. It was printed in three languages and said, 'We wish to state in public that we are sportsmen completely devoted to lawn tennis and in no way connected with politics. We have, therefore, decided to respect Swiss hospitality and shall play to the end of the International Championships at Gstaad. No one can prevent us following our sporting ambitions and with that object we propose to go to the United States.'

At the Press conference which naturally followed we made it clear that this had been our resolve for some time, that we were not Communists, had never been members of the Party but had been used as propaganda for our country. We did not know from one trip to another whether we would be stopped or not and for that, and other reasons, we had decided on flight.

That evening Nemes, the Czech Press Attaché, turned up again and demanded to see us in the hotel. By then we had a guard of Swiss Police and he was refused even telephone communication with us. Eventually he was ordered out of the hotel. He then went down to the club, saw our declaration on the notice board and tore it down. For this the Swiss Government asked for his immediate recall to Czechoslovakia.

From then on we were shadowed everywhere by plain clothes Swiss police, though we did not know it at the time. When another Czech official arrived we were immediately told. This time it was Slansky, brother of the secretary of the Czech Communist Party who was later shot by his own crowd. Slansky registered at another hotel, managed to get Cernik on the telephone and arranged to talk to him at an hotel down in the village, below the Palace. Slansky did not ask to see me as he thought I was the one who had persuaded Cernik to leave. I always smile when I think of Slansky's mistake and the time he wasted talking to the wrong man.

The Swiss police knew about Slansky and the proposed meeting and when Cernik arrived to keep the appointment the hotel was full of plain clothes men. I went to a coffee shop opposite, waiting for Cernik. He crossed the road in twenty minutes. Apparently Slansky had talked to Cernik about his wife and family, had said the Communists knew it was all my fault and if he would go home all would be forgiven.

Cernik let him talk. At the end he got up and walked out without shaking hands. Since then we have never been approached by anyone from what I now call 'the other side'.

The Czech newspapers immediately called us traitors. One of them, the *Rude Pravo*, wrote: 'We accuse Drobny of playing a double game since the war; hiding behind his father, a groundsman, professing loyalty while maintaining links with the bourgeoisie for whom he once chased tennis balls.'

One result of our break was that no Czech tennis players were allowed to travel to the west for five years. Only this year, 1955, has this law been rescinded and Czechoslovakia have re-entered the Davis Cup for the first time since 1949. That was a fateful year for me and for Czech tennis. I lost to Bernard in Paris, my country lost the European Zone championship and Cernik and I made our exit.

Another result was that the Government stopped measures to create Masters of Sport. Later I heard that Zatopek and I were to be the first two. Poor Zatopek had to wait another three years before they passed the law and gave him the status he has so richly deserved.

Champion in Exile, 1955

Levels of the Game
JOHN MCPHEE

It must have cost at least two hundred thousand dollars to produce this scene – to develop the two young men and to give them the equipment, the travel, and the experience necessary for a rise to this level. The expense has been shared by parents, sponsors, tournament committees, the Davis Cup Team, and the United States Lawn Tennis Association, and by resort hotels, sporting-goods companies, Coca-Cola, and other interested commercial supporters. The players themselves paid their way to Forest Hills for this match, though – twenty cents apiece, on the subway. Graebner lives in an apartment on East 86th Street with his wife, Carole; their one-year-old daughter, Cameron; and their infant son, Clark. Graebner spends much of his time selling high-grade printing papers, as assistant to the president of the Hobson Miller division of Saxon Industries, and he is in love with his work. He knows the exact height and tensile strength of the corporate ladder. His boss likes tennis very much, so Graebner's present rung is the handle of a racquet. Ashe is an Army lieutenant, working in the office of the adjutant general at the United States Military Academy. He is a bachelor, and during tournament time at Forest Hills he stays at the Hotel Roosevelt. The Army is almost as tennis-minded as Graebner's boss, and Ashe has been given ample time for the game. But tennis is not, in any traditional sense, a game to him. 'I get my kicks away from the tennis court,' he will say. With accumulated leave time, he plans to go on safari in Kenya. It will be his first trip to Africa.

In 1735, the Doddington, a square-rigger of eighty tons and Liverpool registry, sailed into the York River in Virginia carrying a cargo of a hundred and sixty-seven West African blacks. In or near Yorktown, the ship's captain, James Copland, traded the blacks for tobacco. One young woman, known only by a number, was acquired by Robert Blackwell, a tobacco grower from Lunenburg County. Blackwell gave her to his son as a wedding present – in the records of the county, she was listed only as 'a Negur girl.' According to custom, she took the name of her owner. She married a man who, having the same owner, was also named Blackwell, and they had a daughter, Lucy, whose value is given in her owner's will at fifty dollars. Lucy Blackwell married Moses Blackwell, and their daughter Peggy Blackwell had a daughter named Peggy Blackwell, who married her cousin Tony Blackwell. Their daughter

Jinney married Mike, an otherwise nameless Indian of the Sauk tribe who was a blood relative of Chief Black Hawk. The preacher who married them told Mike to call himself Mike Blackwell forevermore. Jinney and Mike had a son named Hammett, who, in this chain of beings, was the last slave. Hammett was born in 1839. In 1856, he married Julia Tucker. They had twenty-three children. When he became free, he should have been given forty acres and a mule, of course, but no one gave them to him, so he bought his forty acres, in Dundas, Virginia. On the Blackwell plantation, where Hammett had lived, the plantation house – white frame, with columns – still stands, vacant and moldering. The slave cabin is there, too, its roof half peeled away. Hammett's daughter Sadie married Willie Johnson, and their daughter Amelia married Pinkney Avery Ashe. His family line reached back, in analogous fashion, to the ownership of Samuel Ashe, an early governor of the State of North Carolina, whose name, until now, has been kept alive largely by the continuing existence of Asheville. Pinkney and Amelia had a son named Arthur, who, in 1938, married Mattie Cunningham, of Richmond. Their son Arthur Junior was born in 1943.

All these names are presented on separate leaves or limbs of an enormous family tree – six by seven feet, and painted on canvas – that is kept in the home of Thelma Doswell, a cousin of Arthur Ashe. Mrs Doswell, who lives in the District of Columbia and is a teacher of children who have specific learning disabilities, did much of the research that produced the tree, using vacation time to travel to courthouses and libraries in southern Virginia. There are fifteen hundred leaves on the tree, and one leaf – Arthur Ashe, Jr's – is painted gold. Matrilineal in nature, the tree was made for display at annual reunions of the family, which have been held in various cities – Washington, Bridgeport, Philadelphia, Pittsburgh – and have drawn above three hundred people. The family has a crest, in crimson, black, and gold. A central chevron in this escutcheon bears a black chain with a broken link, symbolizing the broken bonds of slavery. Below the broken chain is a black well. And in the upper corners, where the crest of a Norman family might have fleurs-de-lis, this one has tobacco leaves, in trifoliate clusters. Graebner has no idea whatever when his forebears first came to this country.

Levels of the Game, 1969

The Davis Cup
ARTHUR ASHE

In October, our team assembled in Dublin, Ireland, to qualify for the group of sixteen by playing Ireland. Here I saw yet another side of McEnroe. With the Irish emotionally welcoming John as a native son come home, I was prepared to have him play the part, wax nostalgic about the old sod, and milk his visit for what it was worth. As an African American in the 1980s, I knew all about the allegedly magical powers of one's 'roots.' To his credit, however, John refused to indulge in ethnic romanticism. 'I don't have a special feeling competing here because I'm Irish,' he stated bluntly. 'You're playing for your country and trying to win regardless of where you come from.' Many of the Irish loved him for his apparent dislike of British snobbishness as represented by Wimbledon, but he himself was unsentimental. Dublin, he told one reporter, 'looks like London to me, only drearier. I hope the people are nicer.'

The Irish forgave him his truculence; perhaps they considered it characteristically Irish. I myself didn't. In the United States, I have had people say to me about McEnroe and Connors's excesses, 'Gee, what do you expect? That's the Irish in them.' Such ethnic stereotyping makes me uncomfortable. In any event, McEnroe drew a record crowd to watch tennis at the Royal Dublin Society's Simmonscourt Pavilion – a fancy barn, really, where horse and cattle breeders showed their stock. The place had been cleaned out, fumigated, and a carpet set down for play. It was all a little odd. Still, during and after our victory, the Irish were ebullient, gracious hosts. And with his victories in Dublin, McEnroe broke my record of twenty-seven wins for the U.S. in singles matches. I did not begrudge him the record.

For our next match, in the first round of the 1984 Davis Cup, against Rumania, in Bucharest, we finally had the services of Jimmy Connors. Since the last time Connors had played for us, Donald Dell had become his manager. Dell, a former Cup captain, had argued to Jimmy and his mother, Gloria, that no American had ever achieved legendary status in tennis without playing Davis Cup, and so Jimmy agreed to play. But he had evidently heard negative remarks about my captaincy. We had a meeting at a tournament before Bucharest, and he was blunt.

'Look, Arthur, I don't need anyone sitting on the sidelines telling me how to play tennis.'

'I understand, Jimmy.'

'One thing I want to know, though, Arthur. Are you going to fight for me?'

'What do you mean, Jimmy?'

'I mean, am I going to be out there by myself? Will I be doing my own arguing?'

'I'm out there, Jimmy,' I replied. 'I'm on your side. I'm going to be working for you.'

Twice during Jimmy's first match I made sure that I jumped up and made my presence known to Jimmy and the assembled gathering. I am not sure what I accomplished by these moves, except for making Connors happy. But that was reason enough, I suppose.

Connors's effervescence, the stellar quality of his magnetism and drive, lifted everyone. 'That Connors doesn't like losing *in practice*,' Jimmy Arias said to me one day as we watched Connors go after McEnroe on the court. I thought I saw a remarkable spirit of camaraderie, of genuine affection, kindle between Jimmy and John, and ignite among the other players. Then Connors's old discomfort with the Davis Cup began to surface. To Mac and me, that silver cup was the Holy Grail. To Jimmy, it seemed that it might have been made of Styrofoam, he had so little sense of, or interest in, Davis Cup legend and lore.

One day, at practice just before the opening match, he yelled out to me with a question. 'Arthur, this match is best of three sets, isn't it?'

I could hardly believe my ears. 'You mean this practice?'

'No, I mean the matches.' He was serious. Stupefied, I shook my head and looked up into the empty stands.

Once again, as much as he tried, Connors couldn't stomach the fact that everyone was in McEnroe's shadow, as far as publicity and fame were concerned. McEnroe welcomed Jimmy, but I sensed that he also nursed a lingering resentment about the fact that Jimmy had indicated that he would play Davis Cup in 1981 and then changed his mind. Still, John had such a genuine interest in our fortunes as a team that he wanted Connors to play. The previous year, he had even accused me of not being firm enough with Connors. 'He says he's a friend of his,' John told a reporter about Connors and me, 'but I don't think he pushed Connors enough. Arthur doesn't press him.' Of course, I believed that I had pressed Connors as much as I could, or should, have. I was not going to force anyone to play Davis Cup tennis.

Bucharest in 1984 was a dreary city, with shops that had nothing to offer, and with a repressive, intrusive secret police that resulted in our party, including wives, attending a briefing at the US embassy in a room draped with aluminium foil, or some similar substance, to frustrate eavesdropping. The only spark of warmth and friendship emanating from Rumania came from the unforgettable personality of Ilie Nastase. Still a member of the national team, Nastase evoked bitter memories of the Davis Cup tie in Bucharest in 1972 between the US and Rumania, when cheating by local officials reached an abysmal low. In the decisive match between Stan Smith and Ion Tiriac, judges called foot faults to negate Smith's aces, Tiriac orchestrated crowd noises to disturb Smith's game, and a linesman at one point openly massaged Tiriac's cramping legs and urged him on. Smith, always the epitome of self-control, kept his temper in check and eventually won the match. At the end, he gravely shook Tiriac's hand. 'Ion,' Stan said, 'I must tell you that I will always respect you as a player. But I will never again have any respect for you as a man.' Tiriac was left speechless.

Nastase had been, in his prime, fantastically gifted as a player, almost on a level of uncanny ability with McEnroe. He was also given to outrageous behaviour on the tennis court, including crude and vicious teasing of opponents, such as accusations about their sexual preferences and abilities. He liked to call me 'Negroni,' and once, in the heat of battle in a tournament in Hawaii, even called me a nigger. I myself didn't hear the remark but was told about it. In 1975, at the Masters tournament in Sweden, I had walked off the court in a match against him after his taunting had become unbearable. Refusing to answer him in kind, I deliberately defaulted. (The supervising committee decided later that day to award me the match, 6–0, 6–0. After the tournament, which he nevertheless won because its format did not allow for elimination after one loss, Nastase sent me a bouquet of roses.) Since then, I have always counted Nastase as a friend. In 1977, he showed up at my wedding. 'You didn't invite me,' he said, grinning and offering his hand in congratulations. 'But I came anyway.'

Nastase was always a little mad. Now, thirty-seven years old and fifteen pounds above his best weight, he showed flashes of his genius of old, firing thirteen aces past McEnroe in the opening match. He stalled and argued, abused the umpire, and was duly penalized. To our cadre of supporters from the US embassy who waved little American flags to encourage our effort, he genially offered the finger from time to time. He worked on McEnroe, seeking to arouse him; but John remained calm. The Rumanians did not win a set until the last match of the tie.

We beat Argentina and Australia, and then in mid-December, faced the Swedes in the Cup final in Göteborg. This encounter turned out to be one of the more dismal points of my tennis career. From our arrival, nothing seemed to go right. Inside the Scandinavium, the nation's largest indoor facility, the Swedes had prepared a clay court to give themselves an advantage. We needed to accustom ourselves to the surface, but none of us seemed ready to make the supreme effort. Meanwhile, everyone on the Swedish team except Mats Wilander diligently arrived in Göteborg ten days before the tie and worked out hard for four hours daily. Wilander was away only because he was chasing his second Australian Open, which he won. Then, match fit, he hurried home.

In contrast, McEnroe and Connors were both badly off their stride. Unshaven and unkempt, McEnroe looked exhausted and depressed. He had recently been suspended for twenty-one days for outrageous behavior in a tournament in Stockholm. Viewers around the world had seen the film clip of McEnroe engaging in a vile, murderous tirade, smashing racquets and cups and abusing officials. Now, rusty from his enforced rest, he had to return to Sweden to play Davis Cup tennis. With the press he was first testy, then surly, and finally bitter and contentious. Connors, too, hadn't played competitively in a while. With his wife, Patty, expecting their second child any day, he was also distracted. He asked me if he could arrive a day late and I agreed, which was a mistake. When he got there, all his hostility to the Davis Cup and to team play seemed to return. Everything about our arrangements appeared to anger him, and nothing I said made any difference.

Relations between us crumbled after an incident one night. Practice was scheduled for seven in the evening between Connors and Arias, whom I had selected as an alternate singles player all year. Connors, on time, was already at the stadium; I was supposed to bring Arias over. Our car was late in arriving, and we reached the stadium about ten or fifteen minutes after seven. By this point, Connors, who is nearly always punctual (when he shows up for an event), had worked himself up into a sweaty rage. As I walked through a door onto the court, I saw a message he had scrawled in large letters in the soft clay, presumably for me. His message read: FUCK YOU.

I felt exactly as if he had slapped my face. I wanted to replace him on the spot and send him home, but I knew our chances of winning would have dropped precipitously. I swallowed my pride and endured the insult.

In the tie, played before enthusiastic, sellout crowds, the Swedes defeated us decisively, 4–1. Wilander, tanned, lithe, and fleet of foot after his Australian campaign, crushed Connors 6–1, 6–3, 6–3. Jimmy was sadly out of shape, and the clay court set up by the Swedes caused a few odd bounces that frustrated him as he struggled to find his form. At the end of the first set, he resorted to unspeakably vile language, cursing both the umpire and referee Alan Mills (who was also later the Wimbledon referee). Mills was outraged. Connors was fined $2,000 and came within a penalty point of being defaulted. Mills let us know that he was thinking seriously of recommending that Connors be banned from further competition.

Donald Dell, who had come in for the matches, convinced Connors to apologize to Mills. As Donald put it, Jimmy had to apologize to preserve the honor of the United States. I don't know if Jimmy fully appreciated this concept, but he understood it sufficiently to make what Mills called a 'very genuine and personal apology' to both him and the umpire.

By this time, Henrik Sundstrom had defeated McEnroe, who also found the clay surface daunting. McEnroe's rustiness showed, and he had also injured his wrist. The next day, in the doubles, McEnroe and Fleming fell to Jarryd and nineteen-year-old Stefan Edberg in four sets – and we had lost the Cup. We had prepared shabbily, and had paid the price accordingly. For this I bear most of the blame.

The tie now decided, Connors asked to go home to his wife. I gave him permission to do so, and Arias finally had his chance to play. I had named Arias to our team after he had become one of the top ten in the world, then stuck with him when his ranking slid into the twenties. Then I heard from agents for other players who couldn't understand why he was on the team and they were not. I believed that I had to be loyal to Arias, and not dump him simply because he had slipped a little. Meanwhile, Arias himself made it clear that he did not enjoy being a backup player, even to Connors and McEnroe. He wanted to play singles. Now he had his chance in a best-of-three-sets 'dead rubber' match.

Against Sundstrom, Arias took the first set and seemed on his way to an easy triumph. Then, inexplicably, with no sun or wind to contend with, and on his favorite surface, clay, Arias began to hyperventilate. He simply became too excited. As I watched in deepening embarrassment, he began to cramp up badly. Sundstrom won, 3–6, 8–6, 6–3.

Days of Grace, 1993

The Commuter
MARTINA NAVRATILOVA

I was pretty full of myself when George Parma accepted me into his program. Once a week I would hurry from school to catch the commuter train to Prague, usually rushing across the platform with my tennis racquet sticking out, gym bag at another angle, school bag hanging down to my ankles. I always tell people that I developed my strength and my speed running for trains when I was nine and ten years old.

I felt very proud, very mysterious, to be this little pipsqueak of a girl with all the equipment going into Prague to play tennis. You didn't see kids running around Czechoslovakia with tennis gear the way you do in the States, and I would imagine people asking themselves, Who is she? and I would be thinking to myself: Some day you'll know.

I can still recall those slow train rides along the Berounka Valley, through sleepy little villages: Dobrichovice; Vsenory; Mokropsy, where my mother worked in a factory; Cernosice, where my mother's grandmother used to have a farm; Radotin, where my mother's brother, Josef, lived near the station, and sometimes I could see him from the train, working in the garden; Chuchle, where my grandfather lived.

After thirty minutes or so, we'd pull into Smichov, a drab commuter station across the Vltava River from the historic portion of Prague. From Smichov, I'd take the red streetcar to the Klamovka section and walk up the hill to the courts and George Parma. After a few lessons, I would have walked through fire for this tall, handsome man with blond wavy hair. He was like a god to me – cool, intelligent, well educated. He had traveled outside Czechoslovakia many times and knew five languages. He always looked immaculate, as if he were going out to play for the Davis Cup again.

He was the most patient coach a kid could have. He would never shout or downgrade me in any way. All he'd have to say was, 'Come on, Martina,' and I'd chase down every shot. I'd follow every word he said, and if I thought he was going to tell me something, I'd rush right up to the net and stare into his light blue eyes.

If you ever saw a girl get a crush on her teacher, this was it. I used to think to myself that if only I was older, I could have married him. It didn't matter one iota that he already was married, that his wife, Jarmila, was a beautiful and very nice person. I believed George Parma would have been the perfect husband, but that's the way it goes when you're ten.

Once in a while George would come to Revnice to work outdoors with me. It was such a big occasion to have him visit our town that I would wear a white tennis skirt to practice with him. Here was a former Czech Davis Cup player, all decked out in Fred Perry gear, giving lessons to me on the town court. I was so excited to work with him that I'd chase balls until I ran out of breath.

The first thing George did was change my backhand. My father had let me use a two-handed backhand at five and six years old because I'd been too weak to get much on the ball with one hand. But later George could see that all I wanted to do was come to the net and volley, so I was going to need all the reach I could get. So he took my right hand off the racquet and that let me extend my reach a few more inches. If he hadn't, can't you just see Chris and me having the battle of the two-handed backhands?

If I were teaching children now, I would teach a two-handed drive backhand, a one-handed slice, and a one-handed approach and a one-handed volley, to give variety. I wouldn't mind having a two-handed blast for some shots, but I'm not about to retool my game at this point – and also I'm blessed with plenty of power with just the one hand. Kids have more control with two hands, but you're also vulnerable approaching with two hands. Learning both variations is almost like learning an extra stroke, but it's definitely the perfect way to play tennis. Mats Wilander is the best with two-handed or one-handed backhands that I've seen.

George Parma knew what he was doing at the time. His job was to develop good tennis players. Czech women are pretty sturdy and they handle some heavy jobs in factories and shops. He didn't mind working me hard, since there was no sense of tennis being a social outing or a recreation. He had a skill to teach me, and he went at it.

George wanted to refine my game, which made sense. He told me to learn to play the baseline more but still be aggressive. He told me I was like a cat, like a tiger, but that sometimes even a tiger has to be conservative.

I didn't believe in playing conservatively then, and really I still don't. Some of the worst tennis I've played has come when I was too tentative, when I waited for my opponent to make the mistakes – like the time I let myself get talked into sitting back on Kathy Horvath and got zapped right out of the 1983 French Open. But sometimes when I was younger,

I wanted to be too perfect, to hit the perfect winner on the first exchange. I'd try some fancy drop shot and George would raise his eyebrows or say, 'Just hit it back, Martina,' and I'd get in the groove and hit a few forehands. But if I saw an opening, I'd rush the net again, and he'd have to remind me that I was taking a lesson, not playing for the Czech championship.

'Ordinary shots are what make a player,' he would say.

George began to give me tips on how to behave in matches, what to do if people tried to cheat me, how to vary my strokes. I could tell he thought I was developing.

He would talk about the international circuit from his own experience. He once told me how it had been impossible for him to get good training growing up during World War II and right afterward. He undoubtedly could have been a better player if he'd had better coaching, and he thought things would be better for me. By my time, Czechoslovakia was much more open about producing good tennis players to compete on an international basis.

In the mid-sixties, the Communists could see the value of sports as a way of making people proud and keeping their minds off the less pleasant aspects of life. They approached sports the same way they approached the economy: with a plan. You would hear jokes about how the Russians expected Czechoslovakia to produce a certain tonnage of screws every year, so the only way you could achieve your goal would be to produce huge ones that nobody could use. Or if your quota was elevators, you'd produce the proper number – even if they couldn't be serviced.

Sports were easier to plan. The Communists more or less emphasized a different sport in each country: weight-lifting in the Soviet Union, track and field in East Germany, gymnastics in Rumania, tennis in Czechoslovakia.

In my country, sports were one way to show national pride, one of the few safe ways. You could cheer for a Czech hockey team or soccer team, even against the Soviet Union. It was a tradition going back to the nineteenth century when people formed sports clubs like Sokol, to compete in gymnastics. It was the only way you could say to the Hapsburgs, 'Look, we're still Czechs, even if we now belong to the Austro-Hungarian Empire.'

Right after World War II, the Soviet soccer team came to Czecho-slovakia and lost three straight matches – they didn't even show up for the fourth. This embarrassed the Russians so much that when the

Communists took over the country in 1948, they closed down the sports program as a way of curbing nationalism. But by the time I came along, sports were safe again and the government was pouring money into them.

George was a government employee, so he had to follow a certain schedule. Some afternoons he gave lessons and other afternoons he trained a junior team for the government, but he could also make separate deals with people for private lessons, all above-board.

Czechoslovakia had been a Middle European capitalist country until 1948; people were still used to working hard to earn some extra money, and some people still had money to pay for lessons for themselves or more court time for their kids. But George Parma never asked a penny for my lessons and my father never paid him a penny. George saw my talent, and he worked with it.

I also had Madame Kozelska on my side. That little old lady was all over the courts, cleaning out the lockers, dragging the clay, keeping an eye on everybody from her little apartment. She was a regular scuttlebug, and she knew who were the good kids and who were the bad ones. She had taken a liking to me, and she kept telling George to give me more court time. After I had been there a few months, he told me I could have an extra hour for the junior program because I was already at the top of my age group. So I began coming in a second day.

'Work hard, Martina,' he would tell me. 'Compete wherever you have the chance. Get to see the world. Sports is one way you'll be able to travel.'

George never complained about the system, but you could pick up a sense of sadness in him, just like in my mother and other people of that generation. They had been raised by parents who were hopeful for Czechoslovakia's future after World War I, but first the Germans and then the Russians had squashed that hope. George had gone through the dreary Communist game of having his passport withheld or being inexplicably left off a Davis Cup trip he deserved. He would never say anything political, but when he talked about travel, about tennis being one way of seeing the world, you could tell he was thinking about more than just playing a game. He was thinking about being in touch with the world outside our borders, a world to which we belonged, by tradition and by temperament.

He would tell me to set my sights on becoming a good European player – maybe, just maybe, in the top ten in the world. Meantime, my father was telling people I was going to be a Wimbledon champion someday and I wasn't about to disagree with him.

When I was a skinny little girl with the tennis racquets on the train, I'd dreamed of going back on the streetcar to Klamovka and having people recognize me as Wimbledon champion. But I never got the chance, and the Czech government isn't going to let the people know much about me now.

People in Czechoslovakia don't read about most of my tournaments, and my matches are never on Czech television; although you can pick up the West German stations in western Czechoslovakian towns like Pilsen, you're not supposed to watch West German television. I hear that *Rude Pravo*, the party newspaper in Czechoslovakia, is loosening up a little bit and actually printing the results when I win Wimbledon and the US Open. For a long time after I left, I was a non-person in their sports pages.

Even in the souvenir shops of Czechoslovakia you can find a poster of the latest junior hotshots, but you won't see any of Ivan Lendl or Hana Mandlikova, who are still citizens but live mostly in the West. And even if they could make money selling Martina mementoes, they wouldn't do it.

At the Revnice tennis club, where I spent hundreds of hours learning the game with my father and mother, there are only four posters of players taped to the wall: Jimmy Connors, Adriano Panatta, Björn Borg, and Czechoslovakia's sweetheart, Christine Marie Evert. The skinny little runt with the racquets flopping all over on the commuter train? Not a trace.

Martina, 1985

States
MARTINA NAVRATILOVA

'I'm going to America!'

The girl next to me pretended not to hear. Our teacher did not like talking in class.

'I said: I'm going to America!'

She smiled at me patronizingly, either to shut me up or because she didn't believe me. I almost didn't believe it myself. I was going to see Katharine Hepburn and Spencer Tracy walking down Fifth Avenue, Ginger Rogers and Fred Astaire dancing down Collins Avenue.

THE RIGHT SET

I was also going to play tennis against Chris Evert and Evonne Goolagong. That was the most amazing part of all. After I had won the Czech championships in 1972 and the indoor tournament in England, the Czech federation had decided to let me and Marie Neumannova play the US winter circuit early in 1973.

Marie was also going to be my chaperone. She was about ten years older than I, the only Czech player on the Virginia Slims tour allowed to handle her own expenses and travel by herself without any kind of bodyguard. I was thrilled not only to be going to the States but also to be going with somebody who was not 'political,' who was a regular on the tennis tour. For me, that was really the big time.

I was going to play eight tournaments in a row on the United States Tennis Association tour, first in Fort Lauderdale; then in Dallas; Hingham, Massachusetts; Akron, Ohio; New York; and back to Florida for three more. There were two tours in those days: the Virginia Slims tour with Billie Jean King and Rosie Casals and the USTA tour with Virginia Wade, Evonne Goolagong, Chris Evert, and Olga Morozova.

We took off in the dead of Prague winter, snow up to our knees, long nights and short days, and after a long day in the air through Frankfurt and New York, we arrived in sunny Miami, with real palm trees and oranges, to say nothing of cars and interstates, fast-food stands and motels. It looked like Florida to me. I was in America.

Marie Neumannova and I were given an apartment right at the club where we'd be playing in Fort Lauderdale. The man who owned the apartment was staying somewhere else, but every day he would take us for lunch at the club and would insist we have this chocolate-and-vanilla ice cream at the restaurant. You have to be polite when you're in somebody else's country, so I ate more ice cream than I'd ever consumed in my life: mounds of ice cream. Ice cream in the sky. Ice cream on the horizon. Ice cream in the freezer. Ice cream everywhere.

The man's apartment faced the courts, with your typical screened-in Florida porch, so you could watch the matches. Marie and I had some time to explore the New World, so we took a walk down the road and had our first experience with American capitalism: a 7-Eleven store. We bought some food and magazines for $5, which seemed like an amazingly small amount of money for so much. I remember buying a package of ham and sliced bread, and feeling I had made a big financial killing.

My English wasn't very good because I had only taken half a year in school, and I had a hard time translating the words and cost into English.

Even so, I was impressed by the variety of magazines and newspapers and food and cosmetics items. Plus, people could afford them.

Walking back from the 7-Eleven, I spotted a coconut tree. I had eaten canned coconut before but I had never seen a whole one, much less one hanging from a low branch. What can I say? It was a challenge. I plucked it off the tree and carried it back to the apartment, wondering how I was going to open it. We rummaged through the apartment until we found a hammer and a screwdriver, and I went out on the cement patio and whacked away. I was lucky I didn't ruin my hands for tennis, but I finally managed to gash open the coconut and eat a few pieces. After all that, they tasted like the screwdriver.

I had my first hamburger from the grill at the club. After that, they gave us tickets for food, and I'd go back for seconds and thirds. After sampling the American food, I went to work on the English language. My first conversation was with Michelle Gurdal, a player from Belgium, on the way to the courts. It went something like this:

Martina: 'Did you play?'

Michelle: 'Yes.'

Martina: 'Did you win?'

Michelle: 'No.'

Martina: 'Oh, that's too bad.'

I think I do pretty well in English now. I've gotten to the point where I think and dream in English, and enjoy using exotic English words. (One of my friends calls me the Joseph Conrad of tennis; other people suggest I should talk less.) But those first days in Fort Lauderdale, it was hard just trying to understand what people were saying. I couldn't understand why they were laughing.

My first impression of Americans was how friendly they were. In Europe – not just in Czechoslovakia, but in most of Europe – people don't expect to be your best friend right away. There's a little bit of space, until they get to know you. In the States, however, there's the feeling that they can call you by your first name and share secrets with you right away.

I still like that openness about Americans, but I see it a little differently now. They'll tell you about their lovers, about their break-ups, about their problems, how they got pregnant two months ago and had to have an abortion. They'll tell you their life story, and I'm not used to that. But you can also be honest and be yourself with Americans, and that's a big plus. I always felt I could be me, the real Martina, from the first time I came to the States.

Let's face it, in the States anything goes, and not just in New York, either. Coming from Czechoslovakia, where people wear black and gray and *look* black and gray, I almost had to put on my sunglasses when I landed in Fort Lauderdale. People were wearing bright magentas and pinks and lavenders, all this polyester leisure clothing, some of it terrible, but people would wear it. People were expressing how they felt. And as far as I could see, they felt pretty good.

You think about the image of those 'wild and crazy guys' on the old *Saturday Night Live* show, those two swinging Czech brothers wearing plaid slacks and Hawaiian shirts and going out looking for 'foxes.' To me, it was the other way around. I was Miss Conservative off the plane from Prague and here were all these Americans on vacation in Florida wearing Bermuda shorts like Jackson Pollock paintings, golf slacks the color of tomato soup, shirts like TV test patterns. Wild and crazy guys, all right – but from Nebraska and New York, not from Czechoslovakia.

The man who lent us the apartment owned a wig shop, and he gave me one of his $10 specials. I'd been in the States a couple of days and already I had a thick mop of wavy hair to put over my thin, straight hair, which was still brown in those days. I wore the wig to a party in Dallas during the next tournament and thought I looked sensational. Later I brought it back to Revnice and gave it to my mother, who still wears it on occasion.

My first exposure to the American tour was the qualifying round (known as 'the quallies' to one and all), dozens of players competing just to get into the main event. I roared through the quallies, winning three matches, and then won my first round before losing to Linda Tuero, 6–3, 7–6, in the quarter-finals.

In Dallas I lost to Glynis Coles in the first round. Then we flew to Hingham, where I stayed with a family of Czechs who were not very well off by American standards but really wanted us to stay with them. I didn't like it in Massachusetts, perhaps because of the weather, which was as cold as Czechoslovakia but damper.

The climate didn't hurt my tennis, though. I won three straight in the quallies before drawing Evonne Goolagong in the first round of the National Indoors. She was already at the peak of her game then, a lithe, beautiful athlete who had won Wimbledon in 1971 when she was only nineteen. It was all I could do not to stop and stare at her grace and agility, but I got my game together and gave her a match before losing, 6–4, 6–4 – just one service break in each set – probably the best tennis I had ever played.

Right away there were signs that I was going to be better than anybody knew. I was only sixteen and nobody had ever heard of me, so when I was introduced at every tournament, the announcer would say, 'Just sixteen years old, from Czechoslovakia . . .' I wasn't tiny anymore, and I played a big serve-and-volley game, and the fans liked me right away, so I felt at home.

It was just like being a kid, playing with George Parma back at Klamovka. I could run down a lot of balls that many players wouldn't go after. Even when I became overweight at the end of the trip, I could still run down balls. My serve was good. Four weeks into the trip I pulled my stomach muscles and couldn't serve hard, but it was still pretty good. I had a great forehand and an awful backhand. Just by being aggressive, I could win my share of matches on the tour, right from the start. I really didn't know how to play then, but just went out there with fearless abandon.

From playing with Jan Kodes at Sparta, I had learned to love the game of doubles. Marie Neumannova and I beat Evonne Goolagong and Janet Young at Sarasota, Florida, and then we beat Sharon Walsh and Patti Hogan in the finals.

Because of my big game, I came to like the hard American courts, but one of my best early matches was on clay in St Petersburg against Helga Masthoff, a pretty good player at the time. The temperature must have been ninety-five and the humidity about the same, and she had me, 6–1, 4–0, but I kept hanging in with her, and finally won the last two sets, 7–5, 7–5, in a match that took three and a half hours. That match told me something: I knew I could be in the top ten. I really could be one of the best, I told myself. I can beat these people.

I was learning on and off the court. One of the first things I noticed when I came to the States was how people were more openly religious than in Czechoslovakia. In one house where I stayed, the people said grace before dinner. I had never seen that done before and I thought they were kidding.

I'd had no religious training at all back home. My parents hadn't been interested and the government had been trying to downplay religion ever since the takeover in 1948. You'd see the statues on the Charles Bridge or visit the beautiful old cathedrals in Prague to enjoy the architecture, and you'd hear about the old traditions, but religion didn't stay as strong in my country as it did in Poland, for example.

I was raised a basic agnostic. I believe there's something out there, but I don't believe in the Adam and Eve theory. I was brought up on the Darwin theory of evolution; it just makes sense. I believe there are supernatural forces we don't understand, and sometimes I feel my grandmother is really close and I look forward to seeing her again, but I have a hard time believing in heaven and hell.

I couldn't help noticing how many Americans said grace before meals, prayed on television, carried Bibles with them. I had thought Americans were way ahead in science, so I was surprised to see religion so strong. Americans can build computers that put men on the moon but they still say their prayers every day, not just on Sunday. I still don't know if it's the romantic in Americans, the belief in religion.

Now that I live here, I hear so much about this born-again stuff. I was talking with a friend of mine and she was dancing around in robes, going to church four times a week. I believe it's one thing to be religious and another thing to flaunt it in people's faces. School prayer – do it on your own time. In California, a Baptist school canceled a basketball game with a Catholic school. How ridiculous can you get!

To me, religion is fine in moderation. But this 'My God is better than your God' attitude really causes problems. Look at the way Protestants and Catholics used to go at each other in Czechoslovakia, and still do in Ireland. Look at Lebanon, Iran – these people go nuts. If God is such a great guy, why are these people killing each other? Now in the States, a few people are trying to legislate school prayer. It's one thing to have a moment of silence for those who want to pray. But to have an official prayer, out loud? This country was built on freedom of choice.

Sometimes people give me religious booklets, but I just give them back. You believe in what you want; I believe in what I want.

I was a skinny little kid when I left for the States. Ever since I was twelve, I had always eaten a lot and could eat more than my father without gaining an ounce. I was all muscle and bone, as skinny as a stick. Prut, my father called me – 'Stick' – before changing it to Pluto.

Here in the New World, I soon discovered pizza, hamburgers, steak, french fries, pancakes, cereal. I'd see a fast-food restaurant and I couldn't resist sampling the wares. Big Macs. Whoppers. The International House of Pancakes. Howard Johnson's. Lum's. Wendy's. It's a stale joke now, but people used to say I was on a 'see-food' diet. Any food I could see, I'd eat.

My metabolism just couldn't get all that meat organized, and it went straight to my waistline and jowls. Olga Morozova, the Russian player, came up to Hingham the third week of the tour. I knew her from the Communist tournament in Budapest the year before, a really nice person. She looked at me and didn't say a word, just puffed out her cheeks.

I thought, What's her problem? I thought I looked good. I was finally filling out: Martina gets a figure. I thought I looked more like a woman because I wasn't so muscular anymore. I felt more feminine. So I didn't take the hint and kept on Big Macking my way across America, right to Akron, where the new, curvaceous Martina was matched in the first round with a player only a couple of years older.

Her name was Christine Marie Evert.

Martina, 1985

Venus: The Great Experiment
DAVID HIGDON

Here sits Miss Venus Williams, bored out of her beads. We're face-to-face on a canopied cement deck adjacent to a red hard court that has 'Williams' emblazoned in huge white letters across its green backdrop. Behind Venus, two lefties are blasting forehand after forehand at each other on one of the two clay courts. The rest of the Williams family compound – a modest-sized white home, several garages, two lakes, one shattered Yonex racquet, a huge inoperable rusty satellite dish, a half-dozen riding lawnmowers and twice that number of cars, including a blue Impala and white Rolls-Royce – is scattered over 10.6 acres here in Palm Beach Gardens, Fla.

Williams, seventeen, sports the retro cool look – a pink, yellow, purple and mint-green sweater-and-slacks get-up – popular with so many other sixteen-year-olds today. Thanks to her combination of size (6 feet, 1½ inches, last anyone checked), color (black) and sweet sassiness ('That question does not compute'), she reminds me more of the lead character played by Teresa Graves on the '70s TV staple *Get Christie Love* – minus the Afro, of course – than anyone out of *Clueless*. It will be ixnay on this interview, however, if I can't stop Miss Williams from yawning.

Suddenly, we hear a distant shriek. Williams vaults out of her chair and my heart stops beating. I turn around, expecting to find Venus's free-spirited fifteen-year-old sister Serena caught – helpless, mangled – under one of those ubiquitous lawnmowers. Instead, I see her wrestling with two dogs. Venus beams now, her braces brightening up her face. She hops up and down like a kid trying to peer over the candy store counter.

'I haven't seen my dogs in two days,' says Williams, restraining herself from dashing off because she would consider it rude. 'I'm so glad they're back. They go into the woods.' Suddenly, her mood shifts from solace to ire. 'That's their last chance. They don't need to worry me like that. Queen – not the Dalmatian, the other one – taught Chase how to run away. They're not going to teach Star, though, because I'm going to keep them away from Star.'

Star, I discovered earlier in my visit, is a floppy-eared brown puppy the girls acquired a few weeks ago. The dog seems permanently attached to Serena's lap even as she tools around the property at full speed on a beat-up golf cart filled with grass clippings, a baseball mitt, garden tools and a roll of blue tennis strings. It's Serena who later explains why she and her big sis get so worried whenever Chase and Queen disappear.

'This is Lake Inferior,' she says during a tour of the Williams's property, pointing to the smaller of the two lakes. 'If it was up to me, I'd cover this lake up. This lake took my dog's life. Her name was Princess. I would always throw her in the water, and she would always swim back. She was a homebody; she never went anywhere. She loved us. She loved everybody. One day, we were looking everywhere for her, and my Dad saw her here, floating in the water.'

Fledgling tennis pros Venus Williams, hailed as a 'ghetto Cinderella' by her father, Richard, when she first rose out of the gang-ridden Los Angeles suburb of Compton at age ten, and Serena Williams, who some believe will be as good a player, if not better, than her older sister, are home. It's where they cried when their dog died and where they giggle when discussing their father's fear of snakes. It's where they have bike-dived into 'Lake Superior.' It's where they crank up alternative rockers such as Rage Against the Machine, Rancid and The Foo Fighters and turn down countless requests from IMG, Advantage and ProServ agents drooling over representing them. It's where skateboarders are cool but in-line skaters are posers. Explains Serena: 'We don't like in-line skaters, we don't like people who like in-line skaters and we don't talk about in-line skating.'

'Thank you, Serena,' says Miss Williams.

'You're welcome, Venus,' answers Miss Williams.

Silence, for effect, then guffaws. The Williams sisters are home. Here is where they are when they're not on tour, where they haven't been much of the time.

Though Venus has flirted with the WTA Tour since turning pro in 1994, this season will serve as her true coming-out party. 'I think this year will probably be the most fun I'll ever have on the tour,' she says, 'watching my ranking progressively get better.' Venus played three tournaments this past winter, registering her first win over a top-ten player (Iva Majoli) at Indian Wells before falling to eventual champion Lindsay Davenport in a quarter-final match decided by a third-set tie-break. Later at the Lipton Championships, she again produced an upset (Jennifer Capriati) and lost to the eventual champion (Martina Hingis). This month Williams is expected to make her Grand Slam debut at Wimbledon, though the French Open was still a consideration at press time.

Until she travels overseas for the first time in her life, though, Williams will remain at home. It's here where the mysterious Williams sisters transform into two gifted, spirited, bright, goofy, athletic, gutsy, charming kids. They couldn't care less that I believe they're two of the most captivating athletes to surface in women's tennis – no, make that women's sports – this past decade. Big deal that their critics – mostly petrified peers on the WTA Tour – feel they should be competing more often for silver trophies and gold plates than for Gatorade and Snickers bars. Role models? Of course. Child prodigies? Ob. Future burnout victims? Nuh-uh. These girls just wanna be No. 1.

'[Venus] puts a lot of pressure on you,' says Pam Shriver, who has trained with the sisters. 'When we played, she didn't know tactically how to play points yet, but she had weapons and has this natural way of intimidating. If I missed a first serve, I immediately thought: "Criminy!"' Adds Davenport, about her Indian Wells match: 'She was getting some balls back that I guarantee you most girls never get back against me.'

'No one is ever going to back [Venus] up,' says Rick Macci, the Florida pro who jump-started Capriati's career and has worked on and off with the Williams sisters over the last three years. 'She'll have the game to play through Hingis on certain occasions. She's lost more matches in practices than any junior I've coached in my life, but she's going to be a champion.'

Not everyone seems convinced. 'I didn't think she was that great,' said

Majoli after her loss to Williams. Sixteen-year-old Anna Kournikova agrees: 'I have watched both Serena and Venus play, and they're not that good. They don't know how to play points or how to win.' Macci has repeatedly heard juniors with whom he works and their parents dismiss Venus's abilities after watching her play. 'All they see is Venus spraying balls everywhere and looking gangly,' he says. 'Meanwhile, every week, her stock is going up in my eyes.'

There stands Mr Richard Williams, surrounded by a cluster of men. He smokes a cigarette, then another, then another. I am sitting high in the bleachers behind the baseline at the 1995 Acura Classic in Manhattan Beach, Calif. I spot Williams outside the stadium where his daughter Venus is getting thrashed by a nondescript Swede named Asa Carlsson. Daddy ain't watching. 'A psychiatrist told me if I want my daughter to be successful, try your best not to be there when she plays,' Richard tells me later. Venus agrees with such sentiment. 'I would prefer to think for myself,' she says.

Richard Williams has been called a 'liar' and 'genius' and everything in between. Most of the 'in between' is not printable in this family publication. Here is one, however: 'Irascible.' Here's another: 'Insane.'

'He says things people don't like to hear,' says his lawyer, Keven Davis. 'He makes people uncomfortable.'

Not me. I think he's hilarious, unpredictable and delightfully eccentric, the best thing to hit our sport since the days when Pete Fischer, Pete Sampras's mentor, spewed venom at the tennis establishment. That's one reason why I invited Fischer to join me for Williams's match against Carlsson. I also knew that Fischer was coaching a girl, Alexandra Stevenson, who is six months younger than Williams and competed against her in girls' twelve-and-under tournaments in Southern California.

'[Venus] is a great athlete who just happens to be a tennis player,' Fischer said. 'She's tall, muscular and fast. Plus, she's totally coachable. She listens. I've watched her work with coaches and Richard, and she's got terrific concentration.' Fischer claims to have spotted future greatness in Williams back in the days when she would trash his current protégeé in tournaments and then skip off with Stevenson to go swing on monkey bars. 'I said back then,' Fischer claims, 'that these two would be playing in the final of the US Open in seven years.'

That would be 1998, a highly unlikely scenario, considering their limited professional experience, but you never know. Williams stopped playing junior tennis at age eleven, an oft-criticized decision made by the man who says he's been trying to get his daughter to quit playing tennis ever since she was eight years old. 'She's a track runner,' he boasts. Whether or not Williams is serious or simply yanking my chain is unclear, but one thing is obvious: Here is a man who loves to rattle the cage.

'Everyone I've ever met who plays professional tennis is a nut,' he says. 'They're all crazy. And when I say all of them, that includes my daughter Venus. Anyone who picks up a racquet and heads out there and thinks they have a career is a fool. Venus is going to be out of tennis by age twenty-four, twenty-five. And if she lives to be fifty, she has twenty-five more years to be a fool, and I don't want that. I might be doing it the wrong way, but in the end, she will benefit from it.'

Here is the Williams Way: He interrupts carefully scripted workouts to make Venus and Serena study French with practice partner Gerard Gdebey. He seeks counsel from a Seattle-based attorney because, as Davis says with a chuckle, the man 'likes his lawyers as far away as possible.' On the eve of Venus's professional debut, he whisked his family off to Disney World for a few days of roller-coaster rides and Mickey Mouse sightings. Venus told me she hates it when people ask her to describe a typical day in her atypical life. 'It's like the wind blowing,' she explains with a shrug. 'It can change direction.' Richard likes it that way.

Richard Williams grew up in Louisiana, the oldest of five children, the only son of a single mother who picked cotton for a living. He and wife Oracene, whom he met at church, have raised five daughters. He's been surrounded by women his whole life. When Venus was born in June 1980 and Serena fifteen months later, the Williams family lived in Compton. It's a city where, Richard says, 'AK-47s, drugs, PCP, ice and welfare checks are more prevalent than anywhere else in the world.' That's an exaggeration, but you get the drift.

The athletic Williams eventually discovered the joy of tennis. A veterinarian who sat behind me in Manhattan Beach and graciously gave me a tour of the Williams's old stomping grounds the following day said Richard Williams was a 'crafty' player who could hit with both power and finesse. 'He was an expert at all the angles,' said Dr Edward Pygatt, describing Williams's game exactly the same way many people today describe his handling of Venus's tennis career. Williams taught tennis to all his daughters – Yetunde, Isha and Lyndrea as well as Venus and Serena – but Venus showed the most promise.

It wasn't long before Venus Williams, the little girl from the ghetto playing tennis as gang-fire rattled the spray-painted wind screens, started making headlines. Jack Kramer saw her play and proclaimed her a future Grand Slam champion. *Tennis* magazine ran its first article about her in 1991. That year, Richard asked Macci to visit Compton to consider coaching his daughters.

'I hear it all the time: "I've got the next Jennifer," ' says Macci. 'Richard said he'd like to meet me but the only thing he could promise me was that I wouldn't get shot. All I could think of was: "Who is this guy?" ' It was Macci's first lesson in what WTA Tour CEO Anne Person Worcester admiringly calls 'The Richard Williams School of Publicity.' Sure enough, Macci soon was footing the bill for a flight to LA.

'Richard picks me up in this Volkswagen bus that has dents all over it,' Macci recalls. 'There were tennis balls, clothes, McDonald's wrappers, Coke cans, everything scattered throughout this wobbly bus. It was 7.30 in the morning when we arrived at East Rancho Dominguez Park, and there must have been thirty guys there already playing basketball and another twenty lying in the grass passed out.

'We started working out, doing some drills, and after about an hour, I thought I was wasting my time. Then Venus asks to go to the bathroom and as she walks out the gate, she walks at least ten yards on her hands. I was stunned. Then she went into these backward cartwheels for another ten yards. I'm watching this and the first thing I thought was: "I've got a female Michael Jordan on my hands." '

Here crouches Miss Serena Williams, wiping her hands on the front of a Green Day 'Insomnia' T-shirt. Her heavily muscled arms and legs bulge as she reaches for one of two surfboards lying on the floor of a shed that houses 'all our stuff we don't want to clean.' That includes a drum set both ladies admit to having no clue how to play. 'We were going to have jam sessions in there,' says Serena, pointing to a Nirvana poster hanging by one thumbtack on the wall. 'We even bought guitars. But we got preoccupied.'

Surf happens. A hobby one day, clutter the next. There are jet skis near the lake that haven't been used in ages, a basketball court that serves as parking space for another one of those damn lawnmowers. But Serena remains obsessed with riding waves. 'I was at the beach and there was this program going on for little kids,' Serena explains after we hop back into the golf cart. 'They all had surfboards and I had a rotten, ugly, horrible, nasty, funky boogie board. I got a short board, which allows me to rip and shred, but Venus went crazy and got a ten-footer.'

If Mike and Carol Brady had been black, these two could have been Marcia and Jan. (Repeat after me: 'Venus, Venus, Veee-nus!') The two sisters always are trying to one-up each other, but if there's ever animosity between the two, it doesn't surface in public. Venus claims baby sis used to steal things from her when they were little, but they've always been doubles partners. 'I'm a good sister,' Venus says. 'I let her sleep while I'm driving.' On tour, the two always seem to be sharing some kind of inside joke, whispering and then giggling uncontrollably. They never appear more than six feet from each other unless Venus is playing singles matches or seducing the media in interviews.

During those moments, Serena always has seemed a little out of place. She's been described as a pit bull, and at 5-foot-9, she's got the chiseled and somewhat intimidating physique of a sprinter (think Gail Devers with a gap between her two front teeth). 'With Venus, everything comes so easy, whether it's athletic or academic,' Oracene says. 'With Serena, it comes a little harder, but that makes her work harder, too. She's more of a stick-to-it person.'

Unlike Venus, who grasps things quickly yet tires at the same speedy pace, Serena needs time, whether it's learning how to hit a forehand passing shot, adjusting to a move ('I didn't mind the area,' she says about their Palm Beach Garden digs, 'I just didn't like the land and the house') or warming up to strangers. It explains why Serena volunteered to take me for a leisurely spin around their property while Venus darted off into the house to see what was planned for dinner. Venus says Serena is 'kind of a perfectionist, though not neurotic or psychotic.'

Richard Williams likes to boast that Serena 'will be better than Venus.' When you watch her attack the net with the fearlessness and foot speed of Pat Cash, you have to at least consider the possibility. Aggressive, offensive-oriented players always develop slower than your standard base-liners; Serena's middle name, Billie Jean King once joked, is 'Forward.'

Serena devours pro tennis on TV, though she claims not to be too fond of the senior tour. 'All I ever see is [Jimmy] Connors playing [Andres] Gomez,' she complains, 'or Gomez playing someone else.' She would prefer to see more of John McEnroe, a player whose on-court style she always has admired. And, of course, more surfing. Turning the tables near the end of my visit, she asked: 'Don't you want to ask me about my surfing career?' When I acquiesced, she responded: 'I could really be good if I had the time.' Then she challenged me to a game of tetherball and kicked my butt.

Here sits Mrs Oracene Williams, complaining about the decor of her house. 'It's not really me,' she says. A lone blue bead lies on the kitchen floor by her feet. A stack of mail sits precariously on the edge of the table. She wears brown beads in her braided hair, which Serena tugs at during a brief foray into the kitchen.

'That's me, though,' she then says, pointing to some ceramic and wood figurines on the nearby bookshelf. 'I see the collection as old black figures showing how they communicate with their kids. There's a religious one over there, one with a mother spanking her kid . . .' Venus, who also has joined us temporarily, interrupts. 'They come alive,' she says, cringing as she gingerly lifts one figurine off the shelf.

Oracene laughs, then shoos her daughters out of the kitchen. If you think it must be tough for Serena to carve out her own niche with Venus around, imagine what it must be like for Oracene in the overwhelming presence of Richard Williams. Like her husband, Oracene (a.k.a. Brandy) was the oldest child in a large family, though she had seven siblings to Richard's four. She's been nurturing children her entire life. 'Since both Richard and I were the oldest, we're both used to being in control,' she says. 'So that's where we would get a little conflict. I had to learn to back off.'

That doesn't mean she doesn't share her opinion with him. Or put her foot down when necessary. She's even gotten more involved recently in coaching her daughters, shouting out comments during practices and offering advice during water breaks. Like any mother, she worries about her children as they embark on their chosen careers.

'When I first went to a tournament,' she says, 'all the players looked so sad. They look like they hate to be out there, that they're scared. Even the top ones, with the exception of Hingis. They're scared of the competition when they should be inviting it. Venus doesn't worry about winning, because she knows she isn't going to lose.'

Over the last several years, Venus and Serena practiced only with each other or hard-hitting male tennis partners. They learned tae kwon do, worked out with a professional boxer, practiced gymnastic moves, threw a football around. They even did the hula hoop to work on lower-body coordination. But why skip junior tennis? Richard and Oracene believed early competition would hamper their ability to learn and experiment on the court – and figured it would distract them from their education away from it. Venus played Oakland in 1994 – when she beat 59th-ranked Shaun Stafford and was up a set and a break on Arantxa Sanchez Vicario before crashing – solely to avoid falling under the tour's pending age restrictions. Then she played a restricted schedule anyway.

'I think the family should be credited with sticking to their word that they weren't going to push Venus out there and force her to play maximum numbers of tournaments,' Worcester says. 'That had everything to do with family and going to school and learning Chinese and lots of other hobbies and interests which we feel is healthy and try to promote with all our players.'

Oracene Williams expresses no fear that her daughters' limited competition and isolated environment will stifle their professional growth. 'When we moved to Florida from California, it was to make sure we were doing the right things and teaching the right ways,' Oracene says. 'Richard has always supervised their workouts and more or less given them instructions on what he wanted to work on. The only thing I worried about was Venus losing her ability to be natural.' When Venus starts playing tennis full-time, Oracene adds, 'you'll see a new wave of tennis.'

Here come Venus and Serena Williams, eyes blinking in the spotlight. The beads in their braids clatter as they walk. Friends and family follow in their wake. Venus has just lost a professional tennis match. She and her sister are stopped by a stunningly beautiful and familiar black woman. It's Angela Bassett, the Oscar-nominated actress from nearby Tinseltown. 'Oooh Venus, baby,' she coos. 'Give me a hug.' The statuesque Williams, resplendent in a silky Reebok outfit, bends awkwardly to embrace the lithe Bassett. Venus and her sister smile for a photo taken by one of Bassett's entourage. Moving on, Venus rises to her press conference perch above a sea of white faces. 'She doesn't see anything after she loses,' Oracene says, explaining Venus's nonchalant reaction to celebrity. Here is what Richard said: 'Everyone in tennis is a fool.'

Tennis Magazine, July 1997

The Burden of Race

ARTHUR ASHE

I had spent more than an hour talking in my office at home with a reporter for *People* magazine. Her editor had sent her to do a story about me and how I was coping with AIDS. The reporter's questions had been probing and yet respectful of my right to privacy. Now, our interview over, I was escorting her to the door. As she slipped on her coat, she fell silent. I could see that she was groping for the right words to express her sympathy for me before she left.

'Mr Ashe, I guess this must be the heaviest burden you have ever had to bear, isn't it?' she asked finally.

I thought for a moment, but only a moment. 'No, it isn't. It's a burden, all right. But AIDS isn't the heaviest burden I have had to bear.'

'Is there something worse? Your heart attack?'

I didn't want to detain her, but I let the door close with both of us still inside. 'You're not going to believe this,' I said to her, 'but being black is the greatest burden I've had to bear.'

'You can't mean that.'

'No question about it. Race has always been my biggest burden. Having to live as a minority in America. Even now it continues to feel like an extra weight tied around me.'

I can still recall the surprise and perhaps even the hurt on her face. I may even have surprised myself, because I simply had never thought of comparing the two conditions before. However, I stand by my remark. Race is for me a more onerous burden than AIDS. My disease is the result of biological factors over which we, thus far, have had no control. Racism, however, is entirely made by people, and therefore it hurts and inconveniences infinitely more.

Since our interview (skillfully presented as a first-person account by me) appeared in *People* in June 1992, many people have commented on my remark. A radio station in Chicago aimed primarily at blacks conducted a lively debate on its merits on the air. Most African Americans have little trouble understanding and accepting my statement, but other people have been baffled by it. Even Donald Dell, my close friend of more than thirty years, was puzzled. In fact, he was so troubled that he telephoned me in the middle of the night from Hamburg, Germany, to ask if I had been misquoted. No, I told him, I had been quoted correctly. Some people have asked me flatly, what could *you*, Arthur Ashe, possibly have to complain about? Do you want more money or fame than you already have? Isn't AIDS inevitably fatal? What can be worse than death?

The novelist Henry James suggested somewhere that it is a complex fate being an American. I think it is a far more complex fate being an African American. I also sometimes think that this indeed may be one of those fates that are worse than death.

I do not want to be misunderstood. I do not mean to appear fatalistic, self-pitying, cynical, or maudlin. Proud to be an American, I am also proud to be an African American. I delight in the accomplishments of fellow citizens of my color. When one considers the odds against which we have labored, we have achieved much. I believe in life and hope and love, and I turn my back on death until I must face my end in all its finality. I am an optimist, not a pessimist. Still, a pall of sadness hangs over my life and the lives of almost all African Americans because of what we as a people have experienced historically in America, and what we as individuals experience each and every day. Whether one is a welfare recipient trapped in some blighted 'housing project' in the inner city or a former Wimbledon champion who is easily recognized on the streets and whose home is a luxurious apartment in one of the wealthiest districts of Manhattan, the sadness is still there.

In some respects, I am a prisoner of the past. A long time ago, I made peace with the state of Virginia and the South. While I, like other blacks, was once barred from free association with whites, I returned time and time again, under the new rule of desegregation, to work with whites in my hometown and across the South. But segregation had achieved by that time what it was intended to achieve: It left me a marked man, forever aware of a shadow of contempt that lies across my identity and my sense of self-esteem. Subtly the shadow falls on my reputation, the way I know I am perceived; the mere memory of it darkens my most sunny days. I believe that the same is true for almost every African American of the slightest sensitivity and intelligence. Again, I don't want to overstate the case. I think of myself, and others think of me, as supremely self-confident. I know objectively that it is almost impossible for someone to be as successful as I have been as an athlete and to lack self-assurance. Still, I also know that the shadow is always there; only death will free me, and blacks like me, from its pall.

The shadow fell across me recently on one of the brightest days, literally and metaphorically, of my life. On 30 August 1992, the day before the US Open, the USTA and I together hosted an afternoon of tennis at the National Tennis Center in Flushing Meadows, New York. The event was a benefit for the Arthur Ashe Foundation for the Defeat of AIDS. Before the start, I was nervous. Would the invited stars (McEnroe, Graf, Navratilova, et al.) show up? Would they cooperate with us, or be difficult to manage? And, on the eve of a Grand Slam tournament, would fans pay to see light-hearted tennis? The answers were all a resounding yes (just over ten thousand fans turned out). With CBS televising the event live and Aetna having provided the air time, a profit was assured. The sun shone brightly, the humidity was mild, and the temperature hovered in the low 80s.

What could mar such a day? The shadow of race, and my sensitivity, or perhaps hypersensitivity, to its nuances. Sharing the main stadium box with Jeanne, Camera, and me, at my invitation, were Stan Smith, his wife Marjory, and their daughter Austin. The two little girls were happy to see one another. During Wimbledon in June, they had renewed their friendship when we all stayed near each other in London. Now Austin, seven years old, had brought Camera a present. She had come with twin dolls, one for herself, one for Camera. A thoughtful gesture on Austin's part, and on her parents' part, no doubt. The Smiths are fine, religious people. Then I noticed that Camera was playing with her doll above the railing of the box, in full view of the attentive network television cameras. The doll was the problem; or rather, the fact that the doll was conspicuously a blond. Camera owns dolls of all colors, nationalities, and ethnic varieties. But she was now on national television playing with a blond doll. Suddenly I heard voices in my head, the voices of irate listeners to a call-in show on some 'black format' radio station. I imagined insistent, clamorous callers attacking Camera, Jeanne, and me:

'Can you believe the doll Arthur Ashe's daughter was holding up at the AIDS benefit? Wasn't that a shame?'

'Is that brother sick or what? Somebody ought to teach that poor child about her true black self!'

'What kind of role model is Arthur Ashe if he allows his daughter to be brainwashed in that way?'

'Doesn't the brother understand that he is corrupting his child's mind with notions about the superiority of the white woman? I tell you, I thought we were long past that!'

The voices became louder in my head. Despite the low humidity, I began to squirm in my seat. What should I do? Should I say, To hell with what some people might think? I know that Camera likes her blond dolls, black dolls, brown dolls, Asian dolls, Indian dolls just about equally; I know that for a fact, because I have watched her closely. I have searched for signs of racial partiality in her, indications that she may be dissatisfied with herself, with her own color. I have seen none. But I cannot dismiss the voices. I try always to live practically, and I do not wish to hear such comments on the radio. On the other hand, I do not want Austin's gift to be sullied by an ungracious response. Finally, I act.

'Jeanne,' I whisper, 'we have to do something.'

'About what?' she whispers back.

'That doll. We have to get Camera to put that doll down.'

Jeanne takes one look at Camera and the doll and she understands immediately. Quietly, cleverly, she makes the dolls disappear. Neither Camera nor Austin is aware of anything unusual happening. Smoothly, Jeanne has moved them on to some other distraction.

I am unaware if Margie Smith has noticed us, but I believe I owe her an explanation. I get up and go around to her seat. Softly I tell her why the dolls have disappeared. Margie is startled, dumbfounded.

'Gosh, Arthur, I never thought about that. I never *ever* thought about anything like that!'

'*You* don't have to think about it,' I explain. 'But it happens to us, in similar situations, all the time.'

'All the time?' She is pensive now.

'All the time. It's perfectly understandable. And it certainly is not your fault. You were doing what comes naturally. But for us, the dolls make for a bit of a problem. All for the wrong reasons. It shouldn't be this way, but it is.'

I return to my seat, but not to the elation I had felt before I saw that blond doll in Camera's hand. I feel myself becoming more and more angry. I am angry at the force that made me act, the force of racism in all its complexity, as it spreads into the world and creates defensiveness and intolerance among the very people harmed by racism. I am also angry with myself. I am angry with myself because I have just acted out of pure practicality, not out of morality. The moral act would have been to let Camera have her fun, because she was innocent of any wrongdoing. Instead, I had tampered with her innocence, her basic human right to act impulsively, to accept a gift from a friend in the same beautiful spirit in which it was given.

Deeply embarrassed now, I am ashamed at what I have done. I have made Camera adjust her behavior merely because of the likelihood that some people in the African American community would react to her innocence foolishly and perhaps even maliciously. I know I am not misreading the situation. I would have had telephone calls that very evening about the unsuitability of Camera's doll. Am I being a hypocrite? Yes, definitely, up to a point. I have allowed myself to give in to those people who say we must avoid even the slightest semblance of 'Eurocentric' influence. But I also know what stands behind the entire situation. Racism ultimately created the state in which defensiveness and hypocrisy are our almost instinctive responses, and innocence and generosity are invitations to trouble.

This incident almost ruined the day for me. That night, when Jeanne and I talked about the excitement of the afternoon, and the money that would go to AIDS research and education because of the event, we nevertheless ended up talking mostly about the incident of the dolls. We also talked about perhaps its most ironic aspect. In 1954, when the Supreme Court ruled against school segregation in *Brown v. Board of Education*, some of the most persuasive testimony came from the psychologist Dr Kenneth Clark concerning his research on black children and their pathetic preference for white dolls over black. In 1992, the dolls are still a problem.

Once again, the shadow of race had fallen on me.

Days of Grace, 1993

VI Women and Tennis

Tennis for the Ladies

HEINER GILLMEISTER

The first ladies' championship was won by Maud Watson, the local heroine of Birmingham, the very place where Augurio Pereira's lawn pelota had originated. Since she had competed in a public tournament in Edgbaston in 1881 she had not lost a single match.[1] Maud was the daughter of the vicar of Berkswell, a village near Leamington Spa. Before winning the championship, she had played many a strenuous practice match against students from Cambridge who received private tuition in mathematics in her father's home, and lessons in lawn tennis on the adjacent vicarage lawn, perhaps the most important venue in the early days of the sport. Maud left a very interesting (and little known) account herself of how she learnt tennis when she talked shop with Helen Wills at Great Fosters, a small hotel in Surrey where her famous successor had taken up quarters during the All England Championships of 1935:

> My sisters and I took up tennis in our garden, and I didn't find it very difficult because I had played squash racquets with an uncle who was a master at Harrow. This helped my strokes. When I began to play tennis, I hit balls against the wall in our garden. My father was a vicar and a very broadminded man for those days. He let me and my sisters play in a match at Hurlingham, which we won. People thought it scandalous that he should let us play in public! We enjoyed it, though!

Maud was nineteen when she beat her sister Lilian to win the All England championship.

The trophy awarded to the first male champion was the silver cup presented by the journal the *Field*. It was, not unlike the majority of the species, a pot, plain and rather unpretentious artistically, and yet not entirely unsuited for the not too particular male. It was, and still is, worshipped as a precious relic, and William Renshaw took possession of it after three successive victories.[2] Maud Watson's prize was not a cup, but a silver-gilt Rosewater Dish worth twenty guineas. It made visible to everybody that the organizers had very different ideas about the gentleman's lawn tennis and that of the ladies, ideas which, it may be said, still persist.

In 1890 John Moyer Heathcote had given a royal welcome to any lady wishing to honour a Real tennis court with her presence. However, it was only in the spectators' box to the rear of the *dedans* [open gallery at the server's end of the court] where her presence was approved. Her presence on court would have been simply unthinkable. Lawn tennis took a different stance in this respect; it gave the ladies a chance, albeit very reluctantly. At first, the patriarchs of the English family had condoned their wives' and daughters' dalliance with Wingfield's *Sphairistikè*, at least as long as they indulged in the new pastime in the seclusion of their country houses. Then the representatives of the fair sex had asked to be admitted to the lawn tennis club where the former pat-ball had of late been converted to an exacting sport. These activities began to be frowned upon. At last, women came forward with the frivolous request of showing their talent in a public tournament. Such impudence met with a rude rebuff. The All England Club above all would have none of it, and justly so, it was thought.[3] For a game imposing so much strain on the human brain as well as on the body, a woman was simply too weak. As to the brains required in the process, hardly any woman would be capable of even mastering the game's counting method. As to the body, no woman would be capable of playing a game which meant very hard work even to a man.

With smug complacency, the lords of creation nevertheless offered the sporting lady a helping hand. They proposed a smaller court, a lighter racket and a lighter ball in order to reduce the terrible pressure brought to bear on the tender wrist. A deep anguish was caused to them by the fact that the dastardly tennis ball might chance to hit the lady's eye. They advocated a much simplified set of rules. A lady should be allowed to serve from a special service point close to the net; she ought to be conceded the privilege of refusing to take the difficult service as often as she thought fit; and she might expect the gentleman to serve the ball always within her reach. They continued to have their doubts, however, whether lawn tennis suited a lady at all, and badminton was thought by many to be a sport more appropriate to her.

What also aroused the true gentleman's compassion was the frightful burden a woman had to carry in the form of her tennis outfit. Even to his mind it was 'such a drag'.[4] And a drag it was indeed. A tennis dress in the modern sense of the word was, of course, unknown. For playing, the fashionable lady wore the costume which the conventions of the time prescribed for her everyday routine: long skirts which reached the ground; several starched petticoats underneath and the obligatory corset tightly laced. All this was given additional support by a girdle adorned by a silver clasp; it terminated in a stiff whalebone collar around which a necktie or scarf was slung. No dress was without long sleeves. An extravagant broad-brimmed felt hat dominated the lady's head, and a sturdy heeled, elegant boot was considered a must. Perhaps it was thought that a better outlook on the court might thus be obtained.

Under the handicaps of her dress, the lady had developed a lawn tennis style of her own. A 'lady player', writing before the turn of the century, might consider the game itself 'exciting', but this hardly applied to the brand of lawn tennis practised by her own sex:

> The great fault I have to find with the members of my own sex is that they are, as a rule, far too lazy; and how, I should like to know, can they expect to get even the least bit excited over a game when they refuse to move about court at a faster pace than a walk, or, at best, a jogtrot?

And yet: how could the lady tennis player have moved about court at all? The heeled boot made rapid moves to the net and back impossible, since her long skirts caught in it whenever she attempted a dash. If, in order to circumvent this pitfall, she lifted the pendant profusion of cloth, this procedure was questionable from the viewpoint of contemporary morals. The lady, therefore, had no option other than to keep riveted to the baseline. There, the bulging waist of her dress stood in the way of any natural swing of the racket, and this, in turn, greatly promoted the pat-ball variety of lawn tennis. In addition, the lady's impressive broad-brimmed hat (which later was replaced by a flat straw-hat) dissuaded her for decades from using the overhead service.

Worse still, the lady scorned the volley. It was perhaps because she had been told from the very start that this stroke was, as it were, contrary to her very femininity. 'Do not try and volley much', the lady was instructed by Lieutenant Peile who, in 1884, wrote a tennis manual. The 'volley game is not made for ladies! It is too quick, and is too great a strain on the system,' he continued. Abstention from the volleying game might be tolerated in the singles, but how did it affect the doubles game? Here, close to the baseline and in perfect sisterly harmony, the two ladies stood, indulging in rallies which seemed never to end. 'As a game of this description is played at the present time,' Wilfred Baddeley, the masterly representative of the men's doubles game, said full of melancholy in 1897, 'there is but little excitement to be got out of it, either by the players themselves or the spectators; its only useful purpose apparently being the amount of good exercise which all the ladies are forced to take.' Since ladies refrained from volleying, they were in the mixed doubles assigned a role which (according to the philosophy of their gentleman partners) suited them best: that of a charlady. While the bold male, close to the net, was expected to score one splendid triumph after the other, the lady to his rear did the job of a maid of all work by scurrying up and down the baseline.[5] *Faire la femme de ménage* was what the frivolous French called this unattractive and rather humiliating scrounging together of any stray balls that came her way. Because of their inferiority as a sport, the ladies' doubles and the mixed doubles became adopted into the Wimbledon canon only in 1913.[6]

The question why the ladies' utterly inappropriate tennis outfit was not soon replaced (as all 'lady players' hoped) by an improved and more functional one is surely intriguing. Lottie Dod wrote:

> Ladies' dress, too, is a matter for grave consideration; for how can they ever hope to play a sound game when their dresses impede the free movement of every limb? In many cases their very breathing is rendered difficult. A suitable dress is sorely needed, and hearty indeed would be the thanks of puzzled lady-players to the individual who invented an easy and pretty costume.

(The last adjective shows that Lottie was, after all, a woman!)

But whose fault was it that such an individual could not be found? Certainly not the ladies', Lottie exclaimed, but that of their courteous protectors who, in journals such as the *Field*, kept voicing their male chauvinist opinion without ever receiving the slightest rebuke. The editor of the journal is very roundly berated because, 'invested with the prerogative of an irresponsible despot', he had been 'made the ruler of the game as well as an arbiter of fashion, credited with the ability to regulate not only the weight of the lady's racket, but also the length of her skirt'. Lottie here lays bare the true motives of those who considered lawn tennis to be either too exacting or too dangerous for ladies, or who were resolved on confining her, by the introduction of sissy rules, to the secluded atmosphere of the garden party. Rather than conceding to the hated rival a glance at her ankle, these gentlemen would have much preferred seeing their bride or wife collapse under the burden of her tennis attire.

And yet, the ladies' revolt took place at last. 'Ladies should learn to run, and run their hardest, too, not merely stride.' Lottie Dod found fault with those ladies who, with an 'Oh! I can't' on their lips and in feigned despair, used to let pass a ball that might have been returned with a little effort, and who seemed willing to resign themselves to the role of the maid of all work for ever. Shortly before the turn of the century, Herbert Chipp, secretary of the LTA and himself a tennis player of note, had to admit that ladies, and indeed a great many, had taken Lottie's advice to heart. On the time when ladies learnt how to run, which their grandmothers would have called a lapse back into 'pure heathenism', Chipp has to say the following:[7]

> Among the manifold changes and consequent uprootings of preju-
> dices which the latter half of this century has witnessed, nothing
> has been more characteristic of the new order of things than the
> active participation of women in sports and pastimes . . . Lawn
> Tennis must claim a large share of the responsibility for the introduc-
> tion of the new regime. But whether for better or worse, whether
> we disapprove with our grandmothers or approve with our daugh-
> ters, times have changed, and we have to accept facts as we find
> them. And although the present movement may be (and undoubt-
> edly is) often carried to excess, and the athleticism of the *fin-de-siècle*
> woman appears sometimes too pronounced, still it cannot be denied
> that on the whole the changes which have been brought about must
> ultimately prove beneficial to the race at large – at all events physi-
> cally. Whether the benefit will be as great morally is a question
> which only time can settle. But we may surely venture to hope that
> our daughters will not be worse mothers because, instead of leading
> sedentary lives, a great portion of their young years has been spent
> on the river, the tennis lawn, the hockey field and the golf links –
> ay, even on the now ubiquitous bicycle itself.

Even in Germany, the opinions expressed by educators became less severe as time went on. As early as the 1890s, tennis was very strongly recommended for young ladies by August Hermann, a 'Turninspektor' from Brunswick, provided the kitchen, the laundry and the nursery were not neglected. To Hermann's mind, tennis for the German lady was, above all, of considerable value for the German male. Since it was a game for both sexes, he argued, it might lure away young men from their notorious haunt, the *bierhaus*, and from alcohol, tobacco smoke and playing cards, evils to which they had succumbed in the decades past.

A last, but futile, attempt was made by the gentlemen to send the tennising ladies to Coventry, as it were. Having failed to deny them membership of sports clubs, they tried to assign to them the status of a club within the club. This was a practice much adhered to in the United States where, in clubs devoted to the manly game of cricket, for instance, tennis for a long time remained a game exclusively run by the club's womenfolk.[8] When the ladies finally requested to compete in public tournaments along with the gentlemen, this right was, after some hesitation, granted to them, but they had to play their matches at a different venue. In 1879, the first Irish ladies' championships in Dublin (discontinued two years later, in 1881) did not take place in Fitzwilliam Square like the men's, but in Wilton Place, significantly on one of the club's covered (and therefore secluded) asphalt courts. At the first ladies' championships at Wimbledon, the staging of which had been rejected in 1879, the gentlemen in charge of the organization were playing for time: the ladies were admitted to the courts only after the gentlemen had finished their singles championships.[9] To Commander Hillyard, the husband of the Wimbledon champion of 1886, that was not enough. He and others strongly advocated having the ladies' championships played elsewhere, in the provinces and away from gawping crowds.

Tennis: A Cultural History, 1997

1 When Maud was defeated by Lottie Dod in Wimbledon in 1886, she had been victorious in fifty-five successive matches.

2 It is little known that in 1907, after the early death of William Renshaw, his family presented another cup honouring the memory of its famous member. The 'Renshaw Cup' is still awarded, as an additional gift, to the winner of the Wimbledon singles championship.

3 The following points were made by Lottie Dod, the five-times All England champion, who in 1890 contributed a short essay on women's tennis to a volume edited by C. G. Heathcote. This essay, written by an eighteen-year-old girl, is so thoughtful and witty that one easily understands the exceptional role played by its author in contemporary lawn tennis.

4 These are the words of Lottie Dod, ibid.

5 This formation was invented by that great American theoretician, Dr James Dwight, who put it to a successful test around the middle of the 1880s with Blanche Bingley (the All England

champion and later Mrs Hillyard), against William Renshaw who, partnered by Miss Bracewell, stuck to the baseline.

6 From 1899–1907, a women's doubles was added to the Wimbledon programme, and a mixed doubles from 1900–1912, but before 1913 neither of them had championship status. These championships were for a long time held in Buxton (doubles, since 1885) and, by turns, in Liverpool and Manchester (mixed doubles, since 1888).

7 The quotation is from Herbert Chipp's *Lawn Tennis Recollections* which were published in London in 1898.

8 This is the implication of an account of American lawn tennis by the famous Doherty brothers in 1903.

9 This was changed in 1887. From that year, competitions for men and women were held alongside each other.

Always on the Cusp
BILLIE JEAN KING

What troubled me a lot about the revelations [that I had had an affair while I was married, and it was with a woman] was how this would affect the way people would remember me. I'm not, in fact, nearly as hung up on this immortality business as a lot of athletes. Bjorn Borg, for example, was only twenty-three or twenty-four before he was making no bones about how he wanted to go out: acknowledged as the best ever. Now Chris Evert Lloyd has picked up on that. She talks about it regularly in public, which is wise of her because you can't always depend on the press coming up with original notions. So Chrissie says she would like to go out as the best ever, that's what she's striving for, and the press writes that, and they start talking about her as potentially the greatest of all time, and that way she's got a chance to actually end up touted with that top ranking. You've got to win in sports – that's talent – but you've also got to learn how to remind everybody how you did win, and how often. That comes with experience.

But honestly, I've never cared that much for cementing my place in history. Sports is so transitory, so ephemeral. It just seems like so much nonsense comparing me to Helen Wills Moody or Suzanne Lenglen or anybody else from some other time. One lesson you learn from sports is that life goes on without you. As I recall, they didn't cancel the 1970 US Open because I had to miss it on account of a knee operation. In 1973, when almost all the men boycotted Wimbledon, the controversy about their absence helped draw record crowds. There is always someone to put on tennis shoes and fill out the draw if you can't. It goes right on.

Still, what bothered me when I became aware that my privacy would be invaded and the affair would be publicly disclosed in the lawsuit was what people would think whenever my name came up. I feared that I always would be categorized by that, whatever else I have accomplished. I worked hard all of my life to achieve my goals. I will work hard to achieve future goals. I worked hard and became famous for being a tennis champion, and then, because of the disclosure, I was put in the vulnerable position of being remembered and categorized because of this very private and inconsequential episode.

The damage was compounded because the disclosure of my private affair surfaced when it did, right at the time when I was finishing as a player. Now, I have very little time left to play championship tennis to help people forget that insignificant part of my life. There is no way I can get back in the news for winning something on the tennis court, which could send the Marilyn episode back to oblivion. I do have some faith that the world is more understanding now. Still, I fear that, years ahead, when people hear the name of Billie Jean King, they will think of scandal before championships. And that would hurt, hurt very badly. I don't want that.

It worries me more, though, that public disclosure of the affair will come to reflect unfavorably upon women's tennis also. I fear that the sport is in for a hard three or four years. Sponsors will drop women tennis players arbitrarily and without an afterthought. There are just so many worthwhile enterprises – sporting and otherwise – competing for sponsors' support these days, and so they might figure that they do not need anything which they think will create risk.

Most of the men in charge of sponsors' decisions are proud to call themselves conservatives, but I don't believe they are. To me, a conservative is supposed to be someone in favor of individual freedom. But these men will be the first to back away if someone they're associated with exercises that freedom. One of the first ramifications of my situation was that a prominent male corporation executive denied another woman an important public-relations position merely because *he heard* she was a lesbian.

In my case, too, I'm not just a player, not just an ex-champion, but I am, to many people, the personification of women's tennis. So I know very well that this distant episode in my life – one player's life – is going to give a great many nice folks the opportunity to categorize me and some other women tennis players as homosexuals. After all, aren't I the same outspoken women's libber who beat an old ex-world champion in the Astrodome? What can anyone expect from me, anyway?

I am a woman, however, and I will always be. I hope I can take about anything they throw at me – and not necessarily because I'm thick-skinned. But because, in a way, I've had a certain amount of practice at feeling uncomfortable. I've always had the feeling that I was different and that people were critical of that.

In many respects, I like being different. I also like being successful. I somehow always knew that I would succeed. I had a great sense of destiny from the time I was very young. I remember one incident so vividly. When I was only about five or six years old, I was standing with my mother in the kitchen at home in Long Beach. I told her flat out that when I grew up I was going to be the best at something. She just smiled and kept peeling potatoes or doing whatever it was she was doing. She said, 'Yes, dear; yes, of course, dear,' as if I had simply said that I was going to my room or going to eat an apple, or whatever.

So, I have always felt different that way. But it is also true that, as I got older, I could sense that I was different in other ways as well. Of course, I believe everyone is different in some way. I believe that people should not label anyone. I fear that people will tend to categorize me now because of the affair. That is wrong. That affair has nothing to do with my feelings, my perceptions of who I am and what I have done or what I want to do. That does not make me a misfit or anything else. I am still a woman. I am still an athlete.

Of course, much of the reason why I've always felt that I was out of place was because of sports. First, a girl who wanted to excel in athletics was considered to be strange. In the second place, it was all a hopeless dream, anyhow. I think I began to appreciate this when I was only eight or nine, when my father took me to see the old Los Angeles Angels play the Hollywood Stars in the Triple-A Pacific Coast League at Wrigley Field in LA. (The Stars were especially memorable. They wore short pants.)

Right away, I loved it, but it was unfair of me to love it, I understood soon enough, because there was no place for an American girl to go in the *national* pastime. This all came back to me when I saw a commercial on television recently and a whole bunch of kids, boys and girls alike, are all climbing out of a station wagon or getting hamburgers or doing something fun together, and they're all dressed up in baseball uniforms. I'm sure that most people who watch this commercial think how forward it is, how progressive, showing girls on the team, girls in uniform just like the boys. And I have such mixed emotions about that commercial.

It's great that they include girls, but at the same time it's cruel because all it can possibly do is make some little girl somewhere wrongly think that she can be a baseball player, too. And of course she can't. There is no life for girls in team sports past Little League.

I got into tennis when I realized this, and because I thought golf would be too slow for me, and I was too scared to swim. What else could a little girl do if she wasn't afraid to sweat? But as good as I was, and as much as I loved tennis right from the start, I found myself out of place there, too, because it was a country-club game then, and I came from a working-class family. My father was a fireman, and we didn't have any money for rackets, much less for proper tennis dresses. The first time I was supposed to be in a group photograph was at the Los Angeles Tennis Club during the Southern California Junior Championships. They wouldn't let me pose because I was only able to wear a blouse and a pair of shorts that my mother had made for me. All the other players were photographed.

I had some physical defects also. I had bad eyes – 20/400 – in a sport where nobody wore glasses. And, even as quick and as fast as I've been, I've been fat all over at times, with chubby little legs, and there are railroad tracks on both my knees from a number of knee operations. All that has been very apparent, but perhaps what has made it even more difficult for me as an athlete is my breathing problem. I inherited sinus trouble from my mother and chest problems from my father. The worst times of all for me have been in England, where I've played my very best and set all those records. I don't think there was one year at Wimbledon when I was entirely well. I always had a problem breathing there. I guess I am nearly a physical wreck. You see, nothing about me is quite what it seems.

People mischaracterized me even before the affair. I am supposed to be tough, loud, brash, and insensitive. In fact, Larry says I am very shy, and I really dislike being in the company of more than five or six people. I'm really a one-on-one person. So many people thought I was scared and crumbling under the pressure before the Bobby Riggs match. There happened to be a regular women's tournament in Houston that same week, and I was forced to play in it if I played Riggs – can you imagine the best players today getting that treatment? – and so, one day, without warning, I showed up in the locker room, and almost every player there was scrambling to bet against me. Rosie Casals was the only one backing me. That really hurt, that they didn't have any faith in me.

I had warned Margaret Court when she first told me that she had signed to play Riggs (for $10,000 – she thought that was big money) that she was going to have to deal with a whole *season* – not just a day's match. So I knew the build-up would be even greater for Bobby's and my match; we were working off the Court–Riggs momentum. We signed on 11 July for the 20 September showdown, and the hype never really stopped. If it started to slow down, Bobby would whip it back up again.

So all along, my main strategy was not to get swept along in the promotion. Just because I was half of the show on court didn't mean I had to be part of the warm-up act, too. As much as possible, and right up to curtain time, I tried to stay out of the hoopla. After all, it wasn't as if I was needed to sell tickets and hustle the television. We drew 30,472 to the Astrodome and 40,000,000 American TV viewers – plus millions more abroad – so it did well enough without my becoming another carnival barker. Bobby was quite good enough at that.

Nothing he did surprised me. The reception was very much what I expected, and it didn't faze me. I'd played arenas before, and the circus atmosphere Bobby created just made it all of a piece. The only fear I did have was when they brought me in on the litter like Cleopatra. I don't like heights and I was afraid that they were going to drop me. But even my gift of the pig to Bobby and his gift of the big Sugar Daddy to me passed immediately out of my mind. I was really concentrating on my strategy.

The thing that I thought was especially important going in was to volley well. Obviously, I wanted to hit every shot well, and I planned in practice to play an all-court game, sometimes at the net, sometimes back. But I knew Bobby felt that women were poor players at the net, and when I had seen the tape of the Court match, it was apparent that she had reinforced this opinion by playing so badly at net – on those rare occasions when she could get up there. So, to me, it would be psychologically telling if Riggs suddenly realized that this woman could volley.

And I did, too. Five of the first six times he tried to pass me with his backhand, I volleyed away winners. He had me down a service break at 3–2, but by then I knew I could take the net at will, and when I broke right back, that pretty much told the tale. Oh sure, almost right to the end there were all those people who thought Bobby fell behind only to get better odds on his courtside bets, but as far as I was concerned, almost from the first I was amazed at how weak an opponent he really was. All

I ever feared was the unknown, and soon enough he was a known quantity for me.

That match was such madness. How often in this world can you suddenly have something which is altogether original and yet wonderfully classic? And what could be more classic than the battle of the sexes? The only problem for me is that I think everybody else in the world – Bobby included – had more fun with that match than I did. Men's tennis would not suffer if Bobby lost, so he had nothing to lose.

Perhaps people would have known how much it all mattered to me if they could have seen an incident a few days before.

I was practicing down in South Carolina, and I came in for a snack. Dick Butera, my friend, the owner of the Philadelphia Freedoms of World Team Tennis and the husband of Julie Anthony, another friend, was lying on the floor, watching a college football game. It was half-time, and the Stanford band was entertaining, and suddenly, as I watched, the band began playing 'I Am Woman,' and then I realized that they had formed my initials, BJK, on the field, and Dick looked up to share this moment with me, and we both had tears in our eyes. I think that was the happiest the Riggs match ever made me.

But it was never the match itself that upset me. It was all the people clamoring after me. My whole life, I wanted to have mobs of people cheer for tennis, but I really become quite frightened when everybody pushes around me and wants to touch me. I hate it when strangers touch me, even though I understand it is almost always for love, and that they don't mean anything harmful. Still, at the time, when it happens, it scares me.

I have often been asked whether I am a woman or an athlete. The question is absurd. Men are not asked that. I am an athlete. I am a woman. I want all other women to have their rights, because above all else, I'm for individual freedom, but there is very much about the goals and the methods of the women's movement that I disagree with. That is the refusal to recognize that both men and women view each other through sexual bias. Oh, I know this is going to get me in trouble, but I'm going to mention it anyway. I've got a male friend in business, and he told me once that he'd really rather have a good-looking, well-built blonde who can barely manage as his secretary than some old lady who is a secretarial whiz. That's his privilege, I think. And if the blonde takes the job knowing that she's going to get leered at and chased around the desk, fair enough.

I'm still not even absolutely convinced that we need the Equal Rights

Amendment. If it means the end of discrimination on the basis of gender, then I want it. But I don't believe you can legislate people's minds. I believe that it is persuasion you need, not force. Just because you legislate does not mean that people will change. This reminds me of what happened in the waning days of the Roman Empire. Initially, citizenship in the Empire had been one of the most highly prized possessions, but this changed as the Roman Empire began to legislate people's values and behavior patterns. The legislation reached such an extent that in the last days of the empire, Roman citizens were renouncing their citizenship in order to come under the more relaxed alien laws. Citizenship had come to be considered more of a burden than a prize. People simply had become fed up with so much legislation. As another example, there are some countries where people are leaving in droves because of heavy taxation, lack of personal freedom, and overly protective legislation. I do not want that to happen to us.

Sometimes the women's movement reminds me too much of some organized religion, which I can't stand. I was very (quote) religious (unquote) as a kid. Also, I was much less tolerant then. That seems to me to be the trouble with movements, be they Women's Liberation or the Moral Majority or whatever. Then you always have to be against somebody on every issue, and I'm not very good at that. I don't like confrontations. But, of course, I always performed my best when the confrontation was most heightened, in the clutch — the most well-known example being the Riggs match. Nothing ever really fits for me.

I was a virgin when I was supposed to be, and I got married to the right cute boy the way I was supposed to at the time I was supposed to, but then we only had a 'normal' marriage for a couple years — or, anyway, what most Americans presume a normal marriage to be, even if that ideal barely exists anymore. I never feel comfortable with a lot of so-called 'normal' married people because they seem threatened by the way Larry and I live — and this was the case even long before people knew about my affair with Marilyn and could say 'I told you so' instead of just 'I'll bet she's queer.' So I've never really felt at home in that huge world of married people, but I've also never felt at all comfortable when I've been associated with the gay world. Maybe it's mostly that everybody wants reinforcement of their kind of life, and I don't provide that for anybody.

I guess I'm just very much a loner. Except for one thing: I really can't stand to be alone for long. Sometimes I ask myself, Billie Jean, where do you belong? Do you fit in anywhere? Maybe all my life I've just been trying to change things so there would be someplace right for me.

I think the sense – the fear? – of not belonging is greater in my particular case, too, because the ground has kept shifting under my feet. I was born on the cusp – Scorpio/Sagittarius, 22 November; John Kennedy was shot on my twentieth birthday – and maybe that set the stage for my life. In a way, it seems that I've lived on the cusp for a long time, because everywhere, as I approached something, it turned, it changed. Nothing really happened as I had plotted it.

Any woman born around 1943 has had to endure so many changes – in her educational experience, in her working life, in sex, in her roles, her expectations. But with me, it always seemed that I was also on the cutting edge of that change. Any woman about my age – or, for that matter, any person who has had to deal with women, which is just about everybody – has been a part of a great social transition, and just to survive that intact has been an accomplishment for me. I was brought up in a very structured universe – in my family, in school, in tennis, in every part of my world. Then, all of a sudden, the rules all started to change, and it seemed there weren't any rules left. I tried to go with the flow, but always seemed to find myself out in front and on the line.

When I married Larry in 1965, we were going to have babies – lots of them, as far as I was concerned – and I was going to give up tennis, which is the way it was supposed to be. In fact, only two weeks after we were married, I thought I was pregnant. And I was delighted. But even when I found out I wasn't having a baby, I was happy enough just spending so much time with Larry. I'd cook him two meals at home every day and take him his lunch – even when he was on the night shift – to the factory where he worked making ice cream cartons.

As for tennis, it hardly mattered. There certainly wasn't any career for me there. It was just fun, and in those days, before professionals were accepted in the main tournaments, there was no money to speak of. We amateurs – 'shamateurs' was the accepted term – took what we could in the way of 'expenses' under the table, and if it wasn't much, it was still like found money to a young couple, and it helped Larry through law school.

I won Wimbledon three years running, and outside the little tennis community, very few people knew. In 1967 I won all three titles at Wimbledon – singles, doubles, and mixed – and I came back to my country, and there was no one there to meet me, no one at all. And barely six years later, there I was, in the Houston Astrodome, playing prime time to the world in what amounted to the Roman Colosseum, with everyone in civilization chanting my name, hating me or loving me. And everyone wanted – needed – part of me, for tennis or movements or friendship or politics or just for the hell of it – Wouldja, couldja, canya, Billie Jean? – and people were throwing money at me or grabbing at me or calling me a symbol or a leader or a radical feminist. I didn't know where I was. It was so complicated, and one morning I woke up, and where was I? I was in another woman's bed.

So now I know a lot of people will call me a homosexual, but to me that's just another label. As I said, I cannot stand categorization. I'm not concerned for me. I just don't want Larry and my parents and my brother and the other people who love me hurt. And maybe now I can spend some time carving out a place for me in the world around me instead of only in the record books.

Billie Jean, 1982

Ladies of the Evening
MARTINA NAVRATILOVA

The melodic swell of Tchaikovsky's *Swan Lake* poured from the hotel room, for the benefit of all the other players down the hall. In the room, the 150-pound ballerina practiced her pirouettes more diligently than she had ever practiced her backhand. I was that ballerina.

In America, all things are possible – even a ballet line of swans such as you never imagined before: Billie Jean King, Rosie Casals, and yours truly with her own brief solo, a star of sorts in that infamous troupe known as the Ladies of the Evening.

We committed this assault on ballet in 1977, in the third annual Ladies of the Evening performance by the women professionals. We even had an amateur choreographer named Makarova – Dina Makarova, a photographer and translator, not the other Makarova.

We had a lot of fun on the road in those days. From the first time I was allowed out of Czechoslovakia, I sensed the freedom and camaraderie of the women players. They were just building something in those days, and they had a sense of the pioneer about them. They hung out together more than we do today, they had a good time together.

The best example was the Ladies of the Evening. Rosie Casals was the instigator in 1975 on Amelia Island, Florida, at the Family Circle tournament. After most of the spectators had gone home for the day, Rosie set up her own championship match between Peachy Kellmeyer and Vicky (Bird Legs) Berner. There were a few interesting ground rules for this game. Peachy had to drink a beer on every changeover, while Vicky had to drink scotch. That brought the level of tennis to a height nobody had ever seen before. The rest of us got into the act, wearing grotesque outfits of the brightest colors that normally only a tourist would wear.

Chris and I were the coaches. I guess I won't soon forget her outfit: a T-shirt that said BIRD LEGS' COACH, hoop earrings, horizontal striped socks, and an orange baseball cap turned backward like a catcher's. Classy, ya know?

Billie Jean was the umpire, wearing her thickest glasses and making calls as outrageous as the ones she thought had been made against her over the years. Betty Stove and Frankie Durr were the most intrusive pair of ball girls you've ever seen. Oh, yes, and Bird Legs was wearing size forty-eight boxer shorts, to add a touch of dignity to the event.

That started the tradition, and we spent a year planning the next outing. It gave us something to think about on the road for weeks and months at a time. As Shari Barman put it, 'When you always lose in the first round, you need something else to do.' So she had T-shirts made up that said LADIES OF THE EVENING. The tour officials were always a little hesitant about publicizing our group – because of the name, no doubt – but we were not inhibited.

In 1976 we held our bash after the finals of a Virginia Slims event in Los Angeles. Ted Tinling was the master of ceremonies, wearing his best earring. He told the crowd they could stay if they wanted, and most of the 10,000 people sat there and watched Chris play Olga Morozova.

All of us were in a good mood because of the brownies Rosie Casals had baked for the occasion. Billie Jean and Evonne were the coaches this time, and Virginia Wade was the umpire. She did something I've never seen an umpire do: a somersault right in the middle of the court.

Later that night we had a banquet at the Beverly Hills Hotel and Bill Cosby gave out the awards. We made more of a fuss over our Ladies of the Evening contest than about our tournament.

The third version took place in 1977 at a disco in the Hilton Hotel in Philadelphia. By now we were professionals, and we put on a talent show, if you want to call it that. Olga Morozova sang a Russian song;

Chris dressed up as Groucho Marx; Betty Stove dressed as a genie with a Gucci bag; Jeanie Brinkman did a tap dance; Jerry Diamond did an imitation of different players; Frankie Durr danced the can-can; and the lighter of foot performed *Swan Lake*.

Dina Makarova had simplified some ballet steps for Rosie, Vicky, Connie Spooner, our trainer, and me. Billie Jean rehearsed with us, but when the time came, she chickened out. I actually got to the point where I knew the steps so well that they let me perform a solo. I had rehearsed it, much to everybody's displeasure, at odd hours in my hotel room for days ahead. Dum-da-dum, da, da-da-da-da-dum . . . I still remember twirling. If I tried it today, I'd probably break my leg.

That's what life was like when I first joined the tour. It was more fun then because people were more willing to cut up. Even though we competed hard on the court, we had something in common off the court. Nowadays, players go their separate ways, myself included. Kids have parents or coaches or agents with them and don't mingle the way we did then.

In those days we would do things together. I remember, right after I came over, one of those beautiful dry, not-too-hot spring days in Phoenix when the desert was in bloom. Raquel Giscafre, Shari Barman, Fiorella Bonicelli, and I rented four motorcycles, not your little putt-putt motorbikes but 250s and 350s. I was playing Fiorella at eight that night but we figured we'd be getting the same amount of sun and exhaustion, so it didn't really matter. We took off around eleven in the morning, wearing bathing suits and helmets, going eighty-five miles per hour on the interstate. I wouldn't do that on my life today, but then I was eighteen, nineteen, what did I know? We went to this lake, watched people water-ski, almost did that, too, but finally we got on our cycles and roared home. Got back at six and I beat Fiorella in straight sets — just as I would have without both of us having gotten a massive case of sunburn.

It seems to me there was always something to laugh about in those days. On one tour in 1974, I lost to Rosie in three straight tournaments. Billie Jean would come by in the locker room and see me in just a bra and panties and she would tell Rosie how strong I was, that I could pick Rosie up and throw her around. They were pretending they were afraid of me, when the truth of the matter was, I am the biggest pussycat. For the first Ladies of the Evening outing, Rosie had some T-shirts made up that said NAVRAT THE BRAT, a nickname that stayed with me for years. It made me feel part of the gang, better even than back at Sparta.

In the last few years, with all the gossip about lesbianism in sports, I've read some suggestions that mothers of young players were so afraid of their daughters' being accosted in the locker room that they'd accompany them there. That's just so far-fetched. The only mother I ever saw in the locker room was Mrs Austin, and Tracy was so shy she wouldn't walk around in her underwear.

Let's face it, if women are going to become gay, it's not going to happen in the locker room. Yes, in most locker rooms, the lockers are open, and some of us change right out in front of each other. You can also see most of us getting a rubdown from the trainers on a table right out in the open. Some of us are more modest than others, but it has nothing to do with sexual preference. When I first came along, I was petrified to change in front of anybody. I was ashamed of how I looked, too immature at first, then too heavy. I didn't even want to be seen in my underwear, much less the altogether.

After a while, it became too much trouble to change in the shower, to carry a bathrobe with you. It's not like you're an exhibitionist, but you make your living with your body and it stops having a mystique. Now I walk around the house with nothing on sometimes. I don't think Renee Lieberman is ever going to get over my going to the door naked in Far Rockaway to call my dogs back from their walk. Oops, sorry, Renee. Thought I was in the locker room.

But women's sexual preferences are not changed in the lockers. For one thing, I don't think the percentage of gay women on the circuit is that much higher than the national level – 10 percent or whatever. And I'll bet it's about the same in male sports, too. The truth is, men are much more promiscuous about homosexuality. They've got gay bars, gay baths, whereas women have more stable relationships and most don't go in for one-night stands.

While we're talking about the tour, I have never seen a female tennis player who I thought had a dope problem. I've seen some male basketball players go downhill overnight and figured they must be on drugs, and then suddenly they're on rehab. I've heard the same rumors as everybody else about cocaine on the men's tour, but we're two different worlds, meeting only at a few major tournaments, and I've never seen signs of a male player going down like the basketball players. On our tour, there used to be some marijuana, but now you don't even see that. The women are so clean. The extent of their debauchery is drinking a beer or a screwdriver.

Some of the women do have emotional problems – too much, too soon, they have a hard time adjusting to life on the road in their teens. I see mood swings and personality problems in a couple of the most promising young players, but I attribute that to family difficulties, not drugs.

I hate to disappoint people, but the women's tour was much like the old-fashioned image of a college sorority, particularly back in the seventies. We played together, we traveled together, we partied together, we worried about money together.

We also had to compete against our road companions, week after week. Being on the court with an opponent is a strange business. You're totally out for yourself, to win a match, yet you're dependent on your opponent to some degree for the type of match it is and how well you play. You need the opponent; without her you do not exist.

Playing against Chris was always like battling part of your own nature. You know it so well but you can't give in to it. She was not the best athlete in the world, not a pure athlete like Candy Reynolds or Betsy Nagelsen or Hana Mandlikova, but there was always that determination.

I'd be out there on one side of the net and I'd see those eyes squinting and I'd say, 'Oh, no.' I knew she would be steady. I knew she would not make a mistake. She'd whip that two-handed backhand at me. I'd hit the ball back to her, and she would squint again and set her mouth and hit the two-hander, just a little differently this time. She did it so well, for so many years.

Her serve was mechanical, not a weapon. Sometimes I'd wonder why she never improved her serve, considering that she improved the rest of her game. But she had such shot-making ability. Her backhand came back so hard and she never quit on a ball, so you knew you could never quit, either. You'd always have to tell yourself, 'This is Chris. Don't give up.'

Another opponent who really awed me was Margaret Court, because I admired her so much when I was young. I only played her a few times at the end of her career, when she didn't serve that hard, but she was still a wonder. Even when I beat her in the Australian Open at Kooyong in 1975, by a score of 6–4, 6–3, I'd still stand on the other side of the net and watch these bombs come rocketing in on first serve.

She was so tall and formidable that I'd find myself staring at her and wondering what she had been like a few years earlier. I hate to sound like Hana, who's always talking about me being some kind of alien in size and strength, but Margaret actually amazed me with her size and strength.

With Billie Jean, it was different. In my early years, I was totally in awe of her backhand. I would serve her wide and she'd hit it right down the line to my backhand. I'd say, 'Damn, how did she do that?' She wasn't the same player she had been – I never played Billie Jean at her peak – but she was still awesome. She'd try some of those little dinks and I'd think to myself, Cut the crap. But she never let on. She'd just blink at you behind those glasses, and you would wonder, What's she going to do next?

Billie Jean was the leader of the pack, no doubt about it. The queen of the hill. She was such a great player and so proud of women's tennis that she turned the sport into a big-time event. Everything she did was for tennis. She saw this new kid from Czechoslovakia and came over and gave me advice on my backhand. She had advice on every subject. She wanted tennis to succeed so much that she would even try to improve her opponents' games – to prepare us to be professionals.

The only time she didn't give anything away was on the court. I idolized Billie Jean so much that the first few times I played her, I'd get all tense and just give away point after point. I knew my shots were as good as hers, but I also knew how smart she was and I'd start wondering what she was going to do next.

Right in the middle of a match, Billie Jean would totally change her game, and I'd think, Shoot, what does she know? I'd stop playing from strength, and I'd give away a big game to her. Other players did the same thing to me. Tracy Austin, when she came along, would lob for no apparent reason, or suddenly come in behind my ball, or she'd serve-and-volley, and I'd totally lose it. I think they watched Billie Jean play me, and watched me panic.

I've seen Billie Jean practice gamesmanship with other players: stop and argue with the umpire, tie her shoelace, anything to distract her opponent. I knew she could do it, but she never tried it with me – at least I never noticed it.

We played doubles for a while, but we were often on different tours. I didn't beat her until early in 1978, in the finals of Houston, a three-setter. Because I figured I should have done it sooner, it wasn't that big a deal.

I studied Billie Jean so carefully that I even began arguing with the officials at times. After all, I reasoned, if Billie Jean King didn't mind looking like a competitor on the court, why should I? But I don't think people took it as well from me as they did from her. She was special; she was creating modern women's tennis, by force of personality. She set the standard. She made us feel we were all in this together. She made us feel we were building something.

There's not as much of that feeling in the sport now. I know Billie Jean complains that Chris and I don't put enough back into the game. She thinks we should spend our every waking minute promoting tennis. But where do you draw the line? Billie Jean thinks you should play every week, give clinics, make public appearances, talk to the press, because that's what she did. She made this sport what it is today, and I can understand how she feels. But I've got to live my own life, too.

I'm sure Billie Jean wishes she were ten years younger. She built women's tennis up and by the time it peaked, her best years were behind her. It's too bad, but what do you say about Althea Gibson and Maria Bueno, two of the best players in history, who never got any money out of tennis?

Billie Jean had great foresight about tennis. I'm not sure she was that good in following through, in making sound business decisions. She put money into World Team Tennis, softball, a sports magazine, none of which made big profits. I don't think she'll ever have to worry about starving, but she was one of the great champions of all time and the big money wasn't there until she stood up for equal prize money for women.

I look at somebody like Ivan Lendl, who still hadn't won a Grand Slam event until the French Open in 1984, yet he was making millions. And then there was Tony Trabert, who won all the biggest tournaments and probably didn't make a dime. Wrong time, wrong place.

The money today is staggering, I don't even think about it anymore. The amazing part is that I could make even more than I do. I could play exhibitions, like Björn Borg does, and never worry about competing again. But I won't do much of that, and I'll tell you why: I'd rather be on the tour whenever possible. It's as close as I come to having a community.

Chris and I are not as close as we used to be. When Nancy Lieberman and I worked together, there was something of a wedge between me and Chris. Tracy Austin, you never saw or heard much from her. And Andrea Jaeger's got her own problems – half the time she's in a good mood and the other half she's not. But there's still a core of friendship, particularly at the smaller tournaments, where there's less press, fewer business agents around. Some of my best friends are also my opponents.

At the start, I'd have trouble mixing business and friendship. I would lose to somebody I had no business losing to. I played Frankie Durr in 1975, when I had a sore shoulder. They were timing our serves with one of those radar guns, and mine was clocked at 91 miles per hour while hers couldn't even be clocked because the machine wouldn't accept anything under seventy. I was so relaxed enjoying a good hit with her, that she beat me. And it wasn't the only time.

Usually, my competitiveness took over. I remember Kerry Melville Reid complaining that I could get 'obnoxious' on the court, questioning calls. Kerry was quoted as saying: 'She gets that from Billie Jean King, her idol. I guess she figures that if Billie Jean can get away with it, intimidating officials, then she can do it. She copies Billie Jean a lot.' But Kerry added that she liked me anyway, and it was true. Most of us got along.

There were a few players who wouldn't say hello before a match, like Nancy Richey, but I always felt I could socialize and still have the killer instinct. I could do anything with Sharon Walsh before a match, she's so easygoing, or Wendy Turnbull or Betsy Nagelsen or Pam Shriver. I recently played bridge one afternoon with Marcella Mesker and then beat her in tennis that evening.

We took pride in being fair with each other, knowing that the officials were often recruited from local tennis clubs and lacked the reflexes and training needed to call a professional match. When I first came along, the press used to think I complained about my bad calls, but I would argue just as ferociously if I thought my opponent had been shorted. Sometimes I'd even double-fault on purpose if they wouldn't change the call.

Some of the players said I was the fairest one out there. The public thought Evonne was great because she was so serene and beautiful, but she never said anything about a call. Borg never said a word either, even if his opponent was getting screwed by the call. He wouldn't blink an eyelash. But I always wanted the match to be perfect, right down to the officiating.

I've never been able to treat my opponent as the enemy, particularly Pam Shriver, my doubles partner and one of my best friends. I remember only one time being psyched up against her, in Tampa not too long ago in a final, when I was out for a friendly match of tennis on a beautiful

Sunday afternoon. With the score 3–all in the first set, I called a let on her serve, and she disagreed. She got upset and started smarting off, so I thought to myself, Same to you, Turkey, and played my little butt off for the rest of the match. I'm sure I would have gotten my butt in gear anyway, but she helped the cause. Later, we talked about it and cleared the air right away. 'You know me from doubles,' I said. 'If I think it's a let, I'll call it.' I also told Pam that she should be all sweetness and joking around, so she'd have a better chance. Actually, she's given me some of my biggest losses, and she constantly comes up with big matches against me.

At first it was hard being on the road most of the time. I was always glad to see friends like the Hoschls in Chicago or Aja and Paul Steindler in New York. I learned to reach out for friends when I had a free day. One time in Washington, on Super Bowl Sunday, we didn't have a match, so I called Jane Leavy from the Washington *Post* and asked what she was doing. She said she and her husband and some friends were watching the game on television and invited me over. I spent the afternoon with them and we talked football, no tennis, and I felt I had totally escaped from the cocoon for a day.

Ever since I became a pro, I have tried to balance my need for rest with my need for friends. After a while, you have friends everywhere, and you run into some fans who become your friends after you've seen them a few times. It's usually discouraging to both sides because I want to have time with them, yet I don't. On the road, I might want to go to a museum or a movie, but I learned during my time with Rita Mae Brown that I shouldn't be too emotionally spent or physically tired before a match. I now have a policy of never giving a private interview before matches because it might upset me; I don't want to be worrying while I'm on the court, thinking, Gee, why did I say that?

The one thing I learned to appreciate on the road was sleeping right through breakfast. I have a system for when I wake up: order room service, take a shower while waiting for it to arrive, eat with the soaps on television while my hair's drying, and then go out for a walk. I love being in a city like Paris or New York or San Francisco that has a real downtown, where you can drop into a bookstore or gift shop without having to take a car. In a real city, I can walk two blocks and get a lot done, but if I have to drive someplace, it's a drain on my energy. In the hours before a match, I'll read a book or watch TV, and lately I've been playing bridge with Barbara Hunter Estep, my coach's wife.

From the time I joined the tour in 1975, one of my best friends has been Lee Jackson, the chief official. But then again, Lee is a terrific friend to all of us. I know this sounds strange, but it's not like a baseball player saying he's friendly with an umpire, which could never happen. It's hard to imagine John McEnroe or Jimmy Connors hanging out with somebody they've just vilified on the court, but it's different with women's tennis.

I remember the first full year I traveled on the tour, being in New York with nothing to do and calling Lee at her home in the suburbs. She invited me to her club, where I played squash for the first time and gave the club pro a pretty good match. I also played Scrabble with Lee and sat around the club talking with a lawyer about American and European history.

I haven't been doing enough of that kind of thing since I began my full-time exercise and diet program with Nancy, but I know I've got to seek out more friendships, keep learning. In 1976 Lee Jackson's son was killed in an automobile crash and she began to travel more on the tour. She used to organize trips to Disney World or to good restaurants on a night off. I know I missed my mother, not just for her great Czech meals and her sewing, but for her emotional support, and Lee took over that role in my life. I only hope we were as much a comfort to her as she has been to a whole generation of tennis players.

I honestly don't think our friendship has interfered in any way with our work. If Lee is handling my match, and I think somebody is blowing a call on the lines, I'll stamp my foot and say, 'Come on, Lee, look what they're doing.' And Lee will say, right into the microphone, 'That's enough, Martina.' I don't want to embarrass her or her officials, so in a sense she raises our behavior level because we respect her. If that's the difference between men's and women's tennis, *vive la différence*. I will still complain about calls when I think they're wrong, even if the crowd doesn't like it. Tennis is my livelihood. We're not playing for fun like in the old days. But you don't want to humiliate people.

Hana Mandlikova broke my streak in Oakland in 1984, when I was within two matches of tying Chris's record of fifty-six consecutive singles victories. There are no surprises on the women's tour. I know Hana's a great athlete, but she's inconsistent, and if she falls behind she loses confidence. I hadn't been playing much before I went to Oakland, and Nancy was trying to get me to cancel because she wanted me to help her prepare for the Superstars competition. I couldn't get out of it, though, and Hana caught me on a bad day.

That match turned on a call by Lee Jackson. I was serving at 4–all, 15–all in the third set. Hana returned service and I hit a topspin, half-volley forehand that looked as if it would go out, but at the last second it swerved down and landed inbounds. It didn't even touch the line, and the official never even raised a hand to signify it was good, but Lee overruled him and called the ball out.

I asked Lee why she overruled a call that was never made. I mean, even if she thought it was out, she's only supposed to call it out if it's out by a lot. I didn't expect Hana to decline the call but I was annoyed with Lee for making it. I know she's a good official and she's fair, but there was no excuse for that call.

I didn't see Lee for a few weeks, until one day we were practicing in New Jersey and I could hear the clicking of her keys as she walked by. Without looking at her, I started narrating the match with Hana two weeks earlier, talking about the terrible call by the head umpire. Then I turned around and said: 'Oh, hi, Lee, I didn't know you were here.' 'I bet you didn't,' she said. And our friendship went on from there.

I need friends like Lee on the tour. She is as close to family as anybody in this country. But there were times when the tour wasn't enough, when the loneliness was too much. It took about a year for the immensity of defection to really hit me. And when it did, it hit me like a ton of bricks.

Martina, 1985

The Forbidden Zone
MICHAEL MEWSHAW

According to conventional wisdom, male coaches and hitting partners had had a wholesome effect on women's tennis. Players were better conditioned and tactically sounder than in the past, and the circuit was said to be a happier place. Now couples could travel together, and young girls got a chance to mature in a more balanced environment. Supposedly men had also improved the commercial image of the tour, serving as a counterweight to the incessant, exaggerated gossip about predatory lesbians in the locker room.

Yet a number of people expressed misgivings about the situation. They felt that more men meant fewer jobs for female coaches and less input from women officials and executives. This reinforced an antiquated notion that men should be in charge.

Still others saw the arrangement as manipulative and exploitative. 'There doesn't have to be sex for a kind of seduction to take place,' an American player told me. 'When you're sixteen or seventeen, and you have a crush on an older coach, it doesn't take much to get to a girl. The guy will give you a little attention or a hug, or he'll go out to dinner and joke around with you. Maybe he'll rub your back after a tough match. He'll act like he really cares, and pretty soon you're playing your brains out for him. You're running extra laps, doing extra sprints, pumping iron in the gym. You're doing everything you can to keep him happy, to make him like you. But what you're forgetting is that for him it's a business deal. You're paying him and picking up his expenses and here he's got you running yourself ragged to win his approval. It's completely turned upside down, but a girl doesn't realize that until she goes through it a few times – until this coach you thought was so great leaves you because you're losing or leaves you for a higher-ranked girl. That's when you put on your Walkman and put on that old tape of Tina Turner's, "What's Love Got to Do With It?" A girl's gotta learn she's working to make herself a better player, not to get her coach to love her.'

Although she swore she was too smart to be taken advantage of, the girl named a number of players whose careers had been crippled by a 'seduced and abandoned' scenario. In some instances the seduction was literal.

'That's when it's awful,' she said, 'when you have a crush on your coach and you wind up in bed with him. Some of those guys are married and have kids as old as the players they're coaching. It should be clear right off it can't lead to anything good for the girl. Yet I've known players that stayed with a guy for years and the whole time they should have been out dating. Then the coach drops them for another player and the girl goes through like a divorce grieving process.'

The frequency and effects of sexual contacts between male coaches and female athletes – especially between adolescent girls and older men – are matters of dispute. Since everyone involved has a motive to remain silent, very little statistical evidence exists on the subject. For self-evident reasons coaches aren't likely to confess to behavior that might land them in professional or legal jeopardy. In some jurisdictions, sex with an underage girl is a crime. Almost everywhere it's regarded as a serious breach of ethics.

Helen Lenskyj, a sociologist at the Ontario Institute for Studies in Education, has argued in her article 'Unsafe at Home Base' that even when women believe they have been badly abused, they, too, have reasons to remain silent. Like rape victims, they don't relish the prospect of being victimized all over again. 'The process of describing an experience of sexual harassment often feels like reliving it,' Lenskyj writes, 'and that is obviously something that most women want to avoid. In fact, in the chilly climate of sport and physical education, women are perhaps more likely to keep their perceptions private than in other, more supportive contexts.'

As Lenskyj also observes, 'Allegations of lesbianism directed at female athletes deter many women from rejecting unwanted sexual attention or complaining about sexual harassment, since they fear that such actions will confirm that they are not sexually interested in men, and hence, lesbian.'

Kathryn Reith of the Women's Sports Foundation in New York City acknowledges that anecdotal information about the sexual abuse of female athletes reaches her group all the time, but it is difficult to get facts and to get anybody, including victims, to discuss the issue.

'Women's sport is so new,' Reith said, 'and has had to struggle so hard to get where it is, every problem that's brought to its attention is swept under the carpet. Whether it's a question of lesbianism or straight-sex abuse, women in sport are afraid it jeopardizes what they have achieved and so they don't want to deal with it.'

Still, there were those on the tennis tour who didn't shy away from the subject. Early on, at the Italian Open, former player and current Fila executive Marty Mulligan declared it was unethical for a coach to turn a professional relationship into a sexual one. Dennis Van der Meer, who believed most coach/player relationships were now sexual in nature, compared coaches who slept with their players to psychiatrists who had sex with their patients and rationalized this as part of therapy. And Juan Nunez had described how sex destroyed the chemistry that had to exist between a coach and player.

One ITF official wondered whether coaches who had sex with underage players weren't putting themselves and the WTA at legal risk. It was, after all, a litigious age and parents had been known to sue when their daughters were molested by teachers, doctors, and pastors.

Quite often when questions about sexual abuse came up during the course of interviews, the initial response of players, agents, and tour officials was to deny that it was happening. But almost invariably they would acknowledge in the next breath that they were aware of one or two cases, which they considered to be rare exceptions.

For example, Hana Mandlikova said she knew nothing about older male coaches having sex with young players, and she denied that it had happened to her. Yet when asked about a recent case involving a Czech teenager who was rumoured to be sleeping with her middle-age coach, Mandlikova conceded, 'That's true. That was very true, yes. Everybody knew that she was in a relationship with him. I think that's sickening. Especially if he's married or something, I think it's terrible.'

'What if he's single?'

'Even that,' Hana said. 'If he's much older, I think that's not right.'

'Is it just the age or is it the coach/athlete relationship?'

'I think it's just not right. I mean, if you're doing a job, you're doing a job, and you're not looking for something else . . . I just don't understand how this can happen, and that's basically all I want to say about it.'

One former Virginia Slims employee insisted that you could never be sure what went on between people in private. Although she admitted seeing a famous coach come out of a teenage player's hotel room at 3 a.m. in his underwear, she disagreed with the proposition that that itself was inappropriate.

It wasn't simply that some people were reluctant to conclude that where there was smoke there was fire. They refused to concede that fires were any real cause for concern. One player, Andrea Leand, wrote an article describing half a dozen cases of sexual harassment or outright abuse, including an anecdote about a coach who walked in on her while she showered. She also told of a player whose coach was sleeping with the girl and her mother. Yet her conclusion was that these were just isolated incidents. When taken together, however, these 'rare exceptions' and 'isolated incidents' added up to a troubling pattern of widespread abuse. Bob Nideffer, a sports psychologist who wound up marrying Ros Fairbanks, a player he was coaching, told Cindy Hahn of *Tennis* magazine that he knew of many coaches who slept with girls on the circuit. 'The tour is made for it,' Nideffer said.

Overall, dozens of sources said they knew of coaches who made suggestive remarks, fondled girls, gave massages that weren't welcomed, and had sex with players when they could get away with it. Some players admitted that it had happened to them. None wanted to be quoted by name, both because of embarrassment and because they feared repercussions from coaches who were still on the tour. But given the obvious pain it caused them to discuss these matters, I had no reason to doubt their honesty or to press them to give up their anonymity.

A South American said, 'My father handed me over to a man and sent me out on the circuit when I was sixteen. He told me to do whatever the coach said. So when he said we were staying in the same hotel room, then when he moved over to my bed, I didn't know how to say no.'

An Eastern European, a tour veteran ranked in the top twenty, told me, 'My coach has always been my lover.' She didn't mean that she had always had the same coach – just that whoever coached her became her lover. It was a pattern that had started when she left home as a teenager with a Federation coach who controlled her fate. To lose his approval meant losing her place on the national team, losing her passport, her chance to travel to the West, win foreign currency, and help her family. When he demanded sex, how could she refuse?

I interviewed a coach from her country whose attitude suggested what she and other girls had faced as teenagers. He said of a top-ten player he had trained, 'She used to be a great lay. This was back when she was fifteen or sixteen. Then she went off on her own and turned into a lesbian.'

As angry and upset as some women were about what had happened to them when they were young, they continued playing tennis. They had either recovered from these early episodes or had settled into a series of damaging relationships. But other women had suffered such ruinous experiences they had to quit the game.

The worst case was a woman who never had a chance to make it onto the tour. While she was a junior, her parents had opened their home to a touring pro who was in town to play a tournament. One night while she was alone in the house, the man broke into her room and tried to rape her. When she resisted, he roughed her up and masturbated on her.

'I never told my parents,' she said. 'I was ashamed and I was afraid. I knew they'd never believe me, so I didn't try to explain. I didn't explain why I stopped playing either. For years I was a mess.'

Although she had given up the game, she continued to follow the career of the man who had assaulted her. After retiring from competition, he had gone on to greater prominence as a Davis Cup captain and coach. He owned tennis academies, conducted clinics in half a dozen countries, and trained other coaches.

'Every time I watch a tournament on TV,' the woman told me, 'and they show him up in the stands and say what a successful coach he is, I wonder how he treats the women he trains. I don't believe a man like that changes. It's awful to think there might be others like me who were too embarrassed or scared to tell anybody about him.'

Gregory Briehl, a psychologist in Charlottesville, Virginia, has had more than a passing acquaintance with women's tennis. A former college-level player himself, he taught and coached professionally for eight years. When he was in graduate school, he helped pay his tuition by transporting and installing the portable indoor court used at WTA tournaments. In the course of his travels, he came to know a number of the players and served as a hitting partner. (On the wall in his office is a photograph of him on court with Pam Shriver, Hana Mandlikova, and Betty Stove.) Later, by pure coincidence, he found himself treating a few female tennis players who had suffered emotional problems and dropped off the tour because of sexual abuse by male coaches. In addition to his own patients, Briehl, who is an ordained Lutheran minister as well as a psychologist, said he was aware of at least a dozen other players who had become sexually entangled with their coaches.

Before our interview, he suggested I educated myself on the subject by reading *Sex in the Forbidden Zone: When Men in Power – Therapists, Doctors, Clergy, Teachers and Others – Betray Women's Trust*. Written by Dr Peter Rutter of the Department of Psychiatry at the University of California Medical School, the book essentially proposes the extension of the medical profession's Hippocratic Oath to all those arenas where men wield authority over women, and where abuse of that authority can bring 'terrible, life-shattering consequences to a girl or woman when trust is turned to sexual advantage.' Dr Rutter stresses that a man has a professional responsibility to accept the 'expectation that whatever parts of herself the woman entrusts to him (her property, body, mind, or spirit) must be used solely to advance her interests and will not be used to his advantage, sexual or otherwise.'

Although Dr Rutter acknowledges that women can abuse men and other women, '96 percent of sexual exploitation by professionals occurs between a man in power and a woman under his care . . . the male–female power imbalance is reflective of the pattern that exists in the culture at large.' And that imbalance, he believes, prevents a woman from giving informed consent when a pastor, psychiatrist, or employer initiates sexual intimacy.

'My position,' Dr Rutter writes, 'is that *any sexual behavior by a man in power within what I define as the forbidden zone is inherently exploitative of a woman's trust.* Because he is the keeper of that trust, it is the man's *responsibility, no matter what the level of provocation or apparent consent by the woman*, to assure that sexual behavior does not take place.'

During the course of a three-hour interview, Gregory Briehl took the conclusions of *Sex in the Forbidden Zone* and applied them to coach/player relationships. As he bluntly put it, 'Sex abuse is sex abuse.' Since many coaches were acting *in loco parentis*, Briehl believed there was no difference between a man who slept with his player and one who did the same with his stepdaughter.

The tennis tour, Briehl explained, was a fertile ground for all sorts of problems. Unlike team sports, which integrated an athlete into a society of his or her peers, tennis tended to isolate a person from schoolmates and normal formative experiences. 'A kid who really hits the ball is ultimately elevated to a different plane,' said Briehl. 'She's treated differently by her parents. They put more time and money into the child. She's removed from the mainstream of school, taken out of classes for practice, taken away for days to tournaments.' And if she demonstrated exceptional talent, she ended up in the 'artificial environment' of a tennis academy or on the pro tour.

'We talk about what divorce does to kids,' Briehl said, 'but at least they get to stay with one parent. Tennis stars leave both parents and their friends and hometowns. They're removed from a context where they'll be able to develop.'

Feeding into this distortion was the influence of agents and tournament directors and the impact of prize money and enormous endorsement contracts. To an outsider this tidal wave of attention and money might appear to be an enviable bonanza, but to a child, or to a player arrested at a childlike stage of development, the effects could be as devastating as those experienced by a disaster victim.

'People come in and assume parental roles,' Briehl said. 'A tour official or agent serves as a surrogate parent, a mother hen. Some of this is well meaning, but some of it is self-serving.' He named a trainer, now no longer on the women's tour, who was often cited as someone notorious for molesting players.

Experts maintain that sexual abuse exists among all social and economic classes, and Briehl pointed out that he had treated women who had been abused in college, on the satellite circuit, and on the WTA tour. But he remarked that 'the higher the achievement, the more likely girls are to be abused. A kind of diplomatic immunity applies to people in the top echelons of tennis. A college would frown on a coach having sex with a player. But the WTA seems not to notice and to take no position.'

When you cut through the glossy window dressing and discounted the sport's self-congratulatory rhetoric, Briehl said, 'players are commodities. If they don't do well, they're forgotten. A commodity is an object and whenever a person is regarded as an object, the possibility of sexual abuse is great.'

Just how great was difficult to calculate. According to the best estimates, 25 percent of the general female population have experienced some form of sexual abuse. In certain professions the rate is known to be much higher. A 1990 Defense Department study determined that 64 percent of women in the US military have been sexually harassed.

Within what Briehl referred to as 'the skewed population' of the women's tour, he believed the incidence of abuse was quite high. It wasn't just because the players were isolated, subjected to relentless pressure, and sent off for months with male coaches. He said you had to consider the kinds of people they traveled and trained with.

'What type of man wants to be a coach?' Briehl asked. He answered his own question by suggesting that some of them were classic narcissists, guys with big egos and huge appetites for money and approval.

Then, too, most coaches had been tennis pros themselves and had had the same disorienting early experiences as the girls they worked with. The hope was that this made them more knowledgeable, empathetic, and caring, but there was always the opposite possibility. As Briehl put it, some coaches were 'second-generation skewed people.' During their playing careers they had been given to understand that they were above the rules and better than other people. Now they were back on the circuit with an adolescent girl, and 'they think they're entitled,' Briehl said. 'That's a dangerous situation. In psychiatry, it's fifty minutes a week. On the tour, coaches and players are together twenty-four hours a day in what can be a sexually charged atmosphere.'

While Briehl took pains to protect the confidentiality of his patients, he offered some insights into the price young female players had to pay for the delinquencies of their coaches. One of his patients had been in the top twenty and was sixteen years old when her coach crawled into bed with her. She hadn't invited his advances, yet felt powerless to resist and, at the same time, responsible for what happened. Her instinct was to keep things secret to protect herself and the coach, who was a father figure to her. Although she tried to break off the affair, she found she couldn't. She thought she should have been able to control it, but she couldn't do that either. Having been raised to regard herself as exempt from life's rules, she tried to tell herself the relationship didn't really bother her, yet it did.

Finally, the only way out seemed to be to drop off the tour. When the coach couldn't convince her to change her mind, he told her he didn't care whether she quit – so long as she paid him. They had a contract and if she wanted to leave him, she would have to buy it out. In the end, that was what she had been forced to do.

In Briehl's opinion, his patient wasn't the first or last player who had had to pay off an abusive coach to get rid of him. Nor was she the first or last who was so distraught she decided to quit tennis. 'A lot of early dropouts,' said Briehl, 'are girls who've been abused.'

The players he had treated spent lengthy periods in therapy, yet never achieved a complete recovery. They never regained the capacity to trust and never outgrew their tendency to fall into destructive relationships that mimicked the ones they had had with their coaches. Gregory Briehl believed that for those girls and others like them, 'there was trauma just being on the tour. Then the sexual abuse concretized the distortion.'

Ladies of the Court, 1993

VII Artistry and Psychology

Footwork and the Preservation of Rhythm and Balance
SUZANNE LENGLEN

By footwork I do not mean just running about, but the use of the feet.

Your feet are the pivot from which the work is done. You must be easy upon them. Do not allow them to hold the ground flatly, for then movement in any direction will not be instant, and a fraction of time will be lost which cannot be made up.

It starts from the beginning, which is the receipt of service. Be upon your toes, ready to take off in response to the message from your brain.

Not a bad plan in order that this may become natural, and not be forced, is to walk about on your toes when you are dressing in the morning and to go up and down stairs on your toes. Even those who are, by ill luck, flat-footed can in this manner strengthen the arch of the instep.

If you do not start the rally on your toes, you will be apt to be digging your heels into the ground when you run. This jars and throws you out of your stride.

Note carefully whether you are able to move with more ease one way or the other. If that is found to be the case, take every chance of thrusting to the slower side, never dodge it.

Practice moving backward with your face to the net, keeping the weight of the body forward.

When you move sideways remember that it is done by a push or fling of the leg on the side to which you are going, but that the impulse is taken from the foot on the other side.

Never run too fast. Run with short steps or sort of jumps. I cannot emphasize enough the fact that the singles court is not so big as it appears. From the center to the sides it is but 13½ feet, not quite two and a half times your height, between three and four strides. To the net from the baseline it is 39 feet, about ten strides. And so on; you can work out every distance.

Over-running is a thing to which you must pay great heed. Nothing is more calculated to throw you out of your balance and to disturb the preservation of your rhythm.

The secret of rhythm is the joint working of the eye, the brain, and the body, and this is contained in self-control.

Do not permit yourself to be flustered or to become acutely conscious of your stroke production, or to be dreadfully aware of your racket.

Lawn tennis players are constantly catching things like crabs because they allow one portion of their stroke production to get through to their minds above the rest. It immediately exceeds, and balance is gone.

Beware lest the exercise you are giving your right arm should lend it greater weight than the left.

Go through at home, with the racket in the left hand, the movements which you do with the right. At first you will be awkward, but in a very short time you will be able to carry them out. The evening-up of both sides of the body will improve your balance. People are not by nature right-handed or left-handed only. Children are rather prone, I believe, to use the left hand before they are taught that they must use the right.

Correct the tendency you will have to begin all your forward movements by a pressure of your stronger leg. Discover as soon as you can which is the weaker and strengthen it by use.

The arm which does not hold the racket does not for that reason wave idly like a tassel, nor hang rigid like a rod. It has a compensating influence, keeping the racket arm by counter-balance from overdoing the job. It is nearly always held up, across, or at angles to the body, with the elbow bent. If it is not, there is something wrong with your rhythm. It is one-sided. It is ragged. To the spectator you have an awkward appearance. To yourself you have a sense of half-measures.

Never allow any stroke to have a jerk in it. Whenever there is a jerk, there is a jolt to some nerves, as, in another way, when you run or after a jump land on your heels instead of on your toes. A series of such jerks and jolts will tell upon you in a long match and you will tire before you should.

Be careful that the body leans forward, riding upon the hips but deriving its impulse from the feet, upon which you should be able to sway, as from a root or socket.

Practice that sway so that you may be able to throw your whole weight into the blow you give the ball. That blow starts, as I have said, and cannot say too often, through the feet to the center of the racket, which is equivalent to the palm of the hand. In the true understanding of this principle is the foundation of footwork, balance, and rhythm – and good lawn tennis.

Lawn Tennis, 1925

Winning

ALTHEA GIBSON

My tennis trophies, and other trophies like the Babe Didrikson Zaharias Trophy which I won for being picked as the Woman Athlete of the Year for 1957, take up a lot of space in the apartment and make up in a way for the scarcity of furniture, but most of them are still in boxes. I don't dare take them all out because if I did I wouldn't have time to do anything but polish them. I've got enough cups and plaques and statuettes to fill a corner of a warehouse, and I've also got some handsome and useful things like tea sets, butter dishes, cake plates, cocktail shakers, chafing dishes, serving trays, and what not. I'm a guaranteed lifetime customer for the silver-polish industry. Come to think of it, I'll also have to keep a little gold polish on hand. My Wimbledon trophies are beautiful gold salvers, and I am very proud of them and I intend to keep them shining.

Of course, I hope to add some more trophies to my collection before I am through, maybe some more amateur ones and maybe some professional ones, too. That's one thing about the life of a tennis champion; you never can rest on your victories, unless you retire, and I'm not ready to retire yet. With Sydney working along with me, I will keep going right back into training as each new season approaches, just as I did when I got back from the Caribbean and began promptly to prepare for the 1958 Wimbledon and United States championships. I knew I wasn't going to beat anybody with my reputation or my newspaper clippings; I would have to beat them all on the tennis court. If I ever showed signs of forgetting that, Sydney was right there to remind me.

Sydney is not only a fine teacher of tennis, including both strokes and tactics, he is also something of a psychologist. He keeps after me all the time. First, he pounded at me to make me think and act and play with the idea in mind that I had what it takes to become the champion. And after I made it, instead of letting up, he pressed me all the more. 'You've got to hit that ball with pace,' he kept saying, 'you've got to hit with all your strength, and attack forcefully, and overpower your opponent. You've got to hit with pace and with depth, and put that championship power and determination and pride behind every shot. Never let up; don't ever change from the championship way of hitting. You were hitting the daylights out of the ball last year. You were hitting it with force. You've got to hit it even more forcefully, you've got to hit it with daring. You're the champ, you can take chances, you can hit all-out on every shot. You've got the ability and you've got the experience and you've got the control and the power. All you have to do is use it. Stand up there and swing freely and hit with force. Absolutely defy the ball to go anywhere except where you want it to go. That ball isn't going to talk back to you. You're its master.'

It is, you see, Sydney's idea that I should fill my mind with positive thoughts and give no house room at all to negative thoughts, to doubts or fears. 'You're going to win' is the only attitude he will countenance. 'You're going to win, and this is how you're going to win. You're going to hit with force, as forcefully as you can, and never let up, and you're going to hit the ball long, with the kind of depth that keeps your opponent back on her heels on the defensive, just like in a prize fight, and then you're going to open up the court with a forcing shot and then your power is going to take advantage of that opening and put the ball away, and you're going to still be the champion because you're going to play like a champion.'

He psychologizes me, there's no doubt about it. But I like it. It keeps me on my toes. It reminds me that I can't coast, that I mustn't take anything for granted, that I can't give away any games or even points, that I must play power tennis all the time because that's my game and that's what made me the champion.

The subconscious mind acts as a private tape recorder, Sydney says, and then, in a time of crisis, when you're out there all alone on the court and the championship is going to be won or lost in a few swift exchanges of shots, you play these thoughts back to yourself and they mean something to you and you respond to them and they become part of the attacking force you muster and they help you beat back your challenger, because that's the way a champion does. If you have negative thoughts on your private tape recorder, those are the ones that come through at the time of crisis, and they defeat you.

Sydney has something there. He cites, as an example, the night I left

Forest Hills back in 1950 leading Louise Brough, 7–8, in that celebrated third set. Rhoda Smith took me home with her and patted me on the back all the way, and in her apartment that night she wouldn't let anybody talk to me about the match. 'Even if you lose tomorrow, honey,' she told me, 'it won't make a particle of difference. You did yourself proud already.' She meant well, of course. She wanted to ease my mind and relax me and turn away the tension. But Sydney says she did exactly the wrong thing, and I believe he's right. Somebody, Sydney says, should have been talking to me like this:

'You were hitting a great tennis ball out there today. You were hitting the ball with pace, and you were hitting it long. You showed Brough more raw power than she's ever seen come off a woman's racket. You had her on the run. You're going to beat her tomorrow, you're going to finish her off, because you're going to go right out there and do it again. You've got nothing to lose and she's got everything to lose, and you're going to walk out there and tee off with all your strength and power, and she's going to have to play it safe and hope she gets it back and hope you miss and make errors. But you won't. You'll hit the way you hit today, and you'll win, and you'll be on your way to the championship.'

I forced myself to keep those words of Sydney's in my mind every minute when I went back to London for the 1958 Wimbledon tournament. Winning that one meant a whole lot to me. Not only would the championship be an important asset to me whether I became a professional tennis player or a singer, or both, but there was a question of pride involved, too. In sports, you simply aren't considered a real champion until you have defended your title successfully. Winning it once can be a fluke; winning it twice proves that you are the best. I was passionately determined that there wasn't going to be any 'one-shot' tarnish on my Wimbledon championship.

I Always Wanted to Be Somebody, 1958

The Style of Rod Laver
JULIUS D. HELDMAN

Rod Laver was eighteen years old when he first came to the United States to play our circuit. He looked very much then as he does now, although his red hair was usually hidden under a floppy hat and he often had a handkerchief tied around his neck à la Rosewall. He was only of medium build, he looked fragile and he hit the ball a ton. That year he won the US junior title. Six years later he was to become the second man in history to win the grand slam – Australia, France, Wimbledon and the United States championships. Within another two years he became the No. 1 professional and today he is still acknowledged the No. 1 player of the world. He is the only man today who can go through the last rounds of a major international tournament without dropping a set, because he is the only player who can literally crush the opposition with his power. He is capable of being upset (he lost to Cliff Drysdale in the 1968 US open and to Cliff Richey in the 1969 Madison Square Garden open) but only he could win the 1968 Wimbledon open and the 1969 South African and French opens so decisively.

Rod swings at everything hard and fast. His timing, eye and wrist action are nothing short of miraculous. On either side, forehand or backhand, he takes a full roundhouse-loop crack at the ball, which comes back so hard it can knock the racket out of your hand. I saw Rod play Rafe Osuna in the semi-finals at Forest Hills in 1962. It was murder. In the last game, Rafe bravely served and ran for the net. Rod cracked a backhand back full speed, free swing – so hard that Rafe's racket wavered in his hand. Not so amazing, perhaps, but the same scene was repeated four points in a row. Rod literally knocked Osuna down with four successive returns of serve, and Osuna was one of the quickest and best racket handlers who ever played.

On the backhand side, Laver often uses a heavy underspin. Most players who come under the ball slow it up. Not so Rod; he is also moving in and hitting so hard that the shot is deep and attacking and has unusual pace. He often takes high backhands this way, but he is just as liable to come over the ball with a tremendous wallop, ending with wrist turning the racket head over, and the ball going with incredible speed and accuracy.

From the ground, about the only shot that Rod does not clobber is a forehand underspin or chip. I don't recall his using the shot much or at all when he was younger, but as he matured he began occasionally to hold the ball on his racket with some underspin and place it carefully while he ran for the net. But the next time he would literally jump and throw his racket at the ball with all the force he could muster, wrist and arms snapping over at the hit. The shot is unreturnable. It always ends the point, one way or the other, and you can never predict when the lightning will strike, although you know it will be often.

Volleying in top international tennis is more than technical proficiency. Rod is not a great low volleyer, but he is merciless when he gets half a chance. He is competent on low balls, handling them with underspin for control (more on the backhand than forehand, which he can net occasionally), but he will cream any ball at waist level or higher. As time goes on, Laver takes fewer unnecessary big swings at set-up high put-aways; he taps or punches them away. But if he needs to, he can and does hit high volleys with all his might as swinging drives or, on his backhand, sharp underspin angles as well. It is hard to believe a ball can be hit that hard and with that much angle, but Rod does it. No wonder he is the terror of all opponents.

There is not an Aussie netrusher who does not have a great overhead to back his attack. Otherwise he would be lobbed to death. Rod has one of the best, quite flat, angled to his left sharply by preference but capable of being placed anywhere. While Rod is not tall, he is agile and leaps well and is hard to lob over. What is worse, if you do get a lob over him, he will run it down and, with his powerful stiff wrist, rifle a full loop past his helpless opponent. This happens so often that players have begun to say that they prefer to lob short to Rod, at least on his backhand. Actually, if Laver has a weakness, it is on his backhand overhead, on which he does err, but in a way that is silly: how are you going to get in position to play that shot to Rod often?

Some lefties make it primarily by virtue of their serve, John Doeg and Neale Fraser being good examples. Not so Rod. His first serve has always been hard and flat, and he makes his share of aces, but he never had a heavy, deep spin second ball. It was just adequate, at least in the context of world class. In the last year, Rod has made a conscious effort to harden up his second delivery. For a while, all his timing seemed to be affected – he had some eye trouble at the same time – but now he is serving better than ever.

Someone once told Chuck McKinley that he should just try to be steady because he was too small to hit the ball hard. He paid no attention and he won Wimbledon. A few well-meaning coaches advised Rod to temporize more on his shots if he wanted to win a big tournament. It went in one ear and out the other, and Rod rose to the greatest heights in the game. His shots are breathtaking, his talent is enormous and his drive to be the No. 1 has made him the most successful player in the world today.

The Fireside Book of Tennis, 1972

Levels of the Game
JOHN MCPHEE

Ashe returns serve with a solid forehand, down the line. Graebner, lunging, picks it up with a backhand half volley. The ball floats back to Ashe. He takes a three-hundred-degree roundhouse swing and drives the ball crosscourt so fast that Graebner, who is within close reach of it, cannot react quickly enough to get his racquet on it. Hopefully, Graebner whips his head around to see where the ball lands. It lands on the line – a liner, in the language of the game. 'There's Ashe getting lucky again.'

Ashe does a deep knee bend to remind himself to stay low. Graebner hits a big serve wide, and a second serve that ticks the cord and skips away. Double fault. Carole pats the air. Calm down, Clark. Graebner can consider himself half broken. The score is love–thirty. Ashe thinks, 'You're in trouble, Clark. Deep trouble.'

'I'll bet a hundred to one I pull out of it,' Graebner tells himself. Crunch. His serve is blocked back, and he punches a volley to Ashe's backhand. Ashe now has two principal alternatives: to return the ball conservatively and safely, adding to the pressure that is already heavy on Graebner, or to cut loose the one-in-ten shot, going for the overwhelming advantage of a love–forty score by the method of the fast kill. Ashe seems to have no difficulty making the choice. He blasts. He misses. Fifteen–thirty.

Graebner serves, attacks the net, volleys, rises high for an overhead – he goes up like a basketball player for a rebound – and smashes the ball away. Thirty–all.

Now the thought crosses Graebner's mind that Ashe has not missed a service return in this game. The thought unnerves him a little. He hits a big one four feet too deep, then bloops his second serve with terrible placement right into the center of the service court. He now becomes the mouse, Ashe the cat. With soft, perfectly placed shots, Ashe jerks him around the forecourt, then closes off the point with a shot to remember. It is a forehand, with top spin, sent crosscourt so lightly that the ball appears to be flung rather than hit. Its angle to the net is less than ten degrees – a difficult, brilliant stroke, and Ashe hit it with such non-chalance that he appeared to be thinking of something else. Graebner feels the implications of this. Ashe is now obviously loose. Loose equals dangerous. When a player is loose, he serves and volleys at his best level. His general shot-making ability is optimum. He will try anything. 'Look at the way he hit that ball, gave it the casual play,' Graebner says to himself. 'Instead of trying a silly shot and missing it, he tries a silly shot and makes it.' If Ashe wins the next point, he will have broken Graebner, and the match will be, in effect, even.

Again Graebner misses his first serve. Ashe, waiting for the second, says to himself, 'Come on. Move in. Move in. I should get it now.' When Ashe really feels he has a chance for a break, the index of his desire is that he moves in a couple of steps on second serves. He takes his usual position, about a foot behind the baseline, until Graebner lifts the ball. Then he moves quickly about a yard forward and stops, motionless, as if he were participating in a game of kick-the-can and Graebner were It. Graebner's second serve spins in, and bounces high to Ashe's backhand. Ashe strokes it with underspin. Graebner hits a deep approach shot to Ashe's backhand. Ashe hits a deft, appropriate lob. Graebner wants this point just as much as Ashe does. Scrambling backward, he reaches up and behind him and picks out of the sun an overhead that becomes an almost perfect drop shot, surprising Ashe and drawing him toward the net. At a dead run, Ashe reaches for the ball and more or less shovels it over the net. Graebner has been moving forward, too, and he has stopped for half a second, legs apart, poised, to see what will happen. The ball moves toward his backhand. He moves to the ball and drives it past Ashe, down the line. Graebner is still unbroken. But the game is at deuce. It is only the second time Ashe has extended him that far.

After this game, new balls will be coming in – all the more reason for Ashe to try to break Graebner now. Tennis balls are used for nine games (warm-up counts for two), and over that span they get fluffier and fluffier. When they are new and the nap is flat, wind resistance is minimal and they come through fast and heavy. Newies, or freshies, as the tennis players call them, are a considerable advantage to the server – something like a supply of bullets. Graebner meanwhile serves wide to Ashe's forehand, and Ashe hits the return with at least equal velocity. Graebner is caught on his heels, and hits a defensive backhand down the middle. It bounces in no man's land. Ashe, taking it on his backhand, has plenty of time. His racquet is far back and ready. Graebner makes a blind rush for the net, preferring to be caught in motion than helpless on the baseline. But Ashe's shot is too hard, too fast, too tough, too accurate, skidding off the turf in the last square foot of Graebner's forehand corner. Advantage Ashe.

'Look at that shot. That's ridiculous,' Graebner tells himself. He glances at Carole, who has both fists in the air. Pull yourself together, Clark. This is a big point. Graebner takes off his glasses and wipes them on his dental towel. 'Stalling,' Ashe mumbles. While he is waiting, he raises his left index finger and slowly pushes his glasses into place across the bridge of his nose. 'Just one point, Arthur.' Graebner misses his first serve again. Ashe moves in. He hits sharply crosscourt. Graebner dives for it, catches it with a volley, then springs up, ready, at the net. Ashe lobs into the sun, thinking, 'That was a good get on that volley. I didn't think he'd get that.' Graebner reaches for the overhead and smashes it directly at Ashe. Ashe, swinging desperately, belts it right back at him. Graebner punches the ball away with a forehand volley. Deuce. Ashe is rattling the gates, but Graebner will not let him in. Carole has her hand on the top of her head. Unbelievable.

Graebner serves, moves up, and volleys. Ashe, running, smacks an all-or-nothing backhand that hums past Graebner and lands a few inches inside the line. Graebner says to himself, 'He's hitting the lines, the lucky bastard. The odds are ten to one against him and he makes the shot. That bugs me.' Advantage Ashe.

Jack Kramer, broadcasting the match, says that this is the best game not only of this match but of the entire tournament so far. Again Ashe needs just one point and he will be leading four games to two. Graebner serves. Ashe returns. Graebner half-volleys. Ashe throws a lob into the sun. Graebner nearly loses it there. He can only hit it weakly – a kind of overhead tap that drops softly at Ashe's feet. This is it. Ashe swings – a big backhand – for the kill. The ball lands two feet out. Graebner inhales about seven quarts of air, and slowly releases six. It is deuce again.

Donald Dell, the captain of the Davis Cup Team, is sitting in the Marquee. He says, 'Arthur has hit five winners and he hasn't won the game. He looks perturbed.' Dell knows Ashe so well that he can often tell by the way Ashe walks or stands what is going on behind the noncommittal face. But Ashe is under control. He is telling himself, 'If you tend to your knitting, you will get the job done.' Graebner's first serve, which has misfired seven times in this game, does not misfire now. Ashe reacts, swings, hits it hard – a hundredth of a second too late. The shot, off his backhand, fails by a few inches to come in to the sideline. Advantage Graebner.

Carole's fists are up. Clark adjusts his glasses, wipes off his right hand, and bounces the ball. He serves hard to Ashe's forehand. The ball, blasted, comes back. Disappointment races through Graebner's mind. 'I'm serving to his forehand. His forehand is his weakest shot. If the guy returns his weakest shot all the time, he's just too good.' Graebner tries a drop shot, then goes to his right on the sheer gamble that Ashe's response will take that direction. It does. Graebner, with full power, drives an apparent putaway down the line. But Ashe gets to it and blocks the ball, effecting what under the circumstances is a remarkably good lob. Graebner leaps, whips his racquet overhead, and connects. The ball hits the turf on Ashe's backhand and bounces wide. Ashe plunges for it, swings with both feet off the ground, and hits the ball so hard down the line that Graebner cannot get near it. Graebner can be pardoned if he cannot believe it. For the fourth time, the game is at deuce.

'Arthur is just seeing the ball better, or something,' Graebner tells himself. But Graebner sees the ball, too, and he hits a big-crunch unplayable serve. Advantage Graebner.

Serve, return, volley – Ashe hits a forehand into the tape. Ashe has not been able to get out from under. Games are three–all, second set.

Levels of the Game, 1969

The Mental Aspects of Tennis
MARTINA NAVRATILOVA

Concentration

I never used to concentrate on concentrating. The way I had it figured was that whenever I really needed to settle down and focus in for the match, all I had to do was turn it on. It was not long after this cherished belief was shattered that I learned the ugly truth about the Easter Bunny being a phony. The point is, you can be out there in the middle of a tough match pleading to yourself, 'Concentrate! Concentrate!' and it won't happen for you. Concentration is much more elusive than that.

Billie Jean King has spoken about what total concentration is like. 'I can almost feel it coming,' she says. 'It usually happens on one of those days when everything is right, when the crowd is large and enthusiastic and my concentration is so perfect it almost seems as though I'm able to transport myself beyond the turmoil of the court to some place of total peace and calm. I know where the ball is on every shot, and it always looks as big and well-defined as a basketball. Just a huge thing I couldn't miss if I wanted to. I've got perfect control of the match, rhythms and movements are excellent, everything's in total balance. It's just an Aaaaaah.'

Very few people ever get to know this feeling, but then again, few people have trained the way Billie Jean has, disciplining her body and mind to the point where she can achieve this incredible sense of harmony and understanding of the game. I know what Billie Jean speaks of – I have had matches like that as well. I have also lost carelessly because something caused my concentration to wane. It has been a distraction in the audience – someone yelling or shuffling around in the aisles. It has been a case of frazzled nerves in a high-pressure match that has allowed uninvited thoughts to surface. There have been times when I have relaxed my mind after gaining a large lead over my opponent. I would say to myself, 'It's in the bag' and proceed to feel sorry for my soon-to-be-vanquished foe, letting up so as not to cause embarrassment. The wrong person would get embarrassed. Then, of course, there is *this* surefire way to lose concentration: Have a major problem or worry outside of the tennis court. All too often the problem will insist that it accompany you to your match, where it will sit next to you on changeovers, consult with you at the baseline, and nag you at the net. So what do you do at times like this?

Unfortunately, you can do very little at that stage. The concentration that you need has to come to you way before your match. Concentration is born on the practice court, along with your groundstrokes, your foot speed, and everything else. You must mentally treat your practice sessions as matches, concentrating on every ball you hit. Do not be thinking about your practice partner, your upcoming match, or anything else but your own game. You must be keen, alert, and enthused, and as you cover all of your shots, thinking about just one thing at a time, you are making the mental process more and more automatic. When you become a true craftsman at something, having spent long, intense hours of disciplined work, you stop wondering whether your hands will obey what your mind has asked for. It is something you no longer have to think about, because it is second nature to you. This is what a true tennis craftsman achieves. A better-quality practice creates a better-quality match.

I prepare mentally off the court, too. Especially if I've got a grudge match, or I want to prove something, win something big, I will go to sleep imagining what I am going to do. I try to envision the kind of points I want to be playing, the feeling of euphoria after the win, everything. Sometimes I have woken up the next day feeling like it's already happened. That's how real I can imagine the tennis to be.

In practice sessions be certain to do quickness drills, exercises that demand fast thinking and good reflexes. Also, perform drills that demand a minimum amount of balls to cross the net, and if you fail to reach that number, start again from zero. And, of course, practice playing sets against good players, and play to win. Concentration can become a habit. So can winning.

How to Practice Concentration

As I've mentioned, quick drills at the net will aid in prolonging your concentration efforts on the volley and will force you to focus in on the ball off your opponent's racket. Long baseline drills are also a good idea. When I am training with Renee Richards, she will give me specific goals for varying periods of time – five minutes of balls into one corner, perhaps, and then a switch to the opposite end, or every ball past the service line for ten minutes. These drills intensify my concentration and purpose. Renee might also make the rules very specific. If she hits the ball deep into the court, my replies must all land as deep. If her ball bounces high, I must counter with a flat drive. If it's low, I must slice and come to net for the volley. Or she will stay in one corner of the baseline and run me all over the court, but I must play every ball directly back to her. She may stipulate that I must clear at least one hundred shots before the drill is over. Believe me, after the first sixty or seventy shots my concentration is running high, to say the least. These kinds of incentive drills sharpen my concentration more than anything else.

Practicing to Music

Every now and then when I want to relax, lose my inhibitions, and feel more fluid, I turn up the tunes and practice to music. I find that music loosens up my body and mind, and I have waltzed off many a musical practice with sting in my shots and a song in my heart. You should definitely check this out for yourself, especially if you tend to cramp up when you play, getting yourself all pinched and uptight over the game. To those of you who are music lovers, combine two of your favorite things and see how splendidly this duet performs. One note of caution: Do not disrupt neighboring courts with an excess of volume. Not everyone appreciates music. We all boogie to a different drummer.

Attitude

My attitude has been one of the biggest changes in my game, and I credit Nancy Lieberman for the vast improvement in my mental outlook, my work ethics, and the control of my emotions. I truly think that I handle myself in a much better fashion than I did a few years ago. Like John McEnroe, I expect a lot from myself, and when I get angry, I show it. Some players, like us, do, while others don't. One thing is for certain: I'll never give myself an ulcer from holding things in.

Chris Evert Lloyd and Tracy Austin are known for their infinite cool, for never letting things visibly upset them no matter how unjust a call or how poorly they played a ball. They will never let you peek at what's bothering them, so you can never be sure if they are bothered at all. That's a great attitude.

I cannot pull that one off, but my idea is to show my opponents just how relaxed and confident I am feeling, that I, not they, are controlling the match; I do not want my opponent to know that I am upset by something, but if that happens, I try to make my anger work for me. I do not want to be defeated by my own dour outlook. That has certainly happened to me in the past, and Pam Shriver's attitude has caused her to lose matches as well. We are both emotional, high-strung people. Sometimes, channeled correctly, this can be a great advantage. How many times has John McEnroe gotten totally aggravated about a call or a player's stalling or his own mistakes, only to step up to the line on the next point and serve an aggravated ace? I have great respect for anger that is controlled, and I think I have gained a lot of control lately. It is not easy. It shows great strength of character, and mine can stand to get better. Nancy says that I tend to put over this really hostile attitude out on the court, when at number one in the world I should instead be oozing with ease and confidence, and look ready and willing to play at all times.

As I said, that isn't easy for me. At the 1982 Toyota Series Championships final against Chris, my attitude cost me the first set. The match had become a very big deal. Although my 1982 record spoke for itself, there were people who thought that by beating me in this final Chris could be ranked number one. I did not agree at all, but the press had been building up the match all week long. The whole thing had made me very edgy, and it showed. Chris was serving the first set at 4–3, the game at 0–30. I hit a ball to her baseline and I was sure I'd caught the tape. Chris muscled the ball wide off the skid, but my shot was called out. It shouldn't have bothered me so much – I still had chances to break her serve – but the whole thing had unnerved me, and I just couldn't shake it off. I kept thinking of what should have or could have been, and I continued to fume for points and points afterward, causing me to lose the opening set. I bounced back, all right. The episode did not cost me the whole match. But a few years ago it could have. I have come a long way.

To be a better champion than I am right now, my attitude still must improve. This may not be the case with you. You may be gracious in both victory and defeat, and give the benefit of the doubt willingly to the other player. You may never let up for one point and wouldn't think of dogging a match. Your attitude about work could already be a healthy one. Or maybe you just have to work on certain parts of your attitude, such as giving more to a practice session. If your outlook is positive, believe me, that's half the battle.

If you are naturally emotional, this is something you are going to have to work on, because learning a good attitude is not an overnight proposition. That is why a particular story about Bjorn Borg is hard for me to believe. The story goes that Bjorn had a terrific temper when he was younger. He was supposed to have been really emotional, throwing rackets and tantrums all over Sweden, until one day when his father caught his act and told Bjorn that if he kept it up he wouldn't be allowed to play tennis anymore. BOOM! Like that Bjorn cut it out. Now, maybe it happened like that, but I don't believe it, because I know Bjorn off the court, and he just is not that emotional a guy. In any case, he certainly has a style to admire.

I have faced the fact that I will never stop being an emotional tennis player, because I will never stop being an emotional person. But I am tired of losing matches to attitude problems, and it just isn't going to happen that way anymore. I still talk out loud too much sometimes, berating myself long after the fact, but Renee and Nancy have made me better and have convinced me that it is something you really can work on and improve. I try to forget the last point played and go on with the show. I may walk around a little bit, take an extra five or ten seconds to regain my composure, and then proceed. It is a gradual process, but with practice you can actually talk yourself into or out of things.

You can train yourself to handle all sorts of problems on the court by practicing all your shots for hours on end, so that when the moment comes when you must play a big forehand it is not something foreign and scary to you. You can physically take yourself through all of the possibilities in a match, so why not take yourself through the necessary mental processes as well? Renee has shown me how to practice this. She used to throw examples of match situations at me and then explain what I should do, how I should play them, both in terms of execution and mentally, such as play aggressively at break point up, defensively at break point down. She would also explain my opponent's tendencies, weaknesses, and personality to me so that I could anticipate her probable movements. These days Renee does not have to tell me what to do; instead, she asks me what to do in a given situation, and it forces me to think about my mental as well as physical attack. These mental exercises have made me much stronger. If something comes up in a match, I no longer feel angry or confused or embittered by the turn of events. I just pull everything in, breathe deeply, and play the next point.

The Killer Instinct

The killer instinct. Are you born with this? Can you develop it? Can your coach give it to you?

Being competitive and having a killer instinct are two different things. I have always been competitive in everything I do, and until very recently I have never had a killer instinct in anything I've done. There is a vast difference in wanting to beat an opponent and wanting to kill her – that is, really letting her have it, no holds barred, no free points – a real drubbing. When Nancy plays basketball, she plays with total killer instinct. She wants the opposing team to look bad, humiliated. Nancy wants to shut them down. Whenever I played anything I was content to win. What Nancy has instilled in me is the idea that I must never give my opponent the opportunity or reason to believe that they could win the match.

Watch Chris Evert Lloyd or Tracy Austin and you will see the killer instinct at work. They play every point all out, regardless of their lead, and refuse to give their opponents a chance to breathe life into their own chances. What hurt me early in my career was this lack of purpose. I can remember so many three-setters then that should have been straight sets, and so many losses that should have been victories. It was common for me to be up 6–0, 5–1, and proceed to ease things up. I would think I had the match won, lose my concentration, or feel sorry for my opponent, and suddenly I'd be involved in a tie breaker to decide the third set. That's where killer instinct shines. Killer instinct gives you the power to finish the match. When you've got someone down, killer instinct will tell you to beat them and get off the court.

I still think that while you can pick up some killer instinct along the way, it is still just that – an instinct, one you are either born with or not. I think it is a lot like natural talent – you've either got it or you don't. Look at Evonne Goolagong Cawley. She has all the natural talent in the world and no killer instinct, yet she is a wonderful champion. There are those who sigh when they watch Evonne play and say, 'If only she had the killer in her! How much better she could be!' That may be true, but it isn't Evonne. It has got to come, ultimately, from within. You can develop it to a certain extent, as I have, but in the end you must truly believe what you are trying to feel about your opponent. At least that is what happens with me. But what is very important for young players to remember is that when you have them where you want them, you must mentally stay on top of them. You cannot give them the opportunity to think that they can come back and beat you. Hold fast to your leads and play every single point as if you mean it.

How to Handle Winning and Losing

Ideally, you should treat both winning and losing the same way. Knowing that you have given it your best should be as satisfying as any win and as comforting as possible in the face of defeat. The reaction to a win or a loss has got to be balanced – for you, your coach, your parents – and the attitude should always be, 'Let's learn from this match and make the next one better.'

When I was younger and my power game had not yet jelled, I was constantly getting beaten by my peers. I was also a lot smaller than everyone else. I used to have to go up against kids who were two heads taller when I competed in the twelve-and-unders. I had plenty of 6–0, 6–0 losses, but they rarely got me down because I knew how I wanted to play and I believed in my style and my potential. I could have bagged the net game and stayed on the baseline like everyone else was doing with success, but one day, I hoped, my game would work. It took a lot of losses, but at fourteen I started making my mark, and all of those losses had taught me plenty. You must always keep your game in the proper perspective and always look into the future. Remember, the immediate future is not what is important. It is how you wish to play in the end that gets you through the rough spots.

Do not compare yourself to other players around you. Some may be much more physically developed than you are, or have been playing longer than you have. A loss to this person should not devastate you. Some players, such as Billy Martin, peak early, while others, such as Wendy Turnbull, peak late. If you are a serve-and-volley player and your baseline friends keep winning against you, do not despair. You may just have to work a little harder. If you are a baseliner who gets bullied around the court by net rushers, do not get disgusted and refuse to play against them. Instead, play them more often so that you get used to their pace and develop your passes. If you are a hard worker, practicing five hours a day, and you lose to a player who barely warms up before a match, again, do not compare yourself to this player. A parent should not scold one of her children for studying five hours for a test and bringing home a 'C' and praise her other child, who aces courses without cracking a book. These comparisons are unhealthy and unfair, and no one should lay that kind of judgment on you, especially yourself. What is key is that you perform up to your potential.

You must learn from both your wins and your losses. When you win, go over the match in your mind and try to discern what you did right, what you could have done better, and what it took from you mentally to beat your opponent. Sometimes you can win a match and not have played well at all. This has happened to me a lot. I have walked off a win, happy and satisfied, only to have Nancy or Renee say to me, 'What was *that* all about? Where was your mind? Your topspin passing shot? Your lob?' And, of course, they were right. I may not have put much work into the match and won it anyway. Whether I've won or lost, I hate it when people come up to me and tell me that I played great when I know in my heart that I didn't.

You have got to be your own critic, or have people around who will tell it like it is. It's the same with losing a match. There are so many ways to lose a match, and you must take apart your game to find out what had cost you. You could have made mental errors, tactical errors, or technical errors. You might have lost because your forehand broke down, or you played to the wrong side of the court, or you failed to apply the pressure at the right time. Maybe you were just too tired or too sick to win that day. Whatever it is, think about it after the match is over. You may uncover some very telling patterns that you had not realized before. Just the act of putting the match in perspective may help you to sleep better that night.

Reviewing a match helps me immeasurably. Sometimes it takes a while before I honestly come to grips with a loss. I may sometimes have a problem admitting I goofed up a match. Renee will start to say something critical, and I will immediately say, 'No, no, no.' But five minutes later I'll admit to being wrong, and we'll talk. Deep down, of course, I'll have known immediately that what was said had been the truth, but just as deep down I would not immediately have been ready for the harsh reality of the loss. You may be the same way. Sometimes a little breathing room from the loss is all it takes before you can take on the criticism.

Parents and coaches have to be very careful in their treatment of a player's wins or losses. Some parents are all over their kids for losing, or spoil them rotten for bringing home a win. Coaches can be guilty of doing the same thing, and it can really beat up a kid emotionally. My father used to get on my case. Parents and coaches can get in the way too much and place the wrong amount of importance on key issues, thus destroying the 'try' in the child and the love she has for the game. On the tour we've got a couple of parents running around who are just maniacs. They turn their kids into head cases, butting them up against the rest of the tour players, pushing them into too many tournaments when they are down or hurt or tired. There are plenty of players you do not hear about because they have become tennis casualties.

There must be plenty of support and respect all the way around, no matter how the scoreboard reads in the end. Athletes have very delicate psyches. A win should not make them uppity and superior, a loss should not bruise egos or cause a drop in self-esteem. All we are talking about is a game.

Guts

To be a gutsy player you must have a lot of discipline. You have got to be willing to stay out on the court, to scrape and lunge and dive for the ball no matter what the situation. You have to play your hardest even when you know that you are not playing your best. To my mind, 'gutsing out a match' does not happen in the grand arenas like Wimbledon. At Wimbledon there is no question that you are 100 percent willing to win. Lack of nerve is what affects players at Wimbledon, not lack of guts. The gutsy matches I have won are the ones that no one hears about. They may be against someone like Mima Jausevec, a talented Yugoslavian player who is constantly flirting with the Top Ten rankings. Mima may be putting together a real fine game, and I could be way off mine, and it is in these situations that I get truly tested for guts.

I have more discipline than I've ever been given credit for, but there are times when I have not come through. In the 1982 Avon Championships final against Sylvia Hanika I was up a set and leading three games to one in the second. Sylvia began to play all out, and as she surged, my game dipped about 10 percent lower – certainly not so much that I couldn't have pulled through. But I never shook her off, I never pumped myself up enough to finish the match, and by the third set I was no longer playing to win, I was playing not to lose.

Against Chris Evert Lloyd in the 1982 Australian final it was a slightly different case. I had gone down there with a bad attitude – sort of listless and uncaring. I spoke to Nancy during the week and she said, 'What's wrong with you, anyway? It's the Australian Open.' But I didn't get myself up, and during the finals I felt like I was just going through the motions. Don't ask me why, but I just didn't have it. The funny thing is, Nancy knew before I even left for Australia. It was evident in my practice sessions, my attitude, and my general washed-out spirit. Nancy is so disciplined that she would have found some way to win. We spoke about it a lot after I got back, and I understand now that if you do not demand a high level of self-discipline all of the time, you cannot expect to have guts all the time, either. It's a good lesson to learn.

Sportsmanship

In the same way that a player's personality can shine through on a tennis court, her character can as well, and not only when she loses. If there is one thing worse than being a bad loser, it's being a bad winner. Bad winners are the types who will give the impression of arrogant control upon defeating you, depriving you of your self-respect. Bad winners shout for joy upon match point, jump up and down, squeal, yell, the whole scene. Bad winners talk about their feats often and with great relish. Bad winners are a pain in the neck. The 'Do unto others' rule really applies here. You must feel your own joy but be conscious of your vanquished opponent's sorrow. I will never forget how Pam Shriver acted upon defeating me at both the US Opens that we met in. The first victory occurred when she was just fifteen years old, and she had just scored one of the most astonishing upsets in US Open history. You would never have known it by watching Pam. When the last point was over, she didn't scream, she didn't jump or yell – she walked calmly to the net, mindful of my disappointment, and shook my hand. That was it. To have that kind of poise and control at fifteen was pretty impressive. And when Pam stopped my quest for a Grand Slam by beating me in the quarter-finals in 1982, it was the same thing, though we were by then good friends and very close. I hated to lose, but if I had to lose to any player, I was glad it was someone like Pam.

What about the bad losers? I don't have to tell you what they are all about. They are the whiners, the complainers, the cheaters, the ones with the great excuses. To hear them tell it, bad losers have never actually lost a match – it was somehow stolen from them, taken away by a lucky opponent, prejudiced linesmen, deathly illnesses. These people have never heard of a code of honor. They would never give someone the benefit of the doubt on a call. They will certainly not recognize their opponent's superior play. They may be just fine off the court – a good friend, a fun person, sincere. But once they step out on the court to play a match, their good qualities vanish. That is when you can tell who's who, really – when the pressure is on.

Some players will do anything to win, use any scam to disturb their opponents. It can be that they stall continually, have frequent outbursts, pick fights with the linespeople, bounce the ball fifteen times before they serve it. Some players will do anything to get the edge. To my mind that's not part of the game. Years ago I watched Billie Jean King play against a young Russian player, Natasha Chmeryova. I will never forget this match. It was at Eastbourne, England, the warm-up tournament for Wimbledon, and Billie was on court there with this talented teenager. She was talented in more than just tennis. After a while it became obvious that she was going for an Oscar with her performance. I am pretty sure she was playing 'Camille,' because it looked like she could be close to death at any time. The hilarious part of it was that Natasha would be doubled over with seemingly agonizing cramps one minute, and running like a gazelle the very next point. That sort of thing can be unnerving to say the very least. And Billie Jean would look up every now and then and say to the players who were watching, 'What is this?' What it was was a form of cheating.

Your emotions should never lead you to this form of gamesmanship. It could be that you place too much emphasis on winning, no matter the cost, or perhaps you are getting that pressure from your parents. It's okay to be confident, but not to be cocky and abusive. There was more gentility to the game when I was growing up. Now there is a pervading attitude that you are either the best or nothing, and it can create a tremendous conflict inside of you. You must try not to let it bother you if your opponent adopts this attitude, and try not to let it happen to you at all cost. People will think a lot more of you, and not just on the tennis court.

Tennis My Way, 1983

VIII The Modern Personalities

You've Come a Long Way, Billie
GRACE LICHTENSTEIN

It was the day before the battle of the sexes, and the Astrodome complex had turned into one vast gambling casino.

Each night in the practice bubble, Bobby Riggs had taken on a different challenger for an average of $100 a set, first spotting them a few games or setting out rows of folding chairs on the court to liven things up. He had won every time. In keeping with the all-American free enterprise commercialism of the event, spectators were charged $5 admission just to watch the practice sessions. Bobby's victims had included Denton Cooley, the heart surgeon (Bobby had also won from him a free check-up for his brother John, a cardiac patient), and Larry King, who was coaxed onto the court by Jerry Perenchio, the match promoter, as a gimmick to hype ticket sales.

But Bobby was not the only one making book. Perenchio staked $1,000 on Billie Jean with Sid Shlenker, the Astrodome boss. Rosie Casals, who was to do the color commentary on television with Howard Cosell, laid out a few thousand with a Vegas bookie. Bill Moffitt, Billie Jean's ruggedly handsome father, had a few thousand on the line back in California with some fellow firemen. Jimmy the Greek spent hours on the telephone.

The press corps went simply out of control. Writers around the dinner table were like alcoholics let loose in the Jack Daniels distillery – before the appetizers arrived there would be piles of $5 bills stacked between the butter dish and the bread bowl, while some of the most sophisticated reporters in the country sat frantically composing arcane number combinations on scraps of paper. There were pools on how many games the winner would lose, how many games the loser would win – just about the only pool overlooked was one on how many tubas the band would have playing the National Anthem.

When the final, big writers' pool was tallied on Wednesday, the verdict was 22 for Riggs, 10 for King.

There was no way, the experts agreed, that Bobby could lose.

Only one person in town, it seemed, had no betting money on the match: Billie Jean King. 'Gambling doesn't turn me on,' she said calmly, sitting in the practice bubble Wednesday in a lime-green warm-up suit.

Was there something else at stake at this Reno-style carnival besides money? someone asked.

She took a deep breath. 'Pride.'

On all the slips of paper I had contributed to the pools, I had written 'BJK' but it had been with a shaky hand. I wanted her to win more than I had wanted anybody to win anything since Johnny Podres had thrown the last pitch in the '55 Series, not just because I had written a front page paean for *The New York Times* Sunday sports section predicting a four-set King victory, not just because I had gambled half my plane fare home, but because in spite of her faults Billie Jean represented the best that women's sports had to offer. A few weeks before, Nora Ephron (who was putting her money on Bobby now, even though she was the treasurer of our side bet against him) had remarked, 'Billie Jean's not the feminist she says she is.' Nora was right, of course, but who among us was? Billie Jean had come a long way, as an athlete and as a feminist, and I didn't want her to let us down now.

She was not making it easy to pull for her, however. Since playing her two tournament matches at the Net-Set Racquet Club on Monday and working out the next two nights in the bubble briefly, Billie Jean had virtually gone into seclusion. And while Bobby had gamboled, Billie Jean had trained.

Each night, after dinner, she had forced herself to stay awake later and later, so that she would rise later the next morning. The match was scheduled for 7 p.m. and she wanted to be out of bed for seven hours – no more – when that time came. Each day, she did sit-ups, lifted her knee weights, ate a big breakfast of an omelette or ham and eggs, watched television, joked with her father. (One evening they kiddingly compared biceps. Moffitt, who kept reminding everyone he was the same age as Riggs, recalled that he had played three sets of tennis for fun recently against his daughter. He laughed. 'She tired me out so much I had to stay in bed two days!')

The night before the match, Billie Jean and Dennis van der Meer,

King's longtime coach who had also been Margaret Court's coach at the Mother's Day Massacre, sat in King's Houston Oaks hotel suite like Joe Namath and Weeb Ewbank, screening the film of the Riggs–Court match while Marilyn Barnett carefully took notes on their dialogue.

Billie Jean paid particular attention to Riggs's backhand. With typical King *chutzpah*, she had solicited advice on Bobby's game from the woman she had called a 'donkey,' and Margaret had told her his backhand was his weak spot.

The next morning, her mood swung like a pendulum from, as she put it, ' "I'm ready" to "El Foldo." ' She and Marilyn went to a supermarket to buy some Gatorade. An elderly lady spotted her. 'I hope,' she said, 'that you beat his pompous ass!' Billie Jean roared. She returned to the hotel and danced around the suite to the music of *Jesus Christ Superstar*. Larry King told her he figured the match would go four sets. 'No,' she corrected him. 'Three.'

At the Astrodome, a group of celebrities flown in from Hollywood by Perenchio including Jim Brown, Andy Williams and Sandra Giles (Bobby's starlet girlfriend) whiled away the afternoon playing exhibition matches for a sparse crowd. (The evening's tickets entitled them to the afternoon's entertainment as well.) When Billie Jean showed up, she headed straight for the visiting team locker room, which she had requested because her brother, Randy Moffitt, the San Francisco Giants pitcher, used it. The rather bare, cinder-block main room contained a banquet table laid out with food for the women celebrities. Billie Jean dressed in the manager's room, but before she left the Dome that night she tacked a note on locker 20. The Giants would be in town the following week to play the Astros. The note read: 'Hi, Randy – BJK.'

The Old Lady was ready.

Cecil B. De Mille, Walt Disney, Pete Rozelle and the Emperor Nero working as a team could not have staged it better.

A glittering crowd of 30,472 people in everything from evening gowns to dungarees milled around the corridors of the Astrodome, browsing through souvenir stands selling $5 commemorative racquet covers with drawings of Bobby and Billie on either side, tennis sweatbands with the biological symbol for women on them, patches of Astroturf.

Like a green, elongated prizefight ring, the court sat squarely in the infield surrounded by yellow folding chairs, with a champagne bar and a carving board cart offering slices of hot roast beef strategically located in the corners. Midgets dressed as dancing bears frolicked near the dugouts, the University of Houston marching band thumped out 'Jesus Christ Superstar,' a dozen cheerleaders in red hot pants swirled pompons, two dozen women tennis pros in BJK T-shirts lined up along a red carpet outside the field entrance screeching fight songs, and a fortyish woman with a diamond-encrusted cross hanging between breasts bulging out of a white floor-length peignoir slithered into a front row seat.

From the rafters of the middle tiers of red and orange seats hung an array of banners – 'East West North South Ms King Gonna Close Bobby's Mouth,' 'Oconomowoc, Wisc. Says Beat Him Billie Jean.'

Then, to a trumpet flourish, with Howard Cosell giving a play-by-play in a glass-enclosed booth at one corner of the court, a feathered litter right out of *Cleopatra* carried by bare-chested muscle men emerged from beneath the stands onto the carpet. Numero Uno herself, a fixed smile on her face, a lime-green sweater covering her rhinestone-studded blue-and-green Tinling dress, waved at her subjects like an elementary school kid who has suddenly found herself in the middle of the Rose Bowl parade. (Much later, she held a framed photograph of that moment in her hands and muttered, 'At that point, it was El Barfo.')

Another trumpet flourish, and a Chinese rickshaw on gold wheels pulled by a gaggle of girls known as Bobby's Bosom Buddies, their chests heaving against their sweaters like miniature dirigibles, emerged along the second carpet. In it sat the Happy Hustler, cradling a mammoth Sugar Daddy to his own bosom, his small frame practically hidden from view by what seemed like 900 shoving photographers.

Sitting in a tuxedo in the front row next to heavyweight champion George Foreman, Jerry Perenchio ran a steady hand over his Beverly Hills razor cut and said contentedly, 'It's the fight crowd. It's ancient Rome. It's the closest I've come to getting a woman and a man in the ring together.'

A few rows back, Bill Moffitt turned to a reporter. 'I want him shut up,' he said, gesturing at Riggs. 'If he tries anything funny I'm gonna punch him.' Suddenly, out of the corner of his eye, he saw Billie Jean smack a practice volley past Bobby. 'Go, baby, GO!' he shouted, leaping out of his seat.

From the second she won the toss, Billie Jean was in command. All the Barfos, Chokos, Foldos, blood tests and bitcheries were behind her. King was where she belonged, poised on the toes of her blue suede BJK

Adidas sneakers with her upturned little nose nearly hanging over the net, her muscular right arm holding her BJK Wilson racquet cocked for a crunching backhand volley, with 30,000 screaming fans going bananas under the spider-web girders of Houston's gift to architectural vulgarity.

It was tennis the way she had always wanted it, on prime-time television, before a viewing audience of 37 million people, many of them, incredibly, seeing a professional match for the very first time.

In the first game, the two players were feeling each other out. Billie Jean, glancing up nervously at the lights bouncing off the roof, served tentatively, concentrating simply on keeping her balls in play. She wanted Bobby to make the errors, to impress upon him from the outset that she would not crack like Margaret when his chip shots spun off the carpet. She wanted to establish her confidence immediately. At ad-in she hit a crunching high backhand volley, one of her most devastating shots, to win the game. The crowd, which had roared at every practice winner King had hit during the warm-up, bellowed its approval as the two came to the sideline for the changeover.

Bobby Riggs slumped in his chair at the sidelines while his Boy Friday, Lornie Kuhle, massaged his legs. He turned around and spotted Dick Butera, the Hilton Head Racquet Club president, who had tried to talk him into a $10,000 bet at 2 to 1 just before the match. Bobby had refused, demanding 8 to 5. Now, down one game, he sent Lornie to Butera's seat. 'Bobby says he'll take 2 to 1,' Lornie told him.

It was to be his final, quixotic fling. Billie Jean retook the court for the second game with an extra spring in her step. As the set progressed, her strokes grew bolder, more authoritative, as if she were repeating to herself, 'This is where I belong.' Bobby, looking tense and comical at the same time in his Sugar Daddy warm-up jacket, was not where he belonged. He was running like a geriatric jackrabbit from one side of the court to the other, sweeping futilely at a dazzling selection of King spins, chops, smashes. At 4–5, the nerveless wonder, the man with all the angles, the guy who knew how to keep a hold on himself with the eyes of the world on him, choked. Bobby Riggs double-faulted to give Billie Jean the set, and in the first row, George Foreman was on his feet, both black fists in the air.

'Atta boy, Billie!' thundered the champ.

No fans were getting hoarser more quickly than Billie Jean's sister pros, jammed together in a corner of 'ringside,' some in chairs, some squatting on the sideline carpet.

'Kill 'em, kill 'em!' yelled Kerry Melville, the quietest little church-mouse on the Slims circuit. 'Cheat a little!' yelled sixteen-year-old Kathy Kuykendall at Deedee Dalley, the lineswoman nearest the corner. 'My eyeballs are floating,' said Nancy Richey Gunter, once King's arch rival, as she tipsily stumbled to her feet to search for a bathroom. When she returned, weaving, she noticed that there was a discernible stain of red on the seat of Bobby's shorts. 'Maybe he's getting his period!' she howled.

Directly behind the baseline, Gladys Heldman sat with a glass of champagne in her hand next to Teddy Tinling. 'We're all going crazy,' Gladys said with a big smile, her voice an even deeper baritone than usual. 'The hustler out-hustled himself. I'm sitting next to a lovely male chauvinist. What a wonderful time we're having!'

Stella Lachowicz of Virginia Slims passed by, wordlessly handing out small pink pieces of paper with printing on them. They were invitations to a Bobby Riggs Pasadena Bridge Jump.

Easing up just a little at the start of the second set, Billie Jean had trouble with her first serve and let Bobby break her in the first game. It didn't matter. She broke him right back in the next game, and in the glass-enclosed broadcasting booth, Rosie Casals smiled at Riggs's distress. 'Like a duck out of water,' she remarked.

Billie Jean was forcing him now, forcing him to come to the net and play her game, passing him with bullet-like ground strokes down the line, wrong-footing him at the baseline. Huddled in the corner beneath Casal's booth, Bud Collins and Neil Amdur wrote furiously in tiny notebooks, their eyes wide with disbelief. 'Nothing but winners,' murmured Neil. 'She's hitting nothing but winners.'

They stayed even through the seventh game, but the serve-and-volley pace was taking its toll heavily on the old man. His famed lobs had become inviting targets for Billie Jean's unflinching overheads, his first serve refused to stay within the service line and his second serve was skittering straight to King's fearsome backhand. After failing to take advantage of two break points in the fourth game and a third in the sixth game, she carved up Bobby's service in the eighth, first with a sliced backhand, then a topspin forehand, then a backhand return-of-serve passing shot. It was 5–3, Billie Jean.

Marilyn Barnett, in a brown-and-blue paisley halter-dress ('In yoga,' she had explained to me, 'brown is for money and blue is for spirit'), was sitting totally calm next to the Gatorade cooler in Billie Jean's row of sideline chairs. As Billie Jean served for the second set, Marilyn looked across the court at the Slims corner, smiled beatifically, and, with her thumb and forefinger, formed a small circle.

The third set began with Billie Jean breaking Bobby in the very first game, then holding her own in the second game for an insurmountable 2–0 lead. She had won five straight games. Could Billie Jean keep up the pace? She let down enough for him to win the third game and then break back in the fourth. But with the score at 2–2, a rubber-kneed Riggs began running around his backhand and Billie Jean broke his serve again, this time at love. When the score reached 4–2 King, Bobby suddenly stopped the action, coming to the sidelines to have his aching fingers massaged. What no one knew at the time was that Billie Jean herself had suddenly developed leg cramps. 'Oh God – not now!' she thought silently. Bobby returned to the court and won the next game on two unforced errors by King to make it 4–3. Billie steeled herself against the cramps: 15–0, 15–15, 30–15, 40–15, game. The score was 5–3. One more and the circus would be over.

With Bobby serving, the game went to 30–all. Billie Jean dropped a ball right at Bobby's feet on the next serve, and the crowd leaped up in anticipation. Match point. But Bobby wasn't ready to give up, winning the next two points to take the advantage. The game went to deuce twice again before Billie Jean got another chance at match point on a flashing backhand down the line. Still she couldn't finish him off, and twice more they went to deuce.

It ended as it had begun, in Felliniesque pandemonium. Bobby double-faulted to give King her third nerve-wracking, spine-tingling match point. A weak Riggs serve . . . a short exchange . . . and Bobby's high backhand volley sailed harmlessly into the net. The electronic tote-board flashed the numbers 6–4, 6–3, 6–3. A wooden object sailed high toward the roof – Billie Jean's racquet. Before the stampede of fans and reporters could reach her, she shook Bobby's hand, kissed Dennis van der Meer, kissed Dick Butera and fell into Larry's arms. His cherubic cheeks pale, his hands shaking, Larry lifted her onto a table at courtside while Perenchio handed her a trophy and Foreman gave her a check.

Billie Jean blew kisses at the cameras, stuck her tongue out at van der Meer, held up a fist to Marilyn. As the trophy was put in her hands, she spied her father standing in the crush.

Billie Jean shoved the trophy in his direction, holding it over her head. 'Thanks, Daddy!' she shouted above the din.

'Way to go, champ!' he shouted back.

The insane eleven-year-old I had seen at Wimbledon was back.

She unlaced her sneakers, plopped them on top of the table set up on a platform in the home dressing room for the post-match interview, asked for a beer, and marched back and forth like a wind-up tin soldier. 'Gotta calm myself down first,' she told the assembled press corps, a group now large enough to staff four mass-circulation dailies and the three TV networks besides.

I realized that I was having trouble breathing as I put my tape recorder up on the table. Billie Jean looked down at me. 'Didya win a lot of money, Grace?' she demanded.

'Yes, thank you, Billie Jean,' I stammered. Then, remembering a comment of hers, I added, 'But it's not the money, it's the pride.'

'Right on!' She grinned.

The interview began in earnest with someone asking her feelings about the conquest. 'I feel this is the culmination of nineteen years in tennis . . .' she began. I sneaked out of the room to file my story. It was a speech I knew almost by heart, and it was beside the point. The point was that when the chips were down, a twenty-nine-year-old woman athlete, Billie Jean King Superstar, had hung tough. I was so happy I wanted to cry.

While everybody else in Houston stayed up most of the night getting loaded, Billie Jean paid a brief visit to Jerry Perenchio's party in the Astroworld penthouse and then went back to the Oaks with her parents to watch an old Claudette Colbert movie on television.

The next day, she was back at the Net-Set, to play another round in the Virginia Slims tournament. A big bouquet of roses was waiting for her from the players, who only a week before had been angrily talking about having the Women's Tennis Association fine her for skipping too many recent tournaments. They were glad Astrotennis was over; so was she. 'Anyone who had to live with the day-to-day pressure of playing that match wouldn't want to go through it again,' she admitted. 'You can't go out, you can't eat in a restaurant, you stop living.' She smiled. 'Now I want to live a little.'

A knot of people had gathered around her, still wanting to know what Astrotennis really meant.

'Maybe it means that people will start to respect women athletes more,' she said. 'But it's not just me. There are plenty more to take my place.

And in the next decade, I think you'll see women athletes finally getting the attention they've deserved all along.'

It was a fine summation, presented in the tones of a stateswoman. A little while later, I asked her what she thought about one incredible statistic from the Riggs match. She had hit 64 percent outright winners, balls placed so well Bobby never got his racquet on them.

'Wow!' She grinned. 'That's like pitchin' a no-hit game!'

And she did a slow, perfect pantomime of a pitcher, rearing back for the high hard one.

A Long Way, Baby, 1974

Chris Evert: The Cold and Absolute Fire
PETER BODO

It's often said that you can't have it all, but boy-oh-boy, has Chris Evert ever come close. She survived the perils of being a prodigy, amassed a record that makes her one of the top tennis players of all time, and also managed to lead a robust emotional life, unmarred by the kind of scandals that so often haunt celebrities and raise doubts about their judgment and conduct through the unattractive way in which they are played out.

Evert's companions included actors (Burt Reynolds), tennis players (Vitas Gerulaitis and Jimmy Connors, among others), pop stars (Adam Faith), the son of a US president (Jack Ford), at least one talk-show host (Geraldo Rivera, if he is to be believed), and two husbands (not at the same time): British tennis pro John Lloyd and former Olympic skier Andy Mill. Not bad for a young woman who in her heyday was often called the 'Ice Maiden,' and who was repeatedly characterized as an unemotional, repressed, introverted, all-for-Daddy daughter of a strict Irish Catholic, public-park-teaching pro from Fort Lauderdale, Florida, Jimmy Evert.

As a young girl, Evert believed that she would play tennis for a few years, retire to a domestic life, and raise children by the age of twenty-five. She married John Lloyd at just that age, in 1979, but because of her champion's appetite for competition and public performance, as well as her celebrity and emotional independence, her first marriage turned out to be a dry run. As a result of that, Evert was able to wring every bit of potential out of her spare game. She became a beloved ambassador of tennis who spoke to a remarkably broad range of people. A Los

Angeles divorcee who streaked her hair and spent every waking hour in 'work-out' clothes related to her just as powerfully as an eastern dowager who never played tennis on any surface but grass.

All you need to know about Evert's attitude toward tennis was revealed in a brief locker room exchange that transpired at Wimbledon more than a decade ago. Having just lost a match, the amiable pro Paula Smith returned to the locker room and remarked to a friend, 'Thank God that my happiness doesn't depend on winning or losing a tennis match.' Evert, sitting a few feet away, did not miss a beat. She quipped, 'Thank God that mine does.'

Nevertheless, Evert got out just in the nick of time. In 1988, almost a decade after her own estimated time of departure from tennis, Evert married Mill. She was thirty-three at the time, and she would squeeze one more year on the circuit out of her surprisingly durable body. She then beat the biological clock and quickly had two children. All that and filthy rich, too.

As Ted Tinling once told me, the essence of being a star is wanting it both ways: the fame and the privacy, the privilege and the connection with ordinary life, the glamour and a sense of authenticity. But few female players have been able to combine the demands of a long and distinguished career with traditional feminine roles. Two other women who managed to accomplish that were early rivals of Evert's: the Australians Margaret Court and Evonne Goolagong Cawley.

Court, a largely forgotten champion who won more Grand Slam singles titles than any other woman, had no star quality whatsoever. Goolagong had plenty of star quality, but she never shared Evert's enormous appetite for competition, or her hunger for stardom.

'I never really enjoyed everybody making such a fuss over me,' Evert once told me. 'Being able to walk around without a crowd at my heels is just fine. But to be realistic, I also know that I wouldn't be happy if people were shoving me out of the way to get a glimpse of Gabriela Sabatini.'

The key word there is 'realistic.' Evert was the most realistic and self-aware woman pro that I've ever known, but she was also haunted through much of her career by the issue of her image in a way that was often painful for her. She was called prissy, but she became earthy and worldly. She was thought of as cold, but she had a noteworthy capacity for empathizing with those who were different or even threatening to her. (She was, and remains, good friends with her main rival, Martina

Navratilova.) She was accused of being tough, but, well, she *was* tough. At the same time, she was fair-minded and an exemplary sport.

For a long time Evert's only problem was that some people just didn't like what they saw, and so they were predisposed to believe that it couldn't be authentic. Evert certainly sent mixed and provocative signals. She highlighted the difference between two kinds of feminism – the one that accepts, enjoys, and sometimes trades on the fundamental differences between the sexes while still insisting on equality, and the branch whose constituents believe that our traditional concepts of feminity are confining, socially imposed burdens.

Evert took great pride in her status as an athlete and in the strides taken in her time by her profession. She had nothing but contempt for knee-jerk sexism in tennis, of which there was a lot, and she worked arm in arm with the masculinists to get more money and more exposure for women's tennis. At the same time, Evert espoused traditional values and incessantly questioned the conflict between professionalism and her goals as a woman. She carefully avoided defining herself as a feminist, yet she was anything but a boy toy. She lived with one foot planted in each of two different worlds, and it took formidable skill and tact for her to survive and to retain a distinct identity. She was frequently chastised for managing that balancing act.

For instance, when journalist Barry Lorge was working on a tribute to Evert and her legacy, the best thing Billie Jean King could bring herself to say about Evert was: 'Chris is very gracious. She's calculated. She thinks before she speaks. That is the way she was brought up, the way her father is, and the way she plays. She says and does the right thing regardless of how she really feels – unlike me or Martina [Navratilova], who made waves.'

This backhanded compliment is not only curiously bitter, it also leaves the impression that thinking about things before shooting your mouth off is somehow base. But Evert certainly was different from King and Navratilova. She didn't harbor nearly as many controversial opinions, and she often bit her tongue and suppressed turbulent emotions because she didn't trust them, and because she had always believed that keeping them in check was a virtue. The 'clean image' she projected was the result, not the goal, of her modus operandi.

Evert certainly was 'image-conscious.' How could she not have been, given her life experience? You can count on the fingers of one hand the number of times that anybody ever called Evert sensitive, but throughout her entire career she tried to avoid hurting the feelings of others. You couldn't necessarily say this about, say, King, who spent a fair amount of time going around telling other people, including Evert, how they should run their lives. At Wimbledon in 1987, late in Evert's career, King admonished her for not smiling more. She suggested that Evert ought to derive more enjoyment from her waning days in tennis.

'I could have killed her,' Evert told me later. 'I'm not Evonne [Goolagong], who can walk around singing. I told Billie, "Geez, this is Wimbledon, and I'm intense." But the whole incident was really interesting to me because who ever saw Billie Jean King smile when she was still a top player? When she smiled at Wimbledon, you knew it wasn't genuine. And it wouldn't have been genuine coming from me, either. I'm not a fake person, why should I go around smiling or trying to manipulate the crowd's emotions?'

Evert did have a lifelong desire to retain some semblance of privacy. She was especially insistent on the right to make mistakes in private, like the rest of us do. Having been observed, dissected, and analyzed by the media and the public since she skyrocketed to celebrity at age sixteen, Evert became a master not of giving the public what it wanted to see, but what she felt it was entitled to under her uneasy but voluntary pact with fame.

Evert refrained from blasting or criticizing opponents in public, but privately she never refrained from making her feelings known. She never evaded a question unless answering it would embarrass herself or another individual. Even then she would make her point, although she often made you read between the lines to dig it out. Decades of fame also taught her to avoid incriminating herself by taking the fifth amendment on a question. She had a remarkable way of saying a lot without telling you anything at all. She could also tell you all by hardly saying anything. That was good enough for me, but not always for everyone else.

During one period late in her career, rumor had it that Evert enjoyed smoking pot now and then. On one occasion during the Virginia Slims Championships in Madison Square Garden, when Chris was taking a break from tennis, I sat down next to her and said hello. She appeared to barely recognize me. Her eyes were red and lidded, and she had the slightly drowsy look of someone who was high. That was the impression I had, anyway, and the next time I formally interviewed her, I broached the 'P' word in a discussion of her healthy, all-American image, and the conflicts it created in her private life.

'Well, that squeaky clean image was thrust on me at a very young age, when I *was* squeaky clean. And even though I pretty much lived it out, there are things in my life that I'd rather keep to myself. Doesn't everybody? But I won't ever deny something that I know in my heart is true. I don't lie. That puts me in some tough situations because I also believe that a person in the limelight should be free to choose how much he or she wants to reveal. That's a real conflict, and it's taught me to be diplomatic, which some people interpret as being "calculated." At least that's the word that always comes up.

'But to me there's nothing negative about "calculating," which is just thinking ahead. Let's say that somebody comes right out of the blue and asks me if I've tried drugs. Even if it *is* true, I'm not going to jump up and say, "Yeah, I've smoked marijuana." I'm going to think about how many kids I'd let down by admitting that. I'm going to think about fielding a thousand calls from the press. I'm going to think of the context that will appear in. I would say that my attitude about drugs is much more important than whether I've tried them or not, unless I'm doing drugs all the time and going around saying that nobody should ever try them. But we both know that if I come out and say I've smoked pot, that's what is going to be in the headline.'

I believe that this was Evert's way of telling me that she had smoked pot. Whatever the truth, I let her comments stand on their own. Later, another reporter picked up on the theme, and the subsequent story generated just the kind of controversy Evert described and hoped to avoid.

Evert also had a good nose for pretense, an aversion to public displays of sentiment, and enough competitive pride to get herself into occasional bouts of trouble. At Wimbledon in 1986, Evert lost a titanic semi-final struggle to her rival Navratilova, 6–4 in the third set. As usual, Evert showered, put on a new sweater, fixed her hair, and applied a touch of make-up before she walked into the interview room below Centre Court.

After a loss like that, Evert was always loath to face anyone, including her devoted mother Colette. But only the veterans in the tennis press understood how disheartened and prickly she could be under those circumstances. After a few innocuous questions about the match, one of the reporters related the anecdote Navratilova had told in the same room just minutes earlier. She had told the press that near the end of the match, she had tears in her eyes. Those tears were for her friend Evert, Navratilova said, because it had suddenly occurred to her how nice it would have been for Evert to win one more Wimbledon title. For one of the rare times in her career, Evert reacted spontaneously. She rolled her eyes and smacked her lips. Her reply was a simple, incredulous, 'Oh, yeah . . .'

A few reporters exchanged knowing glances. They probably felt that they had smoked out the real Evert – the tough, icy woman lurking behind the gracious, cool image. But I think Evert was showing her sensitivity, not her toughness. She felt that she was being patronized, and it made her angry that Navratilova was callous enough to violate the intimacy of their friendship by sharing the story with the world press. Besides, Navratilova was closing in on a record, nine Wimbledon singles titles. Evert had only three.

Evert's diplomatic ways were also a survival mechanism for a shy girl who became very famous, very quickly, and one who suddenly found herself immersed in a closed society where values different from her own had established a kind of shadow ethic.

At the time, many of the top women players were lesbians. The ethic of this older generation was fiercely professional, and Evert quickly learned that a pecking order existed in the women's game. She would have to learn to play politics with the best of them in order to protect her own interests. I'll tell one sad and weird story to illustrate the degree to which personal and sexual politics play a part in women's tennis a little more often than they should, and how no top woman player can steer clear of them and still be an active force in the establishment that runs the game.

Andrea Jaeger, the gifted prodigy, reached five Grand Slam semi-finals and the Wimbledon final by the time she reached eighteen. We were friends, and I was sorry to see her become something of a lost soul on the tour – a rebellious, discontented, confused pilgrim whose increasingly erratic behavior sent silent but powerful shock waves through the women's tennis establishment. I liked Andrea's punk, rebel-without-a-pause attitude, her fire as a competitor, and her taste in dirt bikes. I didn't even mind that she took to carrying a switchblade. Shoot, I was eighteen once, too.

But the Women's Tennis Association was alarmed by her behavior and the image she projected. The knife proved to be a serious problem, as did the incident in which Andrea shoved another woman, Renee Blount, up against a locker. Jaeger was not only a loose cannon but a top player and potential superstar, a combination that made the WTA establishment (which is dominated by both active and retired players) really edgy. It all came to a head shortly before a shoulder injury sidelined Jaeger for good. When a top woman player with whom Jaeger had a close friendship suddenly took up with a tour official who happened to be one of Evert's friends, Jaeger sensed that she was suddenly getting the cold shoulder from both parties.

Feeling rejected, Jaeger became embroiled in a series of confrontations with her former friend, and other top women on the Tour. The other women closed ranks and, Jaeger said, encouraged her to embark on a lesbian relationship with another player, apparently as part of their damage-control strategy. This really upset Jaeger, who denied having any lesbian inclinations. Jaeger had always admired Evert, and she was crushed by what she described as Evert's complicity in this crude ploy. Feeling betrayed on all fronts, Jaeger caused a fair bit of trouble before it all got sorted out. Among other things, this episode illustrated the dangers of exposing a child who may have been wrestling with typical problems of gender confusion to an atmosphere supercharged with sexual ambiguity and politics.

I was also disturbed by Chris's alleged role in all of this, and I discussed the imbroglio with a number of women players. Most of them said that Jaeger was misinterpreting events and expressing her feelings of rejection in irrational ways. They maintained that Evert was just trying to mediate. And being heterosexual herself, Evert wouldn't be inclined to steer a young player toward lesbianism. Whatever the truth was, I found myself thinking about the whole steamy mess as symbolic of the politics and personal rivalries that cause so much tension on the women's tour. Evert, along with many of her peers, had to contend with those issues every day.

So while Evert may have looked like a tennis player to the manor born, the manor had changed by the time she claimed her birthright. Nevertheless, she was too bright, ambitious, and competitive to stand aside from the battles waged in the new era of women's tennis. She was a player in every sense of the word. And she did such a good job negotiating the quagmire that it's easy to forget how much antagonism and criticism she had to deflect on her way to becoming fully realized as a player, as an activist who played an important role in the governance and promotion of the game, and as a woman whose expectation had always been to be a wife and mother.

When you come right down to it, Evert spent much less time culti-

THE RIGHT SET

vating an image than in dumping one. And, as any celebrity will tell
you, an image is a lot harder to lose than it is to acquire.

The noun 'professional' is commonly used to describe a person who
bears the demands and responsibilities of his or her work effectively, with
grace and consideration for others. In that sense, Evert was the consum-
mate professional. As a result we developed the same kind of fondness
for each other as good neighbours who often meet along the fence
between their properties. Chris always made time to see me privately,
even if she wasn't the subject of whatever article I was about to write.
She also did so during the two or three occasions when she was angry
about something I had written.

Chris was one of the few players who bothered to contact Bjorn Borg
when, less than a year after Borg quit the game but before he officially
announced his retirement, the tennis establishment insisted that Borg
couldn't return to the pro tour without participating in lowly qualifying
tournaments. Evert wrote Borg a letter of support and encouragement.

My friendship with Evert's great early rival, Evonne Goolagong, was
a real obstacle to developing a similar relationship with Evert. She kept
score in such matters and interpreted them as a realist. But while she
thought of me as part of the Goolagong camp, she also appreciated a
spirited defense I wrote about her in one of my first articles for *Tennis*.
She was eighteen at the time, and many people had characterized her as
a chilly bitch goddess who played a lethal but boring game. My take in
that article was that Evert was only boring to boring people who could
not look beyond the conspicuous components of sporting genius – the
athleticism, the flashy strokes, or the sheer power that you expect to see
in tennis champions.

I argued that Evert was a neurological miracle whose consistency was
the product of extraordinary but not necessarily 'athletic' gifts. The signal
sent from Evert's eye to her hand was almost never interrupted by its
passage through her mind, where anxiety or fear or overeagerness so
often blur the message and lead to a flubbed forehand or a weakly netted
volley. Even when she was exhausted, Evert's strokes remained silken,
perfectly timed, and, above all, purposeful.

I still stand by that analysis because, while other women often made
more spectacular shots from difficult positions or reeled off longer strings
of unanswerable winners, Evert had the almost preternatural ability to
avoid having to do those things. In tennis as in life, Evert was first and
foremost about poise and control. She rarely showed an impressive burst

of speed or the kind of acrobatic skill that Navratilova made her stock in trade. Yet you can count on the fingers of one hand the number of times that anybody overpowered Evert, jerked her around the court, or exposed her shortcomings as a pure athlete.

Evert always seemed to be on top of the ball, prepared to make the most use of her riposte. This was partly because of her precision, which enabled her to control any given point from the outset. But it was also due to her powers of anticipation and a unique sense of knowing at all times where she was and where she had to be next. She did not make the game look easy in the way that a natural like Goolagong or Ilie Nastase did, but she sure made the court look small.

Evert had only one technical weakness, and it was the same one that has haunted numerous other women players from successful professionals on down to country club hackers. One of the radical, definitive differences between male and female pros is in the serve. Countless men have survived the pro tour mostly because they had outstanding serves, while countless women have had otherwise sound games hampered by an inability to serve effectively. Evert's serve was effective, but it wasn't good. Her delivery was strikingly labored and self-conscious, as if she had remained an earnest twelve-year-old trying hard to serve exactly the way her father had insisted she should. Nevertheless, Evert shared an interesting quality with other great champions: a formidable ability to blank out any consciousness of a weakness. This is an issue that truly shows the degree to which tennis matches – even whole careers – are played out in the psyche just as much as on the court.

Jimmy Connors never acknowledged that he had real trouble lifting a forehand approach shot from the forecourt over the net. Stefan Edberg pushed his forehand with a bizarre and reluctant shoveling motion but insisted that he felt confident hitting the stroke. Tracy Austin's overhead always looked like an adventure. So it was with the studied serve of Evert. The stroke never really crumbled under pressure because Evert did not dote on its vulnerability or try to do too much with it.

Navratilova did finally develop the confidence to capitalize on Evert's serve, using aggressive returns (including textbook chip and charge tactics) to take control of a point before Evert could do it with her first ground stroke. That was one of the chief reasons the Czech expatriate was able to turn her competition with Evert into the greatest rivalry in women's tennis, perhaps even in all of sports.

Evert and Navratilova stand tied for third place on the all-time list of

Grand Slam singles championships with eighteen titles each. Second place is occupied by Helen Wills Moody, who collected nineteen titles. But the most prolific champion of all time is Margaret Court, whose career spanned both the amateur and pro eras. Court has an untouchable record of twenty-four Grand Slam singles titles, and in 1970 she became the second woman to achieve a Grand Slam, winning all four major titles in the same year (the feat was first accomplished by Maureen Connolly in 1953). There is an interesting footnote to these statistics.

Because of their commitments to World Team Tennis, Evert and Navratilova both skipped the French Open in the mid-1970s. Playing WTT was a particularly unwise choice for Evert, who won two consecutive titles in Paris and then declined to play the event three years running. When Evert returned to Roland Garros, she took up where she had left off, winning the next two titles. She might easily have won the French title in the years that she avoided the event, 1976–78.

Evert once held an enormous head-to-head advantage over Navratilova. In 1977, Navratilova had won only four times out of twenty meetings. But she gradually chipped away at Evert's lead and finally pulled even at thirty wins each in the 1984 Wimbledon final, which she won, 7–6, 6–2. Navratilova then nosed ahead for good and led 35–32 at the time Evert retired in 1985. Not long thereafter, Evert presented her friend Navratilova with an internally illuminated globe featuring a lighted pinhole commemorating every city where Navratilova had captured one or more of her staggering 161 career titles.

Trying to decide whether Evert or Navratilova was the greater player involves many variables. Navratilova dominated Wimbledon to about the same degree that Evert dominated the French Open, primarily because Navratilova was at her best on fast grass courts and Evert was formidable on slow clay ones. Evert's advantage on clay was apparent as early as 1972 when, at age eighteen, she rocked the tennis world by beating Billie Jean King on clay in Florida, 6–1, 6–0. That was one of the most astonishing results of the Open era because that year King won three Grand Slam titles and didn't play for the fourth one, at the Australian Open.

The most interesting way to compare Evert and Navratilova is to break down their head-to-head records on their respective, preferred Grand Slam surfaces as well as on the surfaces that gave each of them the most trouble. Evert went 9–2 against Navratilova on clay, and she holds a 2–1 edge at the French Open. Navratilova's record against Evert on grass was 7–5, with a 4–2 edge at Wimbledon. Overall, Evert enjoys a 14–9 advantage on the combined surfaces, but Navratilova holds a 5–4 lead in their key meetings at Wimbledon and the French Open.

Evert played the French Open thirteen times. Her worst performances at Roland Garros were a third-round defeat in the last year that she played (1988), and three semi-final finishes. She reached the final in nine out of thirteen years, winning the title on seven of those occasions. Navratilova played the French Open eleven times. She missed two more meetings than Evert did during the WTT era, and she stopped competing at Roland Garros after a fourth-round loss in 1988, mostly to improve her chances at Wimbledon. Navratilova's worst performances at the French Open were two fourth-round losses and three quarter-final finishes. She reached the final on six occasions, winning twice.

Now for Wimbledon. Evert played eighteen times, and her worst loss was a third-round defeat suffered in 1983. On every other occasion she reached at least the semi-finals. She played in the final ten times, but she won the title only three times. Navratilova played Wimbledon twenty times. She lost before the semi-finals on five occasions, but she reached the final eleven times, capturing nine titles.

In the big picture, Navratilova has a more glamorous record, while Evert has a more consistent one. Navratilova also played her best at the most prestigious tournament of them all, Wimbledon. Evert's resume at Roland Garros is the capstone of her career, but her record at Wimbledon is a great tribute to her versatility as well as a powerful testament to her competitive powers.

After all, Wimbledon is the domain of the attacking, serve-and-volley player. It is also the domain of the pure athlete. The success of baseliners like Borg, Steffi Graf, and Jimmy Connors at Wimbledon was not predicated on their technical prowess at grass-court tennis but on their mobility, reflexes, anticipation, and a flexibility that allowed them to deal successfully with the unpredictable nature of tennis on grass. Evert was neither an attacking player nor a particularly athletic one. Yet only Navratilova, who was both of those things, prevented Evert from ending up with six or eight Wimbledon titles.

Evert was a surprisingly complete player from day one, but her development into a complete human being was a much more incremental process. The novelist Thomas Mann once said that the best stories were all long stories, which is a natural claim coming from a man who specialized in writing novels as thick as telephone directories. If you take Mann at his word, Chris Evert was one of the best stories in tennis.

One of the chief reasons Evert's career lasted so long is that she paced herself, an ability long lost on successive generations of players. Early on, it was Jimmy Evert who was careful not to expose his teenage daughter to the pressures, demands, and itinerant lifestyle of the pro tour. The most positive feature of her decision to play team tennis was the stability it helped bring to her personal life.

Later on, Evert would take a number of extended breaks from the tour, for preventative rather than curative reasons. At one point in the early 1980s, she decided to skip altogether the dreary, claustrophobic indoor tour that moved from one arena to another, one late night after another, in winterbound cities. Navratilova accused Evert of ducking her in order to protect her World Number One ranking. Evert frostily answered, 'Tell Martina not to worry. She'll have nine whole months to play me.'

Another contributing factor to Evert's longevity was her early training on soft, forgiving clay courts that not only forced her to develop consistency, concentration, and patience, but were less punishing to her developing physique. In stark contrast, Tracy Austin, a Californian whose game was modeled on Evert's, grew up playing on cement courts. Her career was cut short by chronic lower back problems.

Evert could have turned pro at age fourteen, after she first made shock waves by posting wins over perennial top-ten player Françoise Durr and, even more shockingly, Margaret Court, in her first foray onto the circuit. But Evert didn't become a pro until three years later, on her eighteenth birthday. That was more than a full year after her sensational run to the semi-finals of the US Open. By then she had also reached the semi-finals at two other Grand Slam events, the 1972 Wimbledon and US Open tournaments.

One of the main factors in Evert's decision to wait was that she wanted to finish her studies at Saint Thomas Aquinas High School back in Fort Lauderdale, Florida. The other big reason was Jimmy Evert, who exercised complete control over his daughter until she turned eighteen. From the get-go, Jimmy Evert mistrusted the agents of professionalism, from tour officials to racket manufacturers to managers who began to promise him the moon when Evert was fourteen. Even when Evert did turn pro, Jimmy recruited his brother Chuck and a close family friend who lived down the road to help manage her business affairs. His decision to keep it all in the family was not based on a reluctance to give professional managers a piece of the action. He understood the built-in conflict of interest between business managers and the players they represented. Mostly, Jimmy wanted to keep any threat to his daughter's commitment to tennis at bay. As Chris has often admitted, she spent most of her career playing for her father. And he was participating not for his own celebrity or hers, or for money; he was participating merely for distinction. The only big change in Jimmy Evert's material life after his daughter became famous was that, as a result of her prodding, he raised the rates he charged for a tennis lesson at the public courts from $6 to $10.

'There were three big things in my father's life,' Evert once told Curry Kirkpatrick of *Sports Illustrated*, 'family, tennis, and religion. All the other things that came with my success didn't make him happy, they just aged him.'

At that time it was easier to just say no to the temptations of turning pro as soon as possible. Even Jimmy Evert agrees with that assessment. On the other hand, he was a man of absolute values, so I think that even today he would have brought a different sensibility to the table than do most contemporary tennis parents.

One of the best examples of a battle that he lost was Chris's decision to play World Team Tennis. At around age twenty-one Chris wanted to enjoy the camaraderie and security of participating in a team sport. And WTT, with its goofball, quasi-serious ambience and astronomical wage scale, provided the perfect opportunity. But in the end, WTT may have cost Evert an exclusive place behind Court in the Grand Slam record book.

Jimmy also fought hard to keep Evert in the traditionalist camp when the USTA created a women's circuit that was perceived in some quarters as a threat to the new, burgeoning Virginia Slims tour. Many of the pioneering female pros (King, Rosie Casals, and others) were hostile to the embattled amateur establishment and fiercely committed to the new tour. They were critical of the two youngest stars of the game, Evert and Goolagong, when both of them decided to support the USTA tour. The phrase that kept coming up was that they should 'play with the big girls.' The guardians of Evert and Goolagong, Jimmy and Vic Edwards, certainly were old-school types, but each of them was also reluctant to expose his real or surrogate daughter to the pressure and naked professionalism of the Virginia Slims circuit. And the girls – which is exactly what they were at that point – were not all fired up to join the

Slims tour, either. They felt that the 'big girls' were a little scary, a little tough.

In comparison, the USTA circuit was an amiable, low-key operation, and the women who played on it tended to be products of the tennis mainstream. Like Evert and Goolagong, many of them did not see themselves as tennis players for life, and they had a greater interest in the overall social environment of tennis than in the game's potential as a source of income or as a vehicle for social change.

Evert's ambivalence toward the new tour, compounded by her formidable talent, made her a threat to the new order emerging in the pro era. And when I asked the firebrands of professionalism about Evert and what she represented, they spoke guardedly, with a deference demanded by her talent. But if you knew them well enough, they would express their reservations about the apparent 'selfishness' that kept Evert from throwing her weight behind the Slims tour. And any discussion of Evert's girl-next-door image was punctuated with pregnant pauses, colored by thinly veiled cynicism. When the old pros talked about the new kid on the block, they rolled their eyes – often.

Evert's personality did nothing to alleviate the pure fear her game inspired in her older peers. If anything, it exacerbated it. Her sangfroid as a sixteen-year-old during that enchanted US Open of 1971 not only scared the bejesus out of her rivals, it moved the crowd to support her to an extent that automatically turned many people, including many female players, against her.

It certainly wasn't Evert's fault that the crowd cheered her opponent's errors and swept her along on a wave of encouragement. But to many of the other women players it still didn't seem fair. They quickly came to feel threatened by Evert's apparent remoteness, and by the way she seemed to trade on her femininity.

'I know that I wasn't very friendly or warm toward people,' Chris once told me, 'but you know, I was *afraid* of them. Fans and players, too. They were looking at me like I was a little bit of a freak, like how can this girl be so unemotional and cool? People weren't exactly very friendly and warm toward me, either, and for a long time that included many of the other players. I was lucky in that I was the first really feminine, big-name player of the Open era, at least in America. And I carried that to the hilt. I made sure my earrings and makeup were always perfect. But I wasn't trying to intimidate the other women with that, I was just, well, impressionable. It sounds too simple to be true, but my friends in high school had a lot to do with it. My mother had a lot to do with it. I think it also became a little bit of a reaction when people began to say and write that I was kind of cold. That bothered me, it made me feel insecure.'

It did not help that when the reticent prodigy did speak, her comments revealed acute self-consciousness. As a debutante at the US Open, Evert survived six match points in her second-round match to beat Mary Ann Eisel. When she was asked what she had been thinking during the match points, she said, 'I was thinking how I would look during the handshake at the net. Would I be cute? Sad? Tired? Then when the ball came up, it looked so big, just like a huge balloon.'

That remark galled many people, and it helped to implant the notion that Evert was obsessed with her own image. It was easy to forget that in many ways Evert was just another out-to-lunch sixteen-year-old, apt to wonder, 'Who am I?'

The media had a big hand in quickly bending the public's fascination with Evert toward ambivalence. One of the most damning and accurate charges that can be brought against the press is that it is institutionally indisposed toward taking into account the age of its subjects – as if managing to accomplish something newsworthy constitutes a de facto waiver of the right to be young, confused, and stupid. This proclivity has especially hurt tennis, a game full of sheltered, undereducated children and callow prodigies.

Another typical example of the type of problem Chris experienced occurred shortly after she burst on the scene. After a close match with Billie Jean King, who had once again flung herself all over the court trying to intercept Evert's pinpoint passing shots, Evert was asked if she was ever tempted to throw all caution to the wind, abandon her poise, and, as King would put it, 'just go for it.' Evert replied, 'I don't think any point is worth falling down over.'

In an increasingly hot war between the sexes – and among women themselves – that reply was interpreted as a confession of vanity. King was seen as a woman who had the courage to compete with the same abandon that is considered virtuous in men. By renouncing that mentality, Evert seemed to be defining herself as gender inhibited.

Shortly before Chris retired, I found myself sitting with her in some lounge at a tournament, just killing time. I brought up that ancient remark, and she immediately remembered the controversy it had initiated. She told me that the remark had been pumped full of false significance. She had only meant that until match point arrived, no single point in tennis ought to be so important that you would fling yourself after it. And if it was, you just didn't have control of a match.

Evert's extraordinary abilities created an almost immediate backlash. The new American tennis princess soon became the Ice Maiden, once again demonstrating that Shakespeare had it right: Humankind cannot stand too much perfection. The mischievous British press, who at the onset disliked this all-American girl in roughly the same measure that they embraced her after she married the English player John Lloyd, dubbed her 'the Metronome.'

At Wimbledon in 1972, Evert also discovered that the rousing welcome that greeted her just a year earlier at Forest Hills could not be taken for granted. It was different in England, where the Yankeephobes were no less vocal than the Yankeephiles. The press and the public in England were enthralled by Goolagong, and Evert suddenly found herself cast as the villain – the Mary Ann Eisel or Billie Jean King – when she faced Goolagong in a historic semi-final. Goolagong won the match, after which Evert marched into the locker room, let her rackets fall clattering to the floor, and declared, 'Now I hope *they're* happy.'

Evert was acquiring an education quickly. As the realities of her situation sank in, she began to understand that she would not float through life on a magic carpet of adulation, or be spared by virtue of her talent from having to make hard, practical decisions. She would have to learn how to make her way and to take her place in the burgeoning pro establishment represented by the Virginia Slims tour.

The new Slims tour projected glamour that was more evocative of show business than athletics. The media was hot for it, because it appeared to be a social phenomenon, not just another tennis circuit. The commercial expertise of the promoters generated ever-escalating prize money and state-of-the-art administrative and public relations departments. When Evert and Goolagong decided that it was time to play with the big girls, the USTA women's circuit was left dead in the water. Securing the loyalties of Evert and Goolagong put the final stamp of legitimacy on the new Slims tour. While the character and nature of the tour would often be at cross-purposes with Evert's goals and desires, it became the environment in which she was finally socialized.

Over the years she would learn to live in close quarters with a baffling array of characters, including rivals who were apparent clones, lesbians, anorexics, ingenues, unfulfilled heterosexuals, and, as time went on, a parade of flinty, gifted youngsters who would exist outside of the tour establishment in a germ-free atmosphere, under a transparent bubble erected by a family entourage and financed by the tennis bucks that Evert and her peers had helped to generate.

Evert's emotional history may be a long story, but at heart it's the relatively common one of the fairy tale(s) that didn't quite work out. Early in her career Evert allowed that she couldn't imagine being married to a man who wasn't a 'great' tennis player. In what could be interpreted as punishment for her pride, God sent Evert a man named Jimmy Connors. He that was calleth Jimbo. The pairing of Connors and Evert was mortifyingly predictable. Connors was perceived by many as a punk, and Evert's infatuation with him seemed to confirm the suspicion that she was just a silly girl. Cynics delighted in the liaison because it allowed them to vent contempt for two conveniently joined targets. Jimbo and Chrissie were portrayed, in different ways and not entirely without reason, as a pair of tennis brats. Their happiness, while short-lived, really got people's noses out of joint.

In the big picture, Evert's relationship with Connors allowed her to break away from her powerful father without threatening the hopes and dreams that they had invested together in tennis. This loyalty to her father was typical of Evert. When she hired Bob Kain of IMG as her manager, he became her agent for life. She also stayed with the same racket and shoe manufacturers as well, instead of periodically turning herself over to the highest bidder.

Evert made her first, dramatic statement of independence shortly after she began dating Connors at age eighteen. Eager to see Connors, she booked a flight to visit him in Los Angeles. Knowing that her parents would never approve of her actions, she wrote them a tender but firm note explaining what she was doing. Jimmy and Colette Evert were wise enough not to confront Chris when she returned.

It was impossible to expect the romance between Connors and Evert to work out, even though the two were briefly engaged. They were too young, and each of them was brimming with tennis ambitions. Connors was also devoted to his mother and coach Gloria, just as deeply as Evert was devoted to her father and coach Jimmy. The spice in this bubbling Freudian stew was that Jimmy Evert and Gloria Connors themselves had dated briefly, back when they were two young tennis nuts at Notre Dame University.

One of the main reasons the relationship between Chris and Jimmy collapsed was that she was not truly prepared for independence. She tried to transfer her dependence on her family to Connors, but that ultimately made him feel stifled and restless. After the two parted, Connors took up with a colourful assortment of women, a few of whom might still be listed in Andy Warhol's *Encyclopedia of Famous-for-Fifteen Minutes People*. They included someone called Mean Mary Jean (she was in TV commercials for Dodge cars), actress Susan George, and a former Miss World, Marjorie Wallace.

One of Evert's chief talents was her ability to sublimate any personal difficulties she was experiencing in a positive way. When Evert was unhappy, she was a holy terror on the tour – a relentless, unforgiving, highly focused competitor who punished her opponents for the difficulties she was experiencing. In the years between her liaison with Connors and her marriage to John Lloyd, Evert enjoyed a robust emotional life. But tennis always came first, and while a young Evert often turned to other women for her feminine cues, she did not really tolerate anyone's encroaching on her own stardom. These conditions made it difficult to be a genuine and lasting friend to Evert.

The former player Kristien Kemmer Shaw was an important influence when Evert was famous but still socially awkward. Evert took immediate notice of Kemmer at a tournament. She was a very pretty girl, in granny glasses, with her braided hair tied up, reading a book (my guess would be *The World According to Garp* by John Irving). The two quickly became friends, and after Kemmer married New York banker Rick Shaw, she also became Evert's confidante, World Team Tennis teammate (on the Phoenix Racquets), and style counselor. Evert visited the Shaws at their Riverside Drive digs often, and Kristien introduced her to the myriad delights of Gotham. These included shopping at Saks Fifth Avenue, dining at the Palm, having her eyebrows bleached by 'Laszlo,' and getting her hair and nails done by another superstar whose name was hyphenated to boot, Jean-Pierre.

The intense friendship between Evert and Shaw ended quickly, partly because Shaw made some indiscreet revelations to Kirkpatrick in a long profile of Evert in *Sports Illustrated*. Among other things, Shaw apparently told Kirkpatrick that when Connors took up with Mean Mary Jean, a television journalist cornered Evert and broke the news to her during an interview. Evert handled the revelation with aplomb, but according to Shaw, she later broke down in 'a sobbing and moaning fit.' Stung by this indiscretion, Evert had a falling out with Shaw. But, ever the quick study, Evert had absorbed a lot. As her independence and sophistication flowered, tennis remained her hedge. She said, 'My family was my first source of security. But when I started to be truly on my own, tennis became my security. If I couldn't make it work that way, I probably would have become a basket case.'

Evert endured a number of emotional crises and weathered periods of discontent, but instead of negatively affecting her game, they seemed to energize it. But in 1980, at age twenty-five, the basket seemed to beckon. This had less to do with unhappiness (which she could always handle) than joy. In 1978, Evert took a four-month break from the game to refresh her attitude. Soon thereafter she met and began to date her first husband, John Lloyd.

Lloyd was a popular, blond-haired, blue-eyed British heartthrob who had reached the final of the Australian Open at age twenty-three in 1977. He was fleet, skillful, and blessed with a smooth and attractive game. He lacked power, however, and without a weapon, he had to be highly motivated in order to grub out matches and live up to his potential as a Top Twenty player. By that time Evert had done a little more math regarding whom she could marry. He would no longer have to be the number one or three or five player. He didn't even have to be a great player; a good one would do.

As Evert's romance with Lloyd blossomed, she declared that while she would probably continue to play the game after she wed, it was not vitally important for her husband to be a top player. She would be happy with a good ranking, number three or even five.

'How about him being number thirty-two?' she was asked.

She answered, 'Let's not get ridiculous here.'

Looking back on her decision to marry Lloyd, Evert would later say, 'All my life I pictured myself as one day becoming a cute little housewife. It was another variation of the way I saw myself in tennis, as a little, walking, talking tennis doll. So when I grew disenchanted with tennis, I grabbed for that other little idealized image.'

Lloyd recognized and stood in awe of what he would call the 'absolute fire' of champion players, including Borg, Connors, McEnroe, and the woman he would marry. But Lloyd also knew himself well enough to admit that he lacked that fire. He came from a thoroughly middle-class British family of tennis nuts for whom Wimbledon represented the perfect world. But a typically British concept of his own place in the grand scheme of things – a by-product of Britain's class system – inhibited him.

'If I had been born in the States, where it's so much more competitive, where success alone is so much more the be-all and end-all, I might have been forced to work harder and maybe I would have become a better player,' Lloyd once explained. 'On the other hand, I also might have been lost in the shuffle. I was lucky to be born in England where I was among the top two or three players at every level. I was handed things on a plate, and I was very successful in the scheme of things. In the States, I'm not even sure I would have survived the college game to become a pro.'

Lloyd was going great guns when he met Evert. He had reached a career-high ranking of number 23 in July 1978. Less than a year later, he married Evert. He was twenty-six and she was twenty-five, and one of the first issues facing the young couple was just which of them was going to end up the tennis player and which one the significant other.

That decision seemed an easy one at first because Evert was finding it increasingly hard to convert emotions into rocket fuel for her career. And then along came Lloyd to further complicate matters by suggesting that she might draw motivation from a novel source – happiness. Evert had often wondered if she could retain her competitive intensity if she found herself happily married. She soon found out.

There was another important element in Evert's crisis, one that showed the extent to which tennis players can develop the same behavioral habits as fading movie stars or divas. For the first time in her life Evert was hearing footsteps. They were made by a rapidly maturing young woman who had been on the cover of *World Tennis* magazine, racket in hand, at age three, Tracy Austin. Navratilova may have been Evert's lifetime rival, but she was different from Evert in every aspect, from her game to her emotional make-up. This created a pleasant distance between the women and a contrast that both of them enjoyed trading on. But Austin was unnervingly similar to Evert, and she represented the nightmare scenario: being replaced by someone who was a younger, better version of herself.

Austin was so like Evert that she was even forced to deal with similar criticisms. She was frequently described as a cold-hearted tennis doll in gingham. These complaints were transparently sexist (nobody ever slighted Borg or questioned his sexuality when he appeared cold-hearted), but Austin dealt with them differently from Evert. Instead of becoming withdrawn, Austin became more aggressive. She was a regular spitfire, and all her rivals were fearful.

To make matters worse for Evert – but more interesting for others – Austin was also a traditional girl who enjoyed capitalizing on her femininity. To top it off, Austin also played from the baseline, employing a two-handed backhand. The superficial similarities were so striking that Austin was often insultingly referred to as a 'Chrissie clone,' which would be the last android that Chrissie – or anyone else in her shoes – would feel comfortable having to play.

Evert handled Austin's gradual rise graciously, but when the younger girl came within striking distance of her role model, Evert dropped her racket and lit out for the hills. The first important tournament Austin won was the Italian Open in Rome in 1979 when she was sixteen. En route to that victory, Austin ended Evert's record 125-match winning streak on clay.

In September of that same year, Austin beat Evert, 6–4, 6–3, and became the youngest US champion in history at sixteen years and nine months. Early in 1980, Austin demolished Evert in three successive matches in a ten-day span. After the last of those encounters, Evert declared that she was 'burned out' and taking an indefinite rest to reassess her future. In April 1980, Austin was the first woman other than Evert or Navratilova to be ranked number one since 1975.

I'm not cynical enough to suggest that Evert married Lloyd because of Austin, but conjugal bliss did seem to offer Evert a nice way out of a spooky quandary. Evert promised that if her appetite for tennis did not return, she would travel with her husband and provide emotional ballast for him in much the same way that he had through her difficult 1979. So Evert fulfilled her remaining tournament commitments after the three losses to Austin and then joined her husband in Palm Springs, where he was working on his own comeback.

For a while Evert took a whack at what Lloyd called 'the housewife bit.' For three weeks, she swung a mop instead of a racket. Then she began to turn up at the court to watch her husband work out. Then she decided to play for an hour each day, just so she wouldn't get completely out of shape. Soon it was ninety minutes and, by late April, with the Grand Slam season coming up, Evert was once again the lean, mean, fighting machine of yore. Lloyd not only accepted this turn of events, he was magnanimous enough to encourage his wife's aspirations.

Evert entered the Italian and French Opens, and won both events in

1980. At Wimbledon, Evert reached the finals but lost to Goolagong, 6–1, 7–6. Lloyd bombed out in the first round at that same Wimbledon, which brought him to the following realization: 'I was going nowhere fast.' At that point, Lloyd quietly put aside his own ambitions and completed a dramatic and rapid role reversal. Not only did he realize that he was more valuable as the horse than the cart, he flat-out admitted it. And he believed that he could make the marriage work despite the profound change in his role.

Evert won the US Open in 1980, beating the Czech Hana Mandlikova, 5–7, 6–1, 6–1. She turned in a masterpiece of a semi-final victory over Austin in the process. This may have been both the high point and the breaking point of her marriage, because it sealed the issue of whose career would come first in the Lloyd household. As Evert's confidence and ranking grew, Lloyd's declined. The fate that Chris had speculated about so recently was beginning to operate, but not in the way that she had anticipated. (I guess that's why they call it 'fate' in the first place.)

A year of travelling and catering to Chris's needs left Lloyd out of shape and poorly motivated. He couldn't defend the computer points that had created his respectable ranking, and he went into a permanent tailspin. His ranking dropped as low as 356 during his marriage to Evert, and there were numerous painful milestones along the way. At the 1981 US Open, Connors outraged his former fiancée and friend by destroying Lloyd, 6–0, 6–0, 6–2. Chris did not object to the humiliating score (after all, she was a tennis player) as much as the obvious relish with which Connors performed the execution.

Lloyd remained unfailingly amiable, polite, and supportive of his wife, but he was ridiculed by tennis insiders for his fascination with erotic videos. He got great satisfaction out of the success of his wife, but the other players whispered about how completely he had been sucked into the gravitational field of his wife's burning star. When Lloyd did make an effort to rekindle his own career, he became a juicy target for mean-spirited opponents and critics – a habit that wasn't entirely discouraged by John's image as a snappy dresser who, thanks to pastel-mad Ellesse, had matching his-and-hers contracts with his wife. Soon Lloyd was reduced to having to play in the qualifying tournaments held for hopefuls, journeymen, and also-rans vying for a place in upcoming tour events.

'I'd show up for some event with Chris, and we'd stay in the best hotel. I had a nice car, nice clothes, all that. Then, at nine next morning, I'd have to go out and play some guy, and most of the time I could tell what he was thinking: "What's this guy doing here? He's got the coziest set-up in the world, and here he is, trying to take bread out of my mouth. I'm going to whip his ass." '

Lloyd had no appetite for playing under such ugly conditions, and often he merely went through the motions. He failed to live up to his own standards, and he couldn't help but notice that he also failed to live up to those of his wife. 'It hurt Chris more than anything to see me put in a bad performance. It killed her to sit there watching me not put in the effort, even though I was always encouraging her to put in a high degree of commitment. To tell you the truth, I think she felt humiliated.'

Chris, who had drawn great strength and confidence from her husband, was unable to provide the same kind of support for him. That's a tough call, but I'll never forget a remark made by the former tour player and coach Dennis Ralston, who worked with a variety of players including Evert, Sabatini, and Noah. Although he had a fine relationship with Evert, he also knew that she had one thing in common with other great players. 'Every last one of them is a taker,' Ralston said. 'That's just how it is, and you have to live with it.'

Witnesses said that soon little things, such as the fact that Lloyd didn't even know how to drive a car when they married, suddenly seemed emblematic to Evert. During an otherwise idyllic sojourn on Amelia Island Plantation where the Lloyds had a 'touring pro' deal, Evert was disgusted when a harmless snake appeared on their doorstep and Lloyd was too timid to slay the beast.

As Chris's career thrived again, John Lloyd seemed to succumb to the lure of life in the fast lane. The Lloyds went through an unappealing phase together, during which they began to hobnob with a variety of Hollywood celebrities and hipsters.

The Lloyds were invited to dinner at the Beverly Hills home of Ron Samuels, who was the personal manager of his own wife, the star of the popular television series *Wonder Woman*, Lynda Carter. Samuels was a tennis nut, but he also had a reputation as a manipulator of women. Chris was still undecided about her future when she met the Samuelses, but they encouraged her to keep playing. When she decided to do so, they became part of her entourage, although they derived some pleasant – and profitable – side effects from their friendship with the Lloyds. Thanks partly to the offices of Evert, the Lynda Carter/Maybelline Tennis Classic became part of the official calendar of the women's tour, and it attracted many top pros.

Few players have endured a Hollywood phase without ending up looking like guppies in a shark tank, and the Lloyds were no exception. At the time, Navratilova was getting a load of grief for trailing around a bewildering assortment of trainers, advisors, and gofers. Yet after Navratilova beat Evert in the 1983 US Open final, it was Evert who trooped into the press interview room with half a dozen retainers, including Samuels and Carter. I described the scene in some detail in *Tennis* magazine, referring to Samuels, about whom I then knew virtually nothing, as 'some guy in tight jeans and pointy cowboy boots.'

When I next saw Chris a few months later, she sent word through a public relations staffer, Ana Leaird, that she wasn't speaking to me. I wrote Chris a note saying that both of us had been around a little bit too long and had to work together too often to engage in a silly cold war. I gave Leaird the note, but after reading it, she decided that passing it along would only exacerbate the situation. John ultimately broke the impasse by seeking me out and venting his displeasure. He told me that Chris was mostly upset by my characterization of their good friend Samuels. I stood by my point but apologized for any embarrassment I caused Chris by the acerbic way I had made it.

Eventually Samuel and Carter divorced, as did John and Chris. Somewhere along the way their friendships quickly dissolved. Samuels soon took up with fitness-video star Kathy Smith, but by then he was seen less often on the circuit.

The Lloyds also became good friends with the former South African player Johan Kriek and his wife, Tish, a couple of swingers who were part of the nouveau riche scene in Naples, Florida. Tish Kriek was an exhibitionist who used to walk around at tournaments with a serpent in her handbag, and although she knew nothing about tennis, she once sought me out and hit me with both barrels for daring to suggest in print that her husband, who was in his mid-twenties, probably was no longer a legitimate contender for a Grand Slam title. As it turned out, there was no Grand Slam title in Kriek's future, but he did get a Florida ditch named after him (Johan Creek) as well as a reputation for living fast, loose, and loud.

At the beginning of 1982, Chris decided that she and John should spend more time apart, partly so that he could rekindle the flame under his own career. But as she would wryly observe later, 'Absence doesn't make the heart grow fonder. It just makes it grow colder.' At the Australian Open at the end of 1982, Evert had a fling with British pop star Adam Faith. Lloyd, like everyone else in tennis, heard the rumors. He agreed to a trial separation in January 1983, shortly after his wife returned from Australia.

In the ensuing months, John Lloyd became a tennis player again. He reached the round-of-16 at the 1983 Australian Open and the third round at Wimbledon the following June. John and Chris reunited briefly after the 1983 Wimbledon, and Lloyd played a fine US Open. He made the quarter-finals, beating Kriek along the way. Although Lloyd was again punished by Connors in the quarter-finals, he suddenly found himself back in the top twenty. 'He was hurt and angry when he began to play well again,' Chris ruefully told me at the time, 'so if I get any credit for his comeback, it's in a negative way.'

The marriage was on the rocks, even though Lloyd and Evert limped along as a couple until 1986. Apart from being confused, they knew that the staunch Catholic Jimmy Evert, who loved John like a son, would be devastated if they divorced. Both players were also loath to wage an ugly divorce battle. They stayed together long enough to work through whatever resentments each of them felt, and to find a common ground as friends. I don't think that had as much to do with 'image' as it did with their mutual decency and compassion.

Ultimately, the settlement was negotiated by the firm that represented both of them, IMG. The marriage was dissolved gracefully and quietly in 1986, at about the time that an unexpected loss to Helena Sukova in the US Open semi-finals, and a troublesome knee injury, led Evert to take another break from tennis.

That break would last for over five months, a good bit of which Chris spent visiting her friend Navratilova in Aspen. Evert's bum knee did not stop her from skiing and snowmobiling, and her divorce from John had been so slowly and carefully consummated that she was emotionally up to the task when she met the handsome skier Andy Mill.

In a way, Mill satisfied Evert's lifelong desire for a man strong enough to support her without succumbing to domination. He was also full of the classic male qualities that Evert held important. Mill had skied a demanding Olympic downhill race on a painfully injured ankle, finishing sixth. He was also a fly-fisherman, and he not only knew how to drive, he liked racing through the Colorado mountains on a dirt bike. The only thing you could hold against him was his impossibly good looks, which of course many people did.

You could say that it took Evert an entire career to find the kind of man who fulfilled her, or you could say that her career never allowed her to find a suitable man in the demanding environment of pro tennis. You could even say that a deep 'taker's' instinct in Evert ensured that even her traditional desires would not get in the way of her career until she was good and ready – meaning the age at which she had to get out while the getting was good. She did draw new competitive energy from Mill, but the obstacles represented by Navratilova and an assortment of newcomers, including Monica Seles and Steffi Graf, prevented Evert from winning another Grand Slam title. It may have been the best thing that ever happened to her.

Lloyd was unable to sustain his good results in 1984, but he had enjoyed a giddy ride and gotten off the roller coaster set for life. He went on to marry an attractive California girl who would bear him two children, and prove to be a partner in every way that Evert was not. In the end, everybody seemed to win, which is a lot more than can be said for a lot of other people, a lot of the time.

Reflecting on his life with Chris, Lloyd told me, 'Chris is probably the most gracious champion tennis has ever had. But that external sophistication hid the fact that she had a lot of growing up to do. With me, I think she wanted it both ways. And it took her a long time to realize that you couldn't have it both ways – you can't have the macho guy and then the polite, considerate, supportive husband all rolled into one. Jimmy was more the macho guy, and that didn't really satisfy her. I was more the other way, and that didn't do it in the long term, either. She wanted it all, but then she was a person used to having it all.

'But you know, I still don't regret the way I handled it. Sure, I let my tennis go after our marriage. Sure, the celebrity, the publicity, everything suddenly got so much bigger after we became a couple. But the thing is, she had something, that absolute fire, that I didn't. And I truly enjoyed bringing that out in her. Even at the worst of times, I felt satisfied helping my wife. There were wonderful moments at that time when I felt as if we were really a team, accomplishing something that I never could have accomplished alone. I wouldn't trade that for anything. It really was satisfying.'

Don't try to figure it out. You'd have to be a tennis player to understand.

The Courts of Babylon, 1995

Jimmy Connors
RICH KOSTER

If you have ever seen him at his trade, in the flesh, you know immediately that he is special. On the competitive court, he is a small, powerful destroyer. As his coach, Pancho Segura, says: 'The *keed* is a *keeler*.' But his nuclear approach to tennis is best studied, appreciated, when he practices. Watching him hit a tennis ball sets him apart: He is Ted Williams in the batting cage, young Bobby Orr on a rush, Ali displaying all his skill and wile in a sparring session, Jimmy Brown in the broken field.

Jimmy Connors is many things. He is rude, arrogant, foul-mouthed, tasteless, and selfish. On different occasions he has dropped his pants during a practice session, delivered the half-victory sign to a gallery during a match, and gone into the crowd to challenge a fan for remarks made about Christine Evert. He has snubbed the Davis Cup and sued the self-ordained royalty of the sport for millions. He is tennis's Dead-End Kid – with a ton of talent.

He doesn't hit a tennis ball, he explodes it. Like a heavyweight fighter, he seems to put his entire body into every shot. Grunting from the depth of his stomach, he smashes each ball as if it were his last. It is almost frightening to watch him attack. His control is incredible. The ball is blasted toward certain orbit, but rifles to the baseline, into the corners – and seldom lands more than inches over the tape. He has Marciano's lust for practice, staying on the court endlessly. Not since he first picked up a racket at the age of three back in East St Louis has he ever been able to get enough tennis.

His dedication to the game is as much a part of him as his raunchy jokes and deplorable court manners. Indeed, in the years to come, the former may be recognized as his essence, while the other recedes into his maturity. If he is not ranked No. 1 in any given year, it is of little consequence. In the mid-seventies, Connors is the best tennis player in the world. There are hordes who may not like it, but few who would dispute it.

Of course, he is a target of continuing court crusade. He is the white Jack Johnson, the Caucasian Ali. Tennis is in a panic searching for a traditionalist to teach him a hard lesson. The result is a ton of dollars and a forest of headlines for this brash gunfighter who rules international tennis from the unlikely throne of Las Vegas's Caesar's Palace.

While Bill Riordan muses, 'Could there have been a Jimmy Connors without a Bill Riordan? I wonder,' there are those who consider Connors an inevitability – regardless of the Irish Barnum who is generally conceded most of the credit for Jimmy's development. One who doesn't believe Riordan was particularly essential is Dick McGovern, a Belleville, Illinois, attorney and Savings and Loan executive who is Connors' primary financial advisor.

'Riordan?' he says. 'He took a natural and staged a promotion. Segura? He was handed a razor and merely sharpened it. Jimmy Connors was trained to be exactly where he is, exactly what he is. He's supposed to be where he is. Gloria and Too Mom believed it. There was nothing about him which would make you think he'd be the best. He wasn't the biggest or the fastest. He has small hands, almost feminine hands. But she had faith in him. Gloria was determined no one would control or own Jimmy. He was raised to be his own tennis player. He was raised to be the greatest; not just another player. Riordan and Segura like to take credit and Gloria takes a lot of abuse as a stage mother, but she made Jimmy a tennis player.'

McGovern watched the Connors scenario unfold, from the first back-yard court in East St Louis to Wimbledon, Forest Hills, and Las Vegas. He has been Jimmy's money advisor for years, and with Connors more and more on his own, the handling of his finances has eclipsed the need for promoting his image.

To McGovern, Jimmy Connors is 'a big business. His inventory is money. And he has few bad debts.' McGovern refuses to confirm that his client grossed $1 million in 1975, but he doesn't rule it out as a ballpark figure. He readily emphasizes that when Jimmy retires – regardless of when that is – 'He'll easily have $1 million, and more, in spite of taxes, expenses, and everything else. And that's not a sport page figure, not some accounting myth.

'You have to understand,' says McGovern, 'they don't play football in Sweden. This isn't Joe Namath or Kareem Jabbar. With the possible exception of Muhammad Ali and Pele, Jimmy Connors is close to being the best known, up and coming athlete in the world. His opportunities are fantastic. He can play tennis year round. His taxes and expenses are brutal. He pays taxes in ten countries. But he made $300,000 in an afternoon.'

What of the future? Now that Connors has joined the Davis Cup, is the WCT far behind? 'When the numbers are right,' McGovern replies, 'things can be worked out.'

McGovern disputes the accepted belief that it was Riordan who kept Connors out of the union, the ATP. 'Gloria wanted him in tennis on his own terms,' the attorney says. 'She wanted him to be an example to other tennis players. If he could do it, they could. And she didn't want him thrown into week-after-week battles for survival. The design was Gloria's. The money was secondary. Jimmy never had any. He doesn't lead a wild life; he doesn't have wild cars. He doesn't have any extravagances. He doesn't think in those terms.'

Gloria Thompson Connors came up through tennis's barnacled tradition. Like her mother before her, she was a nationally ranked player, and after marriage, she turned most of her energies to teaching. Her mother, Bertha Thompson – Too Mom – taught Gloria, and the two of them taught Jimmy and other young St Louisans. Too Mom would give the instructions, and Gloria would demonstrate. Their classes were overflowing, but when Jimmy and his brother John began to emerge, Gloria and Bertha focused on them.

Gloria Connors is a rather severe woman who doesn't suffer interviews graciously. An active woman in her late forties, she has returned to Belleville and teaching tennis at $12 per half-hour. If there is a contradiction inherent in Connors' court style and the fact that his teachers were women, Gloria can resolve it. 'My teaching theory,' she says, 'has always been to punch the ball. Jimmy was brought up to belt the ball, to punch it, not just paddle it. We emphasized power, not finesse. We made a study of it.

'We didn't teach him the two-handed backhand as a tactic; it was just that he was so little, he needed both hands to pick up the racket. He could hardly swing it. But he had a game by the time he was five. He hits deep and hard, and keeps it in. He plays power tennis. And he learned it from two women. He is the first world's men's champion ever developed by two women.'

The Connors image doesn't particularly disturb Gloria, although she believes it's exaggerated. 'A lot of it is uncalled for,' she says. 'There were others instrumental in creating that image. Jimmy's so different on and off the court. But I taught him he had to be a tiger. If he didn't kill, he'd get killed. When he was a youngster, if I had the chance I'd hit the ball down his throat. "See, Jimmy," I'd say, "even your mother will do it to you." So, I guess I have to take the credit or blame for his court behavior. When he releases pressure, the things he does and says, when he throws a racket or uses bad language – that bothers me to a point. But tennis has become such a big business, there's so much pressure, so much at stake.

'People say that Jimmy just exploded in a year or two, but that's not true. He was nationally ranked at nine, he won the Orange Bowl at ten, the nationals at sixteen, the NCAA as a college freshman. He was a pro at nineteen and No. 1 in the world at twenty and twenty-one. At seventeen, he was beating people like Roy Emerson.

'He began beating me at sixteen. That was the day I had been waiting for. Jimmy was a finished player when we turned him over to Pancho Segura. He had all the strokes. Segura taught him strategy, but he was a finished player. He just needed experience. He had to get more practice, competition. That was why we sent him to California. I felt very early, at the age of nine, ten, or eleven, that he would be No. 1. It always thrilled me to watch him. He's colorful. He does so much on the court. He does thrilling things. He's such a hard worker, and he loves the game.

'Why has he stayed independent? Because he feels he shouldn't have to ask anyone if he can hit a tennis ball. A player's ability should determine if he plays. Tennis shouldn't be ruled. If you have the ability, you should be able to play.'

Gloria Connors seldom allows any softness to show through, but her pride in her mother and son, and their relationship, is an exception. Of Too Mom, she says with uncharacteristic feeling: 'I just don't think she'd have any buttons left. She'd be so proud. She saw Jimmy beat Smith; she saw the beginning of it. She was his biggest booster. She always said, "Jimbo, you're the greatest." '

Almost any way you want to interpret the statement, 'Jimbo, you're the greatest,' it's open to debate. The tennis world is hardly unanimous in its evaluation of Jimmy Connors, his talent, or – especially – his personality.

Connors himself says: 'I like my image. It's me. I'm a louse, but if you're going to be a louse, I say be a good one. I play to win and I play to entertain. It's fun for me and it's fun for the fans. I play tennis for two reasons. I like to hit balls and I like to entertain. My behavior gets people involved, and I think that's what the game needs. A bad guy? I guess people pay to see me get beat.'

If they do, the antagonism only revs up Connors. He is perhaps at his best with his back to the wall. 'I like to have the fans against me,' he claims. 'I want to do everything I can to get them against me more. When they're yelling at me, I really get into the match. I guess I'm trying to tell them that no matter how much they hate me, they have to respect the way I play.'

That respect he has, from his admittedly prejudiced mother to Pancho Gonzales. 'Certainly,' says Gonzales, 'it's premature to go too deeply into that all-time business. But he's already better than Ken Rosewall ever was. For his size, he's the hardest hitter I've ever seen. He has an instinctive knowledge, a feeling for the game that most players don't gain until their late twenties. And he works to his full potential. Nastase, for instance, works to about 85 percent of his potential. You have to be able to put Jimmy on the defensive to have any chance. The times I played him, I had him in trouble a lot with my serve. After that, I was just as afraid of his ground game as the rest of them.'

Segura says of his pupil: 'Jimmy is the closest thing we have to a complete player. He can do everything. When a guy's playing Jimmy, he doesn't know what to expect. Jimmy will stay back and play base line, then rush the net. He can lob you or beat you down the alley with a winner. He's impossible to predict.'

A sampler of opinions on Connors from players would include these observations:

How can you compare Jimmy Connors to Rod Laver? Laver won two grand slams and every other tournament in the world a number of times. – Brian Fairlie

He hasn't got any friends, because he doesn't give a damn about anybody else. – Tom Okker

The guy seems to make himself more unpopular every time he plays. He won't play if he figures there's a chance he might lose in the finals. The sponsors don't like it and the fans will have to be contended with sometime. – Rod Laver

He's always complaining and doing bad things. But not just against the players. He talks against the crowd too much. – Bjorn Borg

I've known him for a long time. I grew up with him in junior tennis. He's always been kind of a loner, him and his mother, and then him, his mother, and Riordan. When the guys are joking in the locker room, he's never part of it. Frankly, because of some of the

things he's done on the court, the guys don't want any part of him.
– Brian Gottfried

I get along with Connors. And there can be no question of his ranking. No one ever dominated tennis like he did the past few years, especially 1974. – Jeff Borowiak

Jimmy spent a night at my house in 1973. It was very pleasant. I could like him. He's a nice kid, but I can't get to him. None of us can. He's been covered up by his mother and his manager. – Marty Riessen

Sometimes, I feel very sorry for him. Maybe 100 percent of the American players don't dislike him, but there must be 98 percent. Before Vegas, people came up to me at cocktail parties and they'd tell me they didn't want me to beat him, they wanted me to kill him. Kill him, mind you, and those were Americans, and I'm an Australian. He never did anything to me, so I was surprised at their viciousness. – John Newcombe

I think the day will come when he outgrows his nasty habits. And I will be the first to say, 'Welcome back.' – Arthur Ashe

Connors, actually, may not be all that different from a host of international tennis stars, especially Americans. If he is, it is more by degree than kind. He is an extreme example of the winning syndrome, of a young man with a narrow focus and a remarkable talent.

'Tennis,' he says, 'has always been the only thing in my life. And it's only recently that I've become aware that it's not the only thing in the world. When other kids were playing baseball and football and running with the guys, I was always in there practicing my tennis. I never had a part-time job. Even when it came to my school work, I just did what I had to, just enough so I wouldn't flunk out. From the time I was a little kid, I knew I had the potential and it was up to me to develop it.

'I grew up in Belleville, Illinois. When I was about seven or eight, the only way I could play was to go to a court in East St Louis, an hour's bus ride from my home. And the only way I could get there was either with my mother or my grandmother. I always felt so uncomfortable, because when I'd get there, none of the other kids would play with me. I wasn't part of their gang. And the only people I could get to play with me were two women. It was like the three of us had our own little gang. I'll always think of my grandmother as one of the greatest women who ever lived. Sometimes I think it bothers people because there has never been another world champion who was groomed by a woman.

'I still respect Bill Riordan, and I will always be grateful for how he promoted my career. It used to be everywhere I went, Riordan went, too. But now I'm at a point in my life where I want to clean my own house the way I want, how I want, and when I want.'

On his image, Jimmy says: 'Whether people know it or not, money is not what makes me happy. If it were the only thing in my life, I would work much harder than I do. I almost bought a Rolls-Royce last year. But when I got behind the wheel, I looked like a little chauffeur. So I didn't buy it.

'Arthur Ashe? I think he's kind of a weird guy himself, and he should keep his mouth shut. With friends like him, who needs enemies? Look, I'm twenty-three and I still have plenty of time. You have to expect to win some and lose some; it's all part of the game. But still, I consider myself very fortunate, and I wouldn't trade my life for anything. I wake up each morning happy to see the sun is still there and shining.

'I've never believed in giving up. People are aware now I have the ability, but they don't know I also have the guts. Sometimes I get carried away and I end up making a fool of myself. In the future, I'm going to try to watch it. I'm not apologizing, I'm just saying I've made some mistakes.

'The fans? Sure, sometimes they make me mad. They hurt my pride. It hurts my ego. You don't think I felt hurt inside when I was playing Manuel Orantes at the US Open and all the people from my own country were rooting for him? You don't think it bothered me that right before that match, a group of people came up and told me how much they wanted me to win, and then I see these hypocrites rooting for Orantes? And whether people know it or not, there's nothing that thrills me as much as when young kids come up and ask me for my autograph. I don't kid myself; I'm thankful for the few friends I have.'

When you listen to Connors, trying to explain himself, grudgingly admitting his vulnerability, his mother's warning keeps coming back: 'See, Jimmy, even your mother will do it to you . . .'

What of Jimmy Connors as he goes his own way? 'Jimmy's over twenty-one,' says Bill Riordan. 'He's still going to play the challenge matches. Basically, I started him out. I wrote the script. Now, he's making a million a year and I want to slow down. I'm fifty-six now. What's going to happen in tennis? I don't know. But I'll be around. If only because of Kramer, I'll stay. He would be the one thing to keep me around. I'm tennis's vigilante. I have no intention of getting out.'

The Tennis Bubble, 1976

Becker

GORDON BURN

'Hit hard, play loud, leave a trail of broken strings,' it says across the sweat-slicked back of the young American player, Luke Jensen. He slips off the practice court straight into the clutches of the little Riviera tennis buds, flaunting their jeans *l'authentique blue* and *le vrai black*, their funkoid *chaussures de basket* and *nouveaux Ray-Ban circulaires*, while their mothers and grandmothers work their Chanel and petition for the best (Rainier-rubbing) positioning on the lunchtime *terrasse* at the Monte Carlo Country Club (MCCC). 'La saison est lancée, et fort bien,' as it will be announced in the following morning's *Nice-Matin*.

The slogan Jensen is wearing is a cheeky reworking of Mark McCormack's perennial exhortation to the suits of the super-corporate International Marketing Group: 'Work hard, work long, work smart.'

Although he earned something in the region of $200,000 in prize money in 1991, Jensen is part of the post-Agassi, fuck-Persil, anti-jock school of grime and grunge. The look is Mickey Rourke as the LA poet Charles Bukowski in *Barfly*, and the skid-row tailoring – the whacked-out T-shirt is matched with shineyed-up chopped-off denims – sits well with the lank hair, the goatee beard, the bitten nails, the bar-bum pallor, the lively gleam in the barely open eyes.

Jensen's face is difficult to read, set as it is against a strip of flashing sea and a bleached-out sky across which hang-gliders drift blithely as they ride the thermals of the high Corniche. His face is blurred away at the edges and smeared looking, the way it would be if you glimpsed it through smoky glass.

But enough remains to see that Jensen, ranked in the low-hundreds on the ATP computer, is still on the up-curve of achievement, hungry for scalps: there are no signs yet of satiety or self-disgust; no hints of jet-droop, fan-fatigue, of the scooped-out jaded look of realized ambition. This by itself is enough to distinguish him from the player practising on a back court whom the crowd is now surging past Jensen in a feeding frenzy to see.

Pat Cash once said that the courts at Monte Carlo made him feel more than usually like a performing animal. 'They're, like, sunk down so people walk along the top, and it's surrounded by a fence and there's two tennis players in there, and the people sort of stroll around and look at you. You feel like a zoo.'

In Boris Becker's case, better make that a monkey menagerie. Becker is out having a hit with his Davis Cup teammate, Michael Stich, the player who demolished him in three sets in last year's Wimbledon final. That match was remarkable for the anguished wailing coming from Becker and for the vituperative verbal punishment he directed at himself; between games he screamed into his towel and even tried to take bites out of it; occasionally between points he smashed himself about the head with his racket or beat his head against the backstop canvas.

It was a performance I'd seen repeated eight days earlier in Barcelona, as Becker found himself going out in the first round to a young Spanish player languishing 200 or 300 places below him on the computer. The match had gone on court twenty-four hours late because of rain, and this was a problem. Then, as he threw the ball up to serve, Becker found that a 'Winston' advertising blimp was in his sightline.

Signboards all over the court, of course, as well as everybody on it, were imprinted with either the Winston name or that of Renault, Perrier, IBM or Reebok, Winston's co-sponsors. Two bims in red Winston livery would flank Becker at the post-match press conference, a further reminder of the ongoing, global, mega-dollar transaction in which he is a star participant. But pursuing their corporate objectives in the air-space where he was struggling to stay in a tennis match was an ad opportunity too many. Becker ditched his racket and kicked the balls away in exasperation.

He has complained loudly over the years about the market-obsessed environment in which he has to play, and about having to be logoed to the eyeballs every time he sets foot in a public place. He has talked of having 'no inner calm, no peace'; about being 'a product, a puppet on a string, a marionette'.

His public statements have echoed John McEnroe's recently expressed opinion that: 'They are trying to turn us into money whores. It's obscene.' Becker's personal worth has been put at around $30 million but it could be greater by a factor of as much as five if he didn't give the finger to most of the commercial opportunities that come his way. 'They say "a

million". And then you say "No",' he has said. 'And then they offer –
because they think everybody has his price – three million. And then you
say "No" again. It feels good to know that I don't come cheap.'

He has contributed to Greenpeace and frequently donates money to
charity. He has spoken up for squatters and the unemployed and helped
Ion Tiriac, his manager, build an orphans' village in Romania which will
be completed by the end of the year.

'I know him very well because he was living in my home many, many
times,' says Nikki Pilic, the German Davis Cup captain. 'And Boris is
one interesting person. He is all contradiction. He is *all* contradiction.
For me he is like the painter Van Gogh. He's not . . . *usual*. He is making
a lot of moves in the very last moment, and always the right moves. He
didn't live at *all* normal life, and now he is thinking recently he wants
to live a normal life.'

'I always tried to live like a normal guy growing up,' McEnroe told
Tennis magazine earlier this year. 'I think that urge for normalcy, together
with getting married and having kids, helped save me from becoming a
burned-out, completely bitter cynic by thirty. That's why I feel for Boris.
One second he can't be better, the next he can't be worse. I can see it –
it's like looking in a mirror.'

Boris-watchers are constantly on the look-out for the outward signs of
fresh stress-cracks in his psyche. The towel chewing and big-match head
banging are easy. Then there's the refusal of eye contact, the rapid
blinking, the stammer . . .

The last three were all in evidence when Becker was eventually persuaded to take questions in the press tent in Barcelona. Unlike Borg who,
in his twilight years, has learned to trot out blandnesses and well-
lubricated generalizations, Becker, desperate to be 'real', still labours
under the misapprehension that he is expected to engage with his ques-
tioner and actually *say something* in these rituals of mutual humiliation.

He sat under the Winston banner, between the Winston bims, behind
a sign that said 'IBM', and gave the appearance of being somebody not
only hemmed in by a business process against which he feels powerless,
but of a man stigmatized by the burry logos he is obliged to wear on
his chest, arms, thigh and ankle: half-bulletin board, half-person. The
scruffiness – ratty hair, smudged forehead, a scurvy three-day growth –
was perhaps in reaction to this. What was he? A survivor of the McDonald's gunman, motorway carnage, the mad axe man, the towering inferno?
A blind diagnosis would be post-traumatic stress disorder. How does it

feel? Sometimes he stared out with what looked like hate in his eyes. Afterwards, on the short walk back to the players' lounge, few felt brave enough to intrude on his particular private grief.

'He's in a foul mood,' Richard Evans reported back. 'He doesn't want to talk the way he's feeling because he thinks he'll probably say something he'll regret.' Evans's card says 'Vice-President, Communications, the Association of Tennis Professionals' and he is one of the few channels of communication Becker has left open to the world.

'Some days he can be very chatty,' Evans says. 'Other days I can walk into the locker-room and he looks like he's never seen me before in his life.' Becker's current coach, Tomas Smid, is forbidden by the terms of his contract from talking to the press. Gunther Bosch, who discovered Becker as an eight-year-old and brought him to the attention of Ion Tiriac eight years later, became an unperson when he put his name to a picture-book of Boris at work and play.

And still the lady from *Hola!* ('I can't go in the restaurant in these old ski clothes,' she said of an outfit that could have done service at Stringfellows) was at a loss to know why Boris refused to throw open the doors of his love nest to her, unlike that sweet Stefan Edberg whose wedding she was covering in Sweden the following week. 'Do you think the new Boris girlfriend is attractive?' she wanted to know. '*Do* you? The black one? I don't think she is good-looking at all.'

Becker once talked about the 'eroticism' he sensed between himself and the people who come to watch him play. 'I know they are silently looking me up and down. I always react in the same embarrassed way. I bend down and tie my shoes although it's unnecessary. They don't only want to see you – they want to have you.'

The gallery crowding round to watch Becker practising with Michael Stich at Monte Carlo is a shifting one: once they have fixed him on their Nikomatics and Akais and Supazooms (the auto-focuses noiselessly shifting and stirring in an oddly sensual way) they get bored watching his power serves and singing topspun back hands and athleticism around the court and wander on.

The girl with the bare midriff, though, has established herself in a prime position at the end of the baseline, just above where Becker is serving, and she's giving way to nobody. She is shaking with the effort of maintaining her posture (no unsightly folding flesh). But she is also shaking with something else. Behind the shield of her dark glasses, her eyes never stray from Becker.

'Bello! . . . Bello!' the middle-aged Italian woman standing next to me croons repeatedly. 'Oh! . . . Boom-boom!'

Unlike Stich, who appears loose, unselfconscious, Becker has the by now familiar look of somebody who feels they are, as he has admitted, 'game to be hunted'; somebody who is finding life 'a lot of hard work for very little fun'.

'Look, my friend,' the manager Tiriac says. 'If you don't want to be there and looked at in the arena, go in the factory where nobody is going to look at you. *Ever*. Make your fuckin' $2,000 a month and shut your goddam big fuckin' mouth. You know, I'm sure that if Boris would go right now to Moscow and work three years in a homeless organization there, he's going to appreciate differently the value of the life when he comes out. You cannot take only the good things and wipe out the other things.'

Tiriac first caught Becker in action on the same court where he has just been practising, in Monte Carlo in 1984. Ilie Nastase was yesterday's papers; Guillermo Vilas's playing days were coming to an end, and Tiriac was sniffing round for hot young blood.

'The guy couldn't run, the guy couldn't do anything,' he says now of the fifteen-year-old Boris Becker. 'It was the worst athlete I ever saw in my life. But he was bleeding on the knees, he was bleeding on his mouth, he was diving all over, he wanted very badly. I mean, I can make an athlete. I don't have a problem. Give him bloody six months on the stairs, three hours a day, comes an athlete and plays like a machine. No problem. I can make him hit a tennis ball from any*where*.

'So. He wanted very badly. He had this will-power; the desire. And I say, okay, I will take another one, then thank you very much, goodbye. Looked like a very determinated kid.'

The hospitality tent where we are sitting, complete with sun divans and a butler butling and a large sign bearing Tiriac's name, is evidence of the progress he has made in the world. He grew up in Romania – 'I started from very, very low, and very hard. I made my way up with my shoulders and my hands' – and has little patience with Becker's carpings about the privations of the celebrity life.

'I know that Boris is just a normal teenager,' he says, 'although he's twenty-five now. I look at him going through *stages*. And he went through a very idealistic stage.'

This is thought to have had its beginnings in a visit Becker made to his former girlfriend Karen Schultz's family in East Germany in the last days of the Cold War. He has recently come out against a reunified Germany staging the Olympic Games in the year 2000, and condemned the growing support for neo-Nazi groups in Europe. 'Stop this hatred, shocked Becker begs Nazi racists,' ran the headlines earlier this year over reports that his girlfriend, Barbara Feltus, a black woman, was facing an 'unbelievable' daily barrage of abuse, 'which has left her feeling terrified'.

'I now experience nationalism,' Becker said. 'So much attention is on my skin and the colour of my girlfriend's skin. It shows me how many extreme right-wing people there are now in Germany.'

'I think Boris is very brave to say all these things,' Nikki Pilic says. 'I think if he lives in a democracy, and Boris Becker is a big product of that democracy, he should express his opinion. I don't have the feeling he goes with a black girlfriend just because he wants to provoke somebody.'

Tiriac would second this. He draws the line, however, at Boris's championing of squatters' rights. 'I think there was *nothing* in it. But what this shows is that Boris is a human being who is much more interested in other things than in a tennis ball.' Pause. 'Very important, though. *Fuckin'* important, tennis balls. If you hit one less, you go, and nobody is talking to you any more.'

I asked him how frustrating it is for him to have Becker giving the thumbs down to virtually all the deals he puts together.

'He doesn't make 10 per cent of his money on the court. [Becker won $1,228,708 in 1991.] He can double that, or triple that. I could make him $2 million tomorrow morning. More.

'So to deal with Boris is not easy. But it is his life. I am very philosophical about this thing. It doesn't matter. The money I make with Boris is almost . . . idealistic. I put forward on the table whatever I think he should take. After that it's his privilege. It is very easy to say no when you make ten times over what you need.

'But to return to your *frustrating* for a moment. I am frustrated because he didn't win another ten Grand Slams by now. I think this guy could have won three times more. Five times more. He has the possibility. Now the question in life is would he have been happier? *I* don't know. He's a very emotional young man. He looks on the outside completely different than he is inside. He's a very mild, sensitive human being, Boris. He's still at twenty-five to find himself. He's trying to *find* himself.'

(269)

And his increasingly erratic behaviour on court and off these days?

'I take it to mean he is a human. I take it to mean that he is going along the same route that they all go along. They cannot cope. They cannot difference the good and the bad; they cannot difference the right and the wrong; they cannot difference the white and the black; they cannot difference when to say no and when to say yes. They're going step by step every day in another life – another level. Then it is very important who you have around. Jeezus. It's much more important almost than your original parents at that stage. Your surroundings, they make you or break you.

'But I can tell you this, my friend. I prefer a Boris to somebody who goes there every day with the same face, comes out with the same face, is going to die with the same face, and doesn't *live*. This guy lives. It's *life* in him. For good or for bad. Boris is a guy that is a fair guy once you get to his heart.'

'Youthful success especially can mean that one becomes symbolic before one is real,' Leo Braudy writes in *The Frenzy of Renown*. 'Created by others before one can create oneself . . . in the course of the twentieth century, the public's ability to create instant fame and thereby satisfy its own sense of fulfilment becomes more powerful, even as the stresses on those so plucked out and ennobled become more severe.'

Becker operates within a forcefield that only his girlfriend, it seems, and Tiriac can safely enter. At home in Monaco, he doesn't answer the phone before ten a.m. and after that it is likely you will have to communicate with him through Barbara Feltus. This applies even to Tiriac.

At Barcelona he didn't want to talk to me because he had a match coming up, and then he didn't want to talk because he was beaten. A meeting in Monte Carlo was set up for the following week and then, twenty-four hours before it was due to happen, cancelled.

Over three days, the time was never judged right to tell Becker that I was hanging around hoping to see him. Tiriac said he would intervene, but then Boris was never available. Kicking my heels in a Monaco bar one midnight I watched Tiriac stroll in with a woman companion. This, it transpired, was the former Monaco police chief's daughter, Benedicte Courtin, whom Tiriac expelled from Wimbledon in 1987, claiming she was 'distracting' Becker from the defence of his title. Tiriac said he would call Boris 'first thing' in the morning. He called first thing, got Barbara Feltus, and I was on the next flight home.

There are two ways of getting to Nice airport from Monaco: by road, along the Côte d'Azur or by helicopter. Within seconds the helicopter is over water, dragging its shadow across the swimming pools and sherbety villas of Monte Carlo, Ville Franche, Cap Ferrat and other places that live, as the brochures have it, where luxury lives; spinning up and out of Boris Becker's life – sphere, star, speck, to quote Updike – like the sweetest-struck ball.

Somewhere down there, Boris still wasn't answering his phone.

Esquire, 1992

Educating Andre
MARTHA SHERRILL

It was a wet, overcast morning in Las Vegas when the journey to Brooke Shields began. The private jet was beaded with desert rain. As Andre Agassi looked out the small porthole, he raised his middle finger, then chuckled a little sweetly. A photographer was on the tarmac, taking pictures for *Sports Illustrated*. The day before, the guy had said something in passing that kind of pissed Agassi off. He made mention of the old days, Agassi's more troubled times, of his misspent youth.

'I work ten times harder than him,' Agassi said softly, shaking his shaved head, 'and he has the nerve to make a crack about something I did as a kid.'

He stretched out on the cool gray leather bucket seats. He was ruminating, philosophizing. His handsome butt settled into one seat. His babyish legs, unformed and not particularly remarkable, were resting in another. He wore a black nylon warm-up. His white-and-gray sneakers were crazy-ugly. On TV, sometimes, he can look a little evil. But now, with his tonsured skull and quizzical expression, he seemed monkish and benign. Even his sharp goatee and two silver hoop earrings – the size of thick wedding rings – weren't lending an air of danger to his overall mien. And he said the most unusual things.

His youth had not been wasted, he said. He had no regrets. He didn't believe in regrets. Regrets, he said, 'make you who you are today.' So, if he did have regrets, he'd be happy about them. Unless he didn't like who he was today or what had become of him. But he does. He does like who he is today, very much.

He is 'the biggest tennis star on the planet,' according to a newspaper in the Bay Area, where he's just won another tournament. He is also a twenty-five-year-old with his own jet and pilot. He needs the jet, he says. It saves him energy.

He competes every other week, with exhibition matches in between. Usually, if he wins, and he's been mostly winning lately – catapulting from a ranking below twenty to number two in the last year – he swiftly removes his baggy Nike T-shirt, balls it up, throws it in the air, and barely waits around to see which screaming teenage girl or middle-aged man catches it. Without too much stopping, except to glance at his Swiss Army watch, he accepts another absurd trophy, smiles amply, utters several profound remarks for the press, and then, almost immediately, showers and changes and gets himself to the local airport, hastens to the sky, and soon winds up – he likes to guess, to the minute, when he'll arrive at her door – in the embrace of his great big love, Brooke Shields.

Everything hits him in the heart, it seems. When he's away from tennis, his eyes turn sweet and rainy. Talking about Shields, he is so open and so unjaded, you have to swoon along with him, hang on for a jet ride through the Land of Earnestness or drown in his spiritual depth. 'It's us on a raw level,' he says, 'that's the most special.'

We rolled slowly down the runway, amid a long, empty landscape, and a pyramid came into view, then palm trees, then a sphinx: the Luxor hotel. We lifted off, rose above the oasis and Agassi's hometown, and it seemed like an exodus of sorts, from a phony fabulous Egypt to New York City, a place that might be just as much so. As soon as the jet reached cruising altitude, Agassi got himself a cup of coffee. He took some milk in it, three sugars, and a packet of Equal.

For years, Agassi did seem determined to waste his talents. He was famous for eating crappy food, for not practicing his game, for getting fat. There were stories about 'tanked' sets, how he lost deliberately and faked injuries. He turned pro at sixteen and seemed exhausted and ambivalent by twenty-three. On a losing streak and injured, he was dumped by his longtime coach. Dumped as a failure.

'Maybe I was rewarded too quickly,' he said. 'I came at a time when tennis needed somebody – when tennis was looking for another American. I had so much notoriety before I really accomplished great things. For me to be doing Nike commercials and Canon commercials and never winning a Grand Slam tournament, that left me with a bad rap – all image, no substance.'

True enough, his clothes got him the attention that his tennis didn't anymore. He wore baggy shorts and black socks and looked like a mall rat. He wasn't grown-up enough to wear white at Wimbledon. And what was with the stringy hair? At a time when American tennis was in a terrific slump, people said he was good for tennis, but somehow, he was bad for tennis, too.

As a toddler, Andre Agassi was initiated into the game as if it were something everybody had to learn, like walking, like holding a fork. His dad, Emmanuel 'Mike' Agassi, was such a fanatical tennis instructor that he had developed an entire routine for learning the game. Day after day, there were as many as eight ball machines on the court at the old Tropicana hotel, shooting out ball after ball after ball at the Agassi kids – Rita, Phillip, Tami, and Andre.

'We loved the rain,' says Phillip Agassi. 'It meant one day when we didn't have to play.'

Mike Agassi is Armenian but was born and raised in Iran. He came to the United States in 1952; he didn't know any English, but he knew how to box. He had been on Iran's Olympic team, and in Chicago, he was a Golden Gloves champ. He was supposed to turn professional one night at the old Madison Square Garden in 1955, but when the boxer he was scheduled to fight backed out, Mike was matched up with an experienced opponent, a guy with forty or fifty fights behind him. It was a long shot, but if Mike fought him, he was told, he'd have a much quicker shot at the championship.

But instead of going into the ring, Mike Agassi crawled out a window. 'He went right into the locker room,' says Phillip, 'and jumped out the window to the street and left. He took a train back to Chicago, and I think that night he bought a tennis racket.'

He panicked?

'No, he didn't panic,' says Phillip. 'He just didn't want to box anymore.'

Tennis became his passion, and Mike Agassi threw himself at the sport, body and soul. With his wife, Betty, he headed west, in the direction of California. He hated the cold and wanted to find a place where tennis was played year-round. When he couldn't find work in California, he backtracked to Las Vegas. Betty found a job at the Nevada State Employment Agency, where she would work for thirty years. Mike drifted from one part-time job to the next, working at casinos at night as a waiter or a showroom captain. During the day, he taught tennis.

The two older kids were 'guinea pigs,' says Phillip. Mike bought ball machines and took them apart, rejiggered them to hold three hundred to four hundred balls, and lined them up along one end of the court at the Tropicana. And they blasted out balls until, at the end of the day, there'd be ten thousand on the court. But that was okay because Mike had gotten huge blowers – those giant fans used to dry baseball fields after rain – to blow all the balls to one side; then he got out his invention that the Agassi brood came to call 'the pusher,' an eight-foot-long beam of steel on wheels that pushed the balls into one corner. Then Mike brought out 'the scooper,' a massive shovel for picking up hundreds of balls at one time.

Andre was the baby and first played tennis for his father at age two and a half, with a racket that Mike had taped to his hand. Before that, a tennis ball had been dangled over Andre's crib to focus his eyes, and he was given a balloon to bat around – hand-eye coordination being everything. Later, he played against his father's students and against the stars who blew through town. At four, Andre played Jimmy Connors. At five, his family moved into a better house, where Mike had built his own tennis court. By six, having spent most days of his life looking over a net, Andre had the Agassi moves down: Hit the ball early, and hit it hard.

'Dad raised me to play,' says Andre. 'I never considered doing anything else. As a kid, all you know is what you see around you, and tennis was all I saw. Why would I want to do anything else?'

Andre started playing in tournaments at seven – early even for tennis – and won his first nine matches. Every other weekend, the family took to the highway in their station wagon and drove to Southern California – ten hours each way – staying all together in one room of a Motel 6, so the kids could play in junior tournaments, where, incidentally, Andre first encountered Pete Sampras and Michael Chang and Jim Courier.

When Andre was sent to live at the Nick Bollettieri Tennis Academy in Florida after eighth grade, he was shocked to learn how bad he could feel. At the famous tennis facility, he was given the chance to challenge other great players his age – and was soon counted among a group of promising Bollettieri protégés that included Aaron Krickstein and Jimmy Arias – but Agassi was homesick. During the day, he was dressing in black, indulging in black moods and tantrums, smashing his racket against a wall when he lost.

'I hated it there,' says Andre, 'hated growing up in Florida, three thousand miles away from home. But the only way I could get out of that academy was to succeed. So that became my inspiration: to do well so that I could escape.'

His brother, Phillip, is a little shorter and darker than Andre and has considerably less hair. He was bald, pretty much, by his late twenties – like a number of his uncles and his grandfather, he says. Now, at thirty-two, Phillip wears a toupee – curly, loose, natural-looking, and soft – but most tennis fans remember him in the stands without it, as the TV camera panned to him during all of Andre's tournaments.

After Andre turned pro at sixteen Phillip traveled everywhere with his brother, sleeping on the floor of Andre's motel room. He booked the hotels and flights, planned meals, rented cars and vans, called the racket stringer, and tended to the endless minutiae of traveling around the world half of the year. 'I've heard that Andre missed his childhood,' says Phillip. 'I did, too.'

And though Andre thought turning pro would be his escape, he still didn't feel any better. There was lots of acting out to do, mostly with his hair. First he shaved his head, then grew a mohawk, then dyed the mohawk blond. At a match in Florida, he turned up wearing jeans, lipstick, and eyeliner. And he'd pierced his ears.

He hid himself, went in disguise. Underneath, of course, Andre was still Andre – competitive and anal, a perfectionist – but outside, he was loose. He told himself that if he looked a certain way, looked cool, he would be cool inside, too. It was a way he could take the pressure off himself. 'I was looking for a break,' says Andre about turning pro, 'but there wasn't a break. I might have gotten away from the discipline of the academy, but then came the criticisms and judgments, getting that nickname: the bad boy of tennis.'

At the end of his first year, he was ranked ninety-one. At the end of his second, he was twenty-five. In 1988, his third year on the tour, he became number three. And around this time, he began wondering what it was all leading to – the matches, the traveling, the ceaseless need to win. Eventually, Andre found God and joined Meadows Fellowship Church in west Las Vegas. On the tour, he got together with Michael Chang to study the Bible. He also talked about religion with reporters. Nowadays, he's generally pretty quiet. He doesn't 'feel the need,' he says, 'to pick up God's slack so much anymore.

'Faith is an important thing. I guess what makes me feel good about all this madness is the sense of peace I have in my daily growing understanding of God's plan for me.'

By 1990, Mike Agassi's plan for Andre was being realized. His ranking stabilized in the top ten – at the end of the year, he was fourth – and Agassi was earning more than $1 million a year in prize money alone. But he was restless with tennis. The years of carrying a tennis bag around the world with an entourage of coaches, agents, and stylists had become an endless grind. He told Phillip to go home, permanently. 'He'd grown up, become a man,' says Phillip, 'and I was still there, his old chaperone. Frankly, I'm surprised he didn't make the decision earlier. I wish I'd been a little more sensitive – so it didn't go on so long that Andre had to say something to me.'

When he wasn't playing his best, he didn't feel he deserved to win. 'It was a perfectionist thing,' says Agassi. When he was finally comfortable playing Wimbledon after skipping it for three years, he did well – lost in the quarter-finals in 1991 and won in 1992. And that same year, his good friend Barbra Streisand even called him a Zen master. But these successes didn't mean much to him.

'I think more than anything, it was childhood stuff,' he says now. 'I didn't want to play, because I felt I had compromised so much of my life to get where I was. I was playing for the wrong reasons, and then all of a sudden, I was forced to understand that and start playing for the right reasons or not at all.'

Things were always up and down with Agassi and Nick Bollettieri – at one point, the two went an entire year without talking – but the end came as a surprise to everybody. It was in 1993, when Agassi started having problems with tendinitis in his right wrist and was losing more and more matches. He got fat on McNuggets and candy, and he slept a lot. When he'd gone pro, he'd weighed 150 but was now up to 180, and *Sports Illustrated* reported that his thighs were rubbing together.

'He used to be a symbol for me of all the kids who didn't ever have to win anymore,' says sportswriter and *Esquire* contributor Mike Lupica. 'Sports used to be talent plus an act. Andre was all act. He was like a rock-star sports celebrity. I used to talk to Connors about this. He'd say, "God, at least we used to win." '

The news that Bollettieri was leaving Agassi came to the tennis star fourthhand. Bollettieri finally admitted in a letter to Agassi that, yes, he was leaving to spend more time with his family. The truth came out a little later: He'd dumped Agassi for Boris Becker.

'He's a selfish person,' says Agassi of his old coach. 'He thought that I wasn't going to do well anymore. But he didn't have the guts to tell it like it was.'

At tournaments now, the two of them run into each other. Agassi says he sees Bollettieri holding court in the lobbies of hotels or surrounded by a group of cronies at restaurants. 'I look in his eyes,' Agassi says, 'and can see that he's not ready to deal with all the things I struggle with about him. So it just passes.'

But when God closes one door, as Andre might say, another door magically creaks open. Two things happened: He started psychotherapy, and Brooke Shields entered the picture. They were set up by Lyndie Benson, the wife of pop saxophonist Kenny G.

'She always had a feeling there was a kinship between us,' says Shields. 'I can't say I was jaded, but I didn't put a lot of stock in it.'

Shields was making a movie in Africa, and after receiving a letter from Agassi, she faxed him back. Soon, they were sending faxes back and forth, every two days for three months. 'We couldn't see each other or speak to each other,' she says. 'So it was this strangely private, very personal way of meeting.'

They had much in common, even talked the same bubbly therapy-speak. It wasn't tennis, in any case. Her grandfather may have been Frank Shields, a US Open finalist in 1930, but Brooke says she never enjoyed the game, 'I've avoided tennis my whole life because of my own stigmas,' she says. 'When I was a kid, there was a lot of pressure to play, and I never would. But my sisters all did. I was the entertainment-industry sister, and I just didn't fit in.'

After she got back from Africa, they talked on the phone every day for six weeks before meeting in December 1993. Shields says she had already fallen in love with Andre by that time but was insecure, sure it wouldn't work. It wasn't their age difference – she's five years older – but mostly what she calls 'my bad track record.'

'It all looked good on paper,' she says. 'Sure, he was smart and nice and called when he said he'd call. He even remembered things I'd told him. All these things – but I was so afraid.'

A month after his own wrist surgery for tendinitis, Agassi stood by Shields when she went through something similar – having all her toes broken and realigned in January 1994, to reverse damage caused by dancing. 'He came and took me to the hospital,' she says, 'and was the first face I saw coming out. I think that was the beginning of a sense of commitment.'

'We've both gone through a lot of the same things,' says Agassi. 'We were both celebrities young. We both were thrown into a strange lifestyle young, and we both got bad raps when we were young, so we have a similar history together. And I think both of us haven't maximized our abilities. But that's changing.'

In order to maximize his own abilities, Agassi formalized a business arrangement with his friend Perry Rogers around the same time. The two have been best friends since they were kids, and Agassi hired Rogers to set up new offices for Agassi Enterprises and help mastermind his contracts. At twenty-six, he is, superficially at least, Agassi's opposite. He dresses in Ralph Lauren khakis and plaid shirts and penny loafers, and comes off more like a Mormon missionary than a sports impresario. He and Agassi are unusually close and spend more time talking about 'relationships and friendships' and 'what you owe God' than money deals, he says. But eighteen months after starting, Rogers pulled off one of the biggest endorsement packages in sports – a contract with Nike that will bring Agassi between $100 million and $150 million during the next ten years.

'We have two rules,' says Rogers during the plane ride to New York. 'We only watch each other's back. I watch his. He watches mine. That way, nobody has to keep watching his own. And if our friendship ever suffers, even this much,' he says, holding two fingers just half an inch apart, 'then I quit.'

His wrist was healing – just an inch and a half of purplish-pink scar – when Agassi began competing again in early 1994. He played well, winning his first tournament in Scottsdale in late February, but it seemed to him there was something missing. His company was coming together. His personal life was finally satisfying – there'd been a couple of serious girlfriends before but nobody like Shields. He'd hired weight trainer Gil Reyes and was finally eating decently. He had bought four lots in a gated community in west Las Vegas and was building a house for his parents, plus a gym and a tennis court for himself. But his game was still unpredictable.

'It was so weird, too,' says Agassi, 'because my tennis was making the rest of my life possible. Perry and I were sitting in my living room one day and just decided I needed a coach.'

He made a list of several guys and took professional player Brad Gilbert to lunch first – without telling him why. Gilbert had written a book, *Winning Ugly*, and was known for being outspoken and having strong opinions about competition. He liked giving advice. The two spoke informally about Agassi's tennis, and Gilbert couldn't seem to help himself from coming up with suggestions. By the next day, they were on the court trying stuff out.

'He had my game diced up like you can't believe,' says Agassi. 'He knew what I did when I was eighteen, what I stopped doing when I was nineteen, what changed in 1990, when I was twenty. I mean, every year, he knew what happened and why my game never got better.'

Gilbert is a dark-haired, smiling kind of guy who looks a little like Richard Gere, with nicely crooked teeth and almond eyes. He is thirty-three and is at the end of his own professional career. Sitting in the Fairmont hotel in San Jose, where he is coaching Agassi to another victory at the Sybase Open, he wears jeans and a moss-green shirt. His feet are planted on the coffee table. And he lights up, two hundred watts, when he starts talking about Agassi.

'Nick felt that if you went out and played well,' Gilbert says, 'that would be enough. I'm more of a strategist.'

Agassi wasn't using his head, Gilbert thought. He wasn't thinking through the whole game. He was misusing his energy, too – he would go into a slump in the second set, then start hitting screaming winners when things got bad. Even though he'd won Wimbledon and reached four Grand Slam finals, he was inconsistent and couldn't be counted on. None of the other players were afraid of him.

So Gilbert gave Agassi his new strategy, his methodology. He didn't hope to improve Agassi's best game – 'few people in tennis have ever hit the ball as hard and deep as Andre,' he says – but he wanted to make Agassi's worst game better. He got him inside the baseline more, serving bigger and dictating play. He also wanted to eliminate Agassi's passive side, the foggy Zen zone he sometimes got into. Gilbert says Agassi was like a boxer who 'couldn't move in for that final knockout punch.'

Agassi also went to Tony Robbins, the motivational speaker, for a little emotional help – like a slightly desperate businessman. He met with Robbins once, professionally, and spent the day with him. 'Tony is an incredible person,' Agassi says, 'and probably one of the most evolved people I've met, in terms of understanding the world and people and human nature.'

But a learning curve is also sometimes a losing curve, initially. Agassi lost the French Open badly and then Wimbledon and then the Volvo Championship in Washington, DC, last July – his ninth consecutive tournament without a title. He wondered if the new plan was ever going to work. And as he did so many other times in his life, when he seemed out of control, he wanted to do something to his hair. 'It was really last summer,' Agassi says, 'that I decided to cut my hair off.'

The upswing came soon enough. He and Gilbert went to Toronto a couple of weeks later, and Agassi won the Canadian Open as Shields watched in the stands. Agassi liked having her there. During his victory at the US Open in September, he stayed with Shields in her Manhattan townhouse. 'And the weirdest thing is,' he says, 'I slept better the night before the finals than ever before.'

A comeback, another peak for the game, seems to be appearing on the horizon, like a dark line way out at sea that becomes a swell that becomes a big perfect wave. You can smell it coming, too, smell it with the energy around Andre Agassi – and the money. He is everybody's hope – and cash cow. In late February, at the Sybase Open, the new San Jose Arena went pitch-black dramatically before his entrance. Disco music, which doesn't agree with him, blared. Spotlights swirled around the ceiling of the dome, searched the stands, then found him, hunted like a movie star at a premiere.

'In promoting this event, the minute we could say that Agassi was coming, it gave us a huge boost,' says tournament director Barry McKay. But even though Agassi promised he'd come almost eight months before the event and was paid a guarantee – top players are paid between $100,000 and $250,000 just to play, which amounts in this case to five times the prize money for first place – McKay still couldn't find a sponsor for the 107-year-old tournament until the weekend before the matches started.

Americans care only if Americans are winning, and, in the last ten years, they mostly haven't been. The attendance numbers worldwide for the sport increased 2 percent last year, but only because tennis is enormously popular in Europe. The golden age of tennis – when McEnroe and Connors and Borg and Chris Evert were in their prime – was so long ago that the kids who started playing tennis then are growing a little old. The night of the finals of the Sybase Open, Agassi versus Chang, there was a handout for a 'Tennis Cruise' – which sounded ominously like something meant to attract senior citizens – stuck in everybody's seat.

While Agassi's image – hot, maybe dangerous – brings teenagers and preteens back to tennis, Pete Sampras's represents something else entirely. In truth, he might be looser and more low-key than Agassi on the court, but Sampras has come to represent a return to classicism and restraint. He wears all white. He modeled his game after Rod Laver's. And until the Australian Open earlier this year – when he sobbed openly during a match against Courier – he displayed very little emotion or personality on the court.

And while Agassi may be 'the biggest tennis star on the planet,' and is rewarded by the clothing and equipment companies for his enormous celebrity – he has deals now with Head, Canon, and Swiss Army as well as Nike – he isn't everybody's favorite tennis player on the planet. Many people still say that Sampras is better.

With the French Open and Wimbledon coming up, the entire world of tennis isn't really rooting for one player over another – for Agassi or for Sampras – as much as it is hoping for a glorious duel between the two men, one that might last for years, one that might, in any case, last longer than Borg–McEnroe. And at twenty-three and twenty-five, Sampras and Agassi are a few years away from the end of their prime, which in tennis is said to be twenty-seven or twenty-eight.

'You gotta keep improving,' Agassi says. 'If you don't, the other guys improve and it's like you de-prove. Number one can't stop there or else you're like Becker or Mats Wilander, and you're there only a month. It's definitely something you have to have a plan for. You have to have a big plan, or else you're just winging it.'

Sweet Pete and the Pirate King slugging it out for number one. Agassi won in Australia, Sampras took Indian Wells. Nike already has the rivalry commercials planned for the summer: Agassi is in one taxicab and sees Sampras passing in another. Both cabs stop. The two players get out in the middle of the street, set up a tennis court, and start going at it.

'You need to have the right ingredients for a rivalry,' says Agassi. 'So many things have to come together for those moments in time: Celtics–Lakers, Dodgers–Yankees, Borg–McEnroe. Me and Pete have the ingredients, and we're starting to make it happen.'

This is what keeps Agassi fired up these days. Just a couple of years ago, he was bored, ambivalent. Dumped by his coach. Left for dead by the tennis world. Now he can't stop thinking about the game. 'It's so alive in me,' he says. 'I can't go too long without thinking about it because I feel like I can improve just thinking about it. Oh, I'm getting better all right. I can see it happen.'

In the very back of the limousine taking him from Teterboro Airport in New Jersey into Manhattan, Agassi seems small – as though lost in a black cave – and young, like a kid wearing a fake goatee and earrings, an Andre Agassi Halloween kit. His wraparound sunglasses are endlessly unflattering. Next to him, on the black leather seat, is a huge white metal box, a bread machine that he has brought from his house in Las Vegas to give to Shields.

'I never use it,' he says, patting the top of the metal box. 'And Brooke said if I brought it here, she'd make me fresh bread.'

For the last six months, Brooke has been starring in the Broadway revival of *Grease*. He's seen it thirty or forty times by now. 'I used to sit in the stands,' he says, as if referring to a sporting event, 'but now I'm backstage, listening to a few skits and sometimes just reading, hanging out in her dressing room, waiting for her there. It's fun to be on somebody else's schedule. I enjoy that. It's so refreshing to me. She's working, and I'm just there, just idling.'

They have a public romance, but they're hardly Liz Taylor and Richard Burton – mixing drinks and throwing ashtrays. It's even hard to imagine them fighting. They talk endlessly about being vulnerable and openhearted and how they are walking the same path to emotional health. They read the same books, C. S. Lewis and Marianne Williamson. But they don't seem, as they might say in California, to be in touch with their rage. 'It's never an accusatory parley of words,' Shields says of their disagreements. 'He'll get quiet, so I'll say, "Let's talk. I think I've said something to upset you. What did I say? How did it affect you? What can I learn from it?" Or he'll say, "I feel I haven't respected you in this area."'

As the limousine approaches Manhattan and Shields's townhouse on Sixty-second Street, Agassi's mind is drifting. 'It's been ten days since I saw her,' he says. He's smiling, peaceful. Scratching himself, he looks eagerly out the window. 'Even if she wasn't an actress,' he'd said earlier, 'it would still be very important for me to have her in my life.'

She's careful not to lean on him, she says, or be too needy. 'He's the hub of the wheel. I see it, day in, day out, in every area of his life. And so, when I came into the picture, I didn't want to be yet another spoke. I want to become my own wheel, with my own spokes. Hopefully, we're on the same vehicle – going in the same direction.'

She'll be moving to California soon, hoping to 'become the actress that I want to become,' she says. Agassi says someday he might be willing to leave Las Vegas, maybe for Marin County. In any case, that's far off. The next three years are for his tennis, for him to do it right. And probably for a wedding. 'Our future together,' she says, 'is our dream.'

The limousine floats to the curb within two minutes of his estimated time of arrival and eases to a stop that's so slow it could almost make you queasy. Agassi has the door open while it's still rolling and scrambles out. Back by the trunk, he loads himself down with his various duffel bags and totes and tennis bags, looking like an undergraduate on semester break. He disappears into the townhouse for a few minutes, then reappears, knocking on the window and pointing. 'The bread machine!' He bends down and hoists it up, smiling like he's home.

Esquire, May 1995

ıx Tradition and the Game

Lawn Tennis
ROBERT D. OSBORN

The scene should be laid on a well-kept garden lawn. There should be a bright warm sun overhead ... Near at hand, under the cool shadow of a tree, there should be strawberries and cream, iced claret mug, and a few spectators who do not want to play but are lovers of the game ... If all these conditions are present, an afternoon spent at lawn tennis is a highly Christian and beneficent pastime.

Lawn Tennis – Its Players and How to Play, 1881

Etiquette
HELEN WILLS

Books have been written on court etiquette, but not about the kind of court etiquette of which I am going to write!

However, hardly less exacting are the rules for conduct and behavior on the tennis court. It is easy to pick out the player who knows what to do and what not to do.

The rules for behavior are very logical and sane. Innate courtesy and sportsmanship have established these. If the player is a gentleman at heart, he does the correct thing on the court whether he knows the rules of tennis etiquette or not. So, I suppose, one should say that in tennis the gentleman makes the rules, rather than rules make the gentleman!

However, no matter what the source of etiquette, it is an important side of the game.

Sometimes amusing incidents occur. At Wimbledon this summer I played against a very sweet and attractive English girl. She was about my own age but had not had very much tournament experience. Naturally, when our match was called for the centre court, she was very excited. We went on the court, played our match, and came off. I noticed nothing amiss. The next day she said: 'Father was so dreadfully annoyed with me yesterday.'

'Why?' I asked.

'When we came on the court, I came through the door first, and you should have, because you are the visiting player.'

Court conduct in England is given even more attention than in this country. The game, during the many years of its growth in England, has produced a certain standard of conduct and procedure among the players, and among the spectators as well, which has been adopted the world over.

I must tell later about gallery etiquette, too, for it is interesting, and very important during tournament matches.

To go on about the player on the court. There are hundreds of little things which stamp the player as a perfect sportsman – things which, in themselves, may sound trivial, yet which, if they are lacking on the court, are very noticeable to one who knows tennis. Since international tennis has become so popular, court etiquette is even more important, because to visiting players every consideration must be shown. The foreign player comes into the court first; he is greeted by the umpire. His opponent spins his racquet, asking, 'Rough?' or 'Smooth?' The 'Toss' made for court, the players take their positions. As they change courts on the odd game, and if they meet at the net, the player who is at home allows the visitor to pass first. Little things like this help the match to run smoothly and pleasantly. They are the expression of a natural feeling of goodwill toward the opponent.

Now and then, surprisingly enough, one discovers players who disregard them entirely.

Everything must be done to make the visiting player's experiences pleasant ones, except, of course, letting him win the match!

Speaking of letting people win. On the Riviera, in southern France, royalty frequently makes its appearance on the tennis court. I have heard players debating whether to lose gracefully, or whether to go out for every possible point. I would answer by saying that the greatest honor that one player can pay another on the court is that of playing hard, and going out for every shot. I know that I never welcome a game or a point that is given to me in a match. An unearned point loses all its flavor. Naturally, any player would have the same feeling.

The matter of 'throwing a point' in a match has come up for discussion times innumerable. One player believes that a bad decision has been made against his opponent. He feels that he should give him the next point, and hits it purposely into the net, or away out of court, or doesn't hit it at all. Some onlookers say: 'How sporting!'

But it is not sporting. First and foremost in a tennis match, the players must abide by the decision of the linesmen and the umpire. It makes an unpleasant feeling if, at any time, their calls are ignored or questioned. The umpire is in the chair, the men are on the lines, to judge the play to the best of their ability. Nine times out of ten they are right.

The player who decides that he must 'throw a point' may very easily have seen the ball incorrectly. From his position on the court he may have thought the ball outside, when it was really in. His resulting generosity serves only to upset his opponent; it breaks into the continuity of his own play, causes discussion among the audience, and worries the linesman and umpires.

In one match that I recall, three points in a game were thrown away by the two players. The characters 'Alphonse et Gaston' were brought to mind. Great confusion resulted. The audience ended by rocking with laughter, and it was some moments before either of the players steadied down to his regular game.

Sometimes some one in the audience, lacking in knowledge of how to act at a tennis match, has risen out of his seat and 'booed' the umpire when a situation of this sort has come up. It was really the player who deserved it for having caused the trouble.

If the decisions are bad, as they cannot help but be sometimes – no one is infallible – they should be ignored by both players, unless the umpire decides that a 'let' should be called. Then the point is played over again and it is fair to every one.

If your opponent slips on his feet, are you to hit the ball easily, so that he will have a chance to return it? This is a difficult question to answer. Obviously, the situation determines what a player shall do. Of course it is a part of the game to stay on one's feet. If the rally gets going so fast that the opponent can't keep his footing then it means that he has less claim to the point than has his adversary. I think, in this case, that the ball should be returned in the regular way of play. Of course if the slip turns out to be a real accident, then the player would not care much what happened to his ball, because he would fear that his opponent was injured.

However, a slip, or a fall, doesn't always mean that your opponent has lost the point or his playing ability! He may be even more dangerous! I have been against players who have recovered themselves and made aces off my gentle returns. One of my partners in mixed doubles took advantage of our opponents' kindness and won a point off their easy return when he was sitting on the ground. So, you see, a point is never won or lost until the ball bounces twice, no matter whether a player is sitting or standing.

When the match is over, it is the custom in this country to shake hands across the net. In England this is not done. But when an American player takes part in English tournaments, the English player, if he is accustomed to international play, shakes hands with him afterward, knowing that the visitor is used to it.

Being a good loser is a part of correct court behavior. There are few players who let their feelings run away with them. Now and then, however, there is one. I heard about one match where the loser refused to shake hands with her adversary, but walked off the court after the match. Fortunately, this sort of thing happens rarely.

Sometimes a player allows his temper to get the best of him after a bad shot. Several players that I know have the habit of muttering to themselves after a particularly bad shot. Another player that I have seen in action several times, once became so angry over the way the game was going that he threw his racquet over the backstop and walked off the court. But you can follow many tournaments and see nothing as surprising as this!

The necessity for correct behavior does not end on the court. The player who habitually has a good number of 'alibis' with which to explain his defeat is very tiresome. The man who is the best on that particular day wins the match. His opponent may have played better on some previous occasion, or may plan to play better in the future, but, at the time of the match, the winner played the winning game.

The spirit of good sportsmanship and correct behavior that tennis demands on the court is no less important on the part of the gallery. Whenever tournaments are played and there is promise of keen competition between players, onlookers will be found on the sidelines.

The tennis audience has always been supposed to be a discreet and refined one. There are correct times for applause if a shot or rally has been particularly brilliant. No one 'boos' the umpire or hurls pop bottles. Tennis has thrills for the onlooker, but no noisy thrills.

The person who takes it upon himself to berate the umpire, to utter comments on the turns in the game, is at once conspicuous in the grand stand. The one who understands tennis is never conspicuous. It is only the one who doesn't know who calls attention to his own ignorance.

Tennis audiences that I have known both here and abroad vary but little. Tennis attracts an intelligent and well-bred group of people. Of course, when you play away from home, it is not surprising to find that the greater part of the audience wants its own players to win. In this country it is the same. We applaud generously the visitor, but we hope that our own player will be the victor.

Youth has a great appeal to the onlooker in tennis. Youth has eternal attraction, the world over, of course. Its spirit is irresistible. The young English girl Betty Nuthall was perhaps one of the best liked visitors that we have ever had. Young, pretty, with fair hair and rosy cheeks, good-natured, she won the favor of the gallery immediately. Her efforts were encouraged frequently, even more than those of the home players.

With the great growth, recently, of interest in tennis, the number of people who come out to see the more important matches has doubled and trebled. Thousands gather to see the Davis Cup matches and the men's and women's National Championships. With such enormous galleries it is more difficult to preserve the dignified atmosphere that has so long been associated with the tennis audience.

Several seasons ago I participated in a tournament in which the committee made clever use of the backs of the programmes. There was printed a list of suggestions and hints for the audience.

1 Do not applaud except at the end of rallies. Sudden noise disconcerts the player.
2 Do not move about during actual play. It is hard to see the ball against a moving background.
3 Parasols interfere with the view of other spectators.
4 Do not try to attract the attention of a friend who is engaged in a match, or about to go on the court.
5 Do not make remarks about the players. Their friends or relatives may be sitting near by.
6 Do not question the decision of umpire or linesmen. They are in a better position to judge the ball than you are.

These hints may well be called the six fundamentals of etiquette for the tennis audience.

Each one of them recalls incidents, amusing and otherwise, which I have experienced or witnessed.

I have seen an enthusiastic friend rise and call out encouragement to the player about to come on the court. The player might have been nervous and trying to brace himself for the coming match. The enthusiasm of the friend might have served only to make it more difficult for him.

Once I was watching from the grandstand a match in which a young and rather awkward girl was taking part. The mother was sitting near by. The girl's strokes were all wrong, but I happened to know that she had had little experience in tournament play, and that she was doing, under the circumstances, quite well. Several women a few rows back had begun to talk about the players and their strokes.

'Have you *ever* seen such an awkward girl? So gawky! I ask you, *why* do such people play in matches?' – and so on.

Sometimes during a thrilling match, it is next to impossible to smother an outburst of enthusiasm. Especially in international matches do interest and excitement run high, and sometimes demonstrations of one sort or another are unavoidable. The woman who emits little shrieks over every long rally, however, should be either muffled or else asked to leave the grandstand. Nothing can be more disconcerting to the player on the court, or more tiresome to those around her.

During the tennis at the Olympic Games in 1924, there were a number of amusing incidents. The American tennis players who went to Paris that year still laugh about one occurrence. During the matches, until there was much complaint, a woman vender went through the stands crying out in a high wailing voice: 'Glaces! Glaces! Qui veut des oranges, des banans? Glaces! Glaces!'

There would be a tense rally on the court, the players in the thick of a thrilling moment, the spectators with their eyes glued on the ball, complete, tense silence – then the wail: 'Glaces! Glaces!'

Parasols are another menace to the enjoyment of the spectator. If a parasol is hoisted, the person behind gets his view cut off. I think that parasols are a necessity on hot days at tennis matches. If you have a little patch of shade to sit in, you enjoy the game much more. You can be sure that your hat is not going to lose every bit of its color in the sun. Without a parasol, you are unhappy; with a parasol, you make others unhappy. I have discovered a solution of the problem. I have a small sunshade just large enough to keep the sun off my head and shoulders. It is about the size of the ones that used to be so popular years ago with old ladies. But mine is not adorned with lace and ruffles as those of the days gone by.

It has a smart wood handle, which can be adjusted, long or short, and is checked with blue and orange in a plaid design. It is ideal for sport, cuts off nobody's view, and makes the hot afternoon at a tennis match quite bearable.

Every sport has its own particular gallery. An enthusiast goes to a football or a baseball game and applauds wildly. He goes to watch a golf match and prays that he will not sneeze just as a stroke is being made. He goes to the tennis and sits sedately, and applauds at correct intervals.

While the etiquette of the grandstand at tennis may seem conservative, it is based on sane and logical reasons. Tennis is a conservative and dignified sport. The etiquette of both gallery and court conforms to the spirit of the game.

Tennis, 1928

Court Manners and Etiquette
ROD LAVER

Sportsmanship is the essence of the game, and yet you don't want to be too good a sport. Or what I call a false sportsman.

I will give you a couple of examples. In 1966 at Forest Hills, Clark Graebner, the American, and Jan Leschly, the Dane, were in the fifth set of an exciting semi-final. Leschly hit a ball that sailed over the baseline, apparently Graebner's point at a time when every point was golden. But Graebner said no. He called to the umpire that his racket had ticked the ball. Nobody noticed, nobody heard, but Clark knew it wasn't his point, and he wouldn't take it. In such a case the umpire accepts the player's refusal of the point and awards it to his opponent. Graebner won the match anyway, so maybe being a good sport pays off.

Now, in 1967 I was up against Andres Gimeno in the final of the US Pro Championship in Boston. On set point for me in the second set, I knocked a ball just wide of the sideline. That should have made it deuce and kept Andres alive. Instead the linesman signaled that the ball had hit the line. Point, game, and set to Laver. Gimeno fussed. I asked the umpire to check with the linesman to make sure. I didn't want the point that way. I made it clear that I hoped the linesman would change his mind. He wouldn't.

I thought of a similar instance three years before on the same court. I was playing Pancho Gonzales for the title and I hit a winner on an important point. The linesman called it out. Pancho wanted that point badly, but not on a bad call. He pointed to the spot where the ball had landed six inches inside the baseline, but he couldn't convince the linesman. In such situations players benefitting from outrageous calls have been known to throw the next point or the next game to demonstrate their so-called sportsmanship.

Did I? Did Pancho? Not on your life. Once we had registered disapproval and asked the linesman to reconsider (they can change their calls, you know), we brushed that point out of our minds. On to the next point. In a tournament match you must play the calls, as we say – accept what comes. There will be bad calls when humans are involved, but I think the supposedly noble gesture of giving away a point is a grandstand play. Further it's an out-and-out insult to the officials who are unpaid volunteers graciously giving their time and effort to aid in the presentation of a tournament.

In a match without linesmen and umpire, you're on the honor system. Make your calls quickly and fairly. If there's any doubt, give your opponent the benefit of that doubt. Don't let your opponent take advantage of you. If he's serving before you're ready, tell him politely. You don't have to get into a screaming match about quick-serving as Gonzales and I once did.

In a club match you can be pretty casual, but if your opponent cramps or injures himself and wants to resume three hours later, you may have to remind him about the play-is-continuous rule. You're not being a bastard by expecting a default if your opponent can't continue after a brief rest. Fitness is part of the game, and if a player breaks down physically, then he's the loser.

This rule is stretched badly, even at the top level. At the Philadelphia Indoor in 1970 Butch Buchholz was going at John Newcombe in a quarter-final. One of Butch's shots skipped off the net and struck Newcombe in the eye. Newcombe was carted off to the dressing room for examination and treatment. Long delay. Buchholz thought he was being a good sport by not demanding his rights: a default. By the time they returned to the court Butch had gone cold, and he was in a mental stew about whether he should have insisted on the victory. He lost. It cost him money that night and possibly the $10,000 first prize.

Butch was wrong in not speaking up. The officials were wrong in allowing the delay. Newcombe was a bigger name than Buchholz. Everybody felt sympathetic, but it should have been Newc's tough luck, a break of the game.

It happens all the time, but don't accept it in a tournament. The rule says nothing about extenuating circumstances, only that play must be continuous.

Like Graebner, in that match with Leschly, you are expected to call infractions against yourself such as touching the net, double-hitting (a 'carry'), or hitting the ball when it is 'not up' (having bounced twice).

If you suspect someone of giving you the business consistently on bad calls, you can refuse to play him again. Or break his rackets over your knee. I never resort to the latter because I weigh only 147, and hardly anybody I play with is smaller.

The Education of a Tennis Player, 1971

'You *Cannot* be Serious'
JOHN FEINSTEIN

It was Sunday in Melbourne. Hot, breezy, humid. A typical late-January, Australian summer day. Day seven of the Australian Open was winding down to an uneventful conclusion. There had been some minor upsets but nothing that was going to knock the Melbourne trolley-car strike off the front page.

In the pressroom, the Australian tabloid writers glanced nervously at the clock again and again, hoping that John McEnroe would make short work of Mikael Pernfors. An easy McEnroe victory would get Rachel McQuillan, the country's latest female hope, on court to play her match in time to make first-edition deadlines. Rachel McQuillan was nineteen, blond, and ranked fortieth in the world. Headline stuff for the tabloid boys.

There was no reason for any of them to believe that McEnroe and Pernfors wouldn't cooperate. McEnroe had been the talk of the tourna-ment for three rounds, dropping just fifteen games in nine sets. He had looked very much like the old untouchable McEnroe, losing as many as three games in a set only once.

It wasn't only the numbers that were impressive. McEnroe looked relaxed on court, happy with himself, his game, and the Australian public. Everyone was reveling in seeing him produce a brand of tennis that many, McEnroe included, had wondered if they would ever see again.

One of the people who had marveled at McEnroe during his second-round victory over Austrian Alex Antonitsch was Gerry Armstrong. He had umpired a match early that afternoon and, with the rest of the day off, had done something he almost never did: gone to watch a tennis match on his own time. 'If there's one player I'll go out of my way to watch play tennis when I'm not working, it's McEnroe,' Armstrong said. 'The guy is an artist. There's no one in the game quite like him.'

On this Sunday afternoon it was not McEnroe's artistry that was on Armstrong's mind as he walked to the umpire's chair to work the match between the artiste and Pernfors. Armstrong had been a full-time professional umpire for a little more than three years. He had worked the men's final at Wimbledon in 1988 and the women's final in 1989. By any account, he was one of the top two or three umpires in the game — which is why he was in the chair for this match. In making the umpiring schedule, Ken Farrar, the supervisor of officiating at all Grand Slam tournaments, was keenly aware of which matches might be troublesome and, no matter how well he had been playing or how smoothly his previous matches had gone, any McEnroe match was worrisome. Armstrong, a thirty-four-year-old Englishman who had spent most of his adult life as a soccer goalie before a chronically separated shoulder had forced him to retire, had assumed he would get McEnroe in the fourth round or the quarter-finals, and that was fine with him. He had worked McEnroe matches often in the past, not without problems, but he'd never encountered a situation he couldn't handle. As he walked onto court that afternoon, Armstrong had no reason to suspect this match would be any different.

'What you learn about the job, though, is that you can never predict what will happen,' he had said earlier that week. 'The most innocuous, innocent match can blow up anytime, anywhere. You always have to concentrate totally because you never know where a problem is going to come from.'

Certainly, no McEnroe match was ever considered innocuous or innocent. In his ten years as a supervisor, Farrar had always made certain to be nearby whenever McEnroe was playing. He had assigned himself to center court that Sunday and, as the match began, he was seated across the court from the umpire's chair, hoping he wouldn't be needed. 'To be honest,' he would say later, 'the way things had been going, there was no reason to expect a problem.'

What Armstrong and Farrar couldn't know was that McEnroe had awakened that morning feeling uneasy. He knew how well he was playing. He also knew that Ivan Lendl was not at the top of his game. He had spent enough time with Boris Becker during the week to know that Becker was still emotionally wiped out from the Davis Cup final and wanted to go home more than he wanted to play tennis. He respected Stefan Edberg, but he certainly didn't fear him. And he knew beyond a shadow of a doubt that if he stayed at this level, those were the only players in the field who had any chance of beating him.

Once, McEnroe would have been so focused on winning the tournament that his mind's eye could have seen only Pernfors that morning. He would have seen a combative, pesky ground-stroker, talented enough to have been a French Open finalist in 1986 but who, after various injuries and setbacks, had come into this tournament ranked sixty-third in the world. But McEnroe had let his thoughts wander into the future. 'I got myself messed up,' he said later. 'I knew how well I was hitting the ball. I wasn't serving as well as I can, but I was hitting the ball as well as I ever have. But instead of thinking about winning the Australian, I started thinking about my schedule.

'I had already been on the road for almost four weeks. It hadn't been so bad, because I had my family with me. But if I made the semi-finals, which I was almost sure I would, it meant I would barely have a week at home before I had to leave for Milan. And then there was Toronto and Philadelphia right after that.

'That should have been the last thing in the world I was thinking about, especially in the middle of a Grand Slam tournament. But it was almost like I wasn't prepared to play as well as I was playing. I had always had trouble getting ready that soon after Christmas. All of a sudden, there I was. I couldn't handle it.'

Almost from the start of the match, it was apparent that this was a different McEnroe. He won the first set 6–1, but that was deceptive. Every game was close. Pernfors had all sorts of chances, starting with three break points in the first game of the match. McEnroe, however, kept coming up with the important shots, and there was every reason to believe that even this less-sharp McEnroe could wear his opponent down.

Pernfors's reputation on tour was not exactly that of a blood-and-guts battler. He was Swedish born and American educated, having played tennis at the University of Georgia. Unlike most of the other top-rated Swedes, it had been in college, not as a junior in Sweden, that he had come of age as a player. He fit none of the Swedish stereotypes. He wasn't blond or bland. He spoke perfect English – with a Southern accent – and was known as someone who enjoyed a good party at least as much as he might enjoy rolling in the dirt to win a five-setter.

He had come to Melbourne, however, with new resolve. He would turn twenty-seven in 1990, and he knew time was running out. He had been ranked as high as tenth in the world, in 1986, but had done little since then. So he had made the long trip to Australia ten weeks early to work and play himself back into top shape. This work had paid off for three rounds. Pernfors had lost just one set and came into the match with McEnroe convinced he was capable of winning.

The first set did little to change his mind. It had been closer than 6–1. Pernfors is the kind of player who chases down so many balls that no point is easy, and that made McEnroe uptight and nervous. He had complained about a couple of calls and had whined about photographers moving during points. To Armstrong, in the chair, and Farrar, sitting across the court, those weren't good signs.

Early in the second set, Pernfors finally converted a break opportunity, aided by a close call on the baseline. When Pernfors then held serve to go up 4–1, McEnroe came out of his chair after the changeover and walked directly over to the lineswoman who had made the close call against him two games earlier. Standing a few feet from her, he repeatedly bounced a ball on his racquet strings and stared at her. The crowd began to hoot, but McEnroe never said a word, just stared balefully.

In the chair, Armstrong made a decision. He thought McEnroe might be headed for an explosion. 'A lot of times when John is edgy early in a match, a warning will calm him down,' Armstrong said afterward. 'It's as if you're saying to him, "Okay, John, you've had your say, now let's just play tennis." I was hoping that would happen here. What he was doing was intimidation, there was no questioning that. So I gave him a warning.'

A warning is step one in tennis's code of conduct. Prior to 1990, the code had four steps: a warning, a point penalty, a game penalty and a default. But in the Byzantine world of tennis politics, the men's sport had been split at the start of the year into two separate governing bodies. One of the ramifications of the split was a tighter code of conduct. Step three – the game penalty – had been eliminated. Now tennis players were like baseball batters: Three strikes and they were out.

Still, the warning was hardly cause for concern. McEnroe had been only one step from default many times in the past and had always kept himself under control from that point on. Now, he was still two strikes away. A long way from serious trouble.

'The strange thing about it,' he said later, 'is that I've been *so* much worse in the past. There was no reason for him to give me that warning. No reason at all. I never said a word to the lady.'

But Armstrong had made a judgment call, guided by his instincts. 'Something just tells you that the right thing to do is to warn a player,' he said. 'I was hoping John would understand what I was doing and that would be the end of the trouble.'

Farrar was hoping the same thing. When Armstrong warned McEnroe, he sat impassive as always, arms folded, his eyes hidden behind his ever-present sunglasses. Farrar never lets anyone see him sweat – but he does plenty of sweating. 'The last thing in the world I wanted was to have to go out there on court,' he said. 'But once Gerry warned him, I had to be ready in case John started to argue.'

Farrar is a latecomer to tennis, a New Englander who grew up playing hockey. Later, while working in the Midwest, he became a hockey referee, but when he moved back to Boston in the 1960s, he found it tough to break into the establishment world of hockey officiating.

When a friend told him he could get into the annual tennis tournament at Longwood for free if he was willing to work as a linesman, he jumped at the chance. 'They gave you two tickets and a hot dog in those days,' he said. 'I thought it was a great deal.'

Farrar quickly fell in love with his new avocation. He began working at any junior tournament he could find, driving around with a stepladder in his trunk that he would set up as his umpire's chair. In the 1970s, he went to work for World Team Tennis and, in 1981, was offered the chance to become one of the first professional supervisors for the Men's Tennis Council (MTC). He was in the construction business at the time and a little bit bored, so he took a shot.

At age fifty-five he had been named head supervisor for the Grand Slams. This was his first tournament in that capacity, although his role was the same as it had been when he had been an MTC supervisor. Seeing McEnroe in a snit was nothing new for Farrar but, as had always been the case in the past, he could feel his palms beginning to sweat when he heard Armstrong call the warning.

McEnroe's argument was brief, though. The danger passed. Pernfors went on to win the second set and, as Armstrong had hoped, McEnroe dug in to play tennis. There were distractions: a baby crying in the stands, a few stray fans trying to bait McEnroe by yelling when he threw the ball up to serve, a few others telling him loudly to 'just shut up and play' whenever he argued a call. The match kept evolving from a curiosity into one filled with excellent tennis. Pernfors looked a little like the Pernfors of 1986, slugging his ground strokes, chasing McEnroe's volleys, passing him at key moments. McEnroe seemed equal to the task. When he won a taut third set 7–5, it looked as if everything was going to work out. Rachel McQuillan would be on court in time for the Aussies to make their deadlines.

And then, all hell broke loose.

Serving at 2–3, deuce in the fourth set, McEnroe pushed a forehand approach wide. Frustrated with himself, he hurled his racquet to the ground. The crack could be heard throughout the stadium. Farrar heard it and stiffened. 'That's an automatic,' he explained later. 'If a player throws his racquet, it's up to the umpire to decide whether to penalize him – *unless* it cracks. Then he has no choice. He *has* to call it.'

Armstrong did just that. 'Racquet abuse, Mr McEnroe,' he announced. 'Point penalty.'

The timing could hardly have been worse for McEnroe, because the point penalty gave Pernfors the game and a 4–2 lead. If Pernfors could now hold serve twice, the match would come down to one set. McEnroe certainly didn't want that. So he tried to talk his way free, saying he really hadn't thrown the racquet that violently.

'You broke the racquet,' Armstrong told him. 'That's automatic, John.'

'All I did was crack it,' McEnroe said. 'I have every intention of continuing to play with it. Look, it isn't broken, it's just a crack.'

McEnroe wasn't going to win the argument, but he continued anyway. Armstrong let him go for a while before saying, 'Let's play.'

Those two words are a code. They mean 'I've heard enough.' Players know it as well as umpires do. McEnroe couldn't let go, though. As he had often done in the past, he demanded to see the referee.

The referee for the Australian Open was Peter Bellenger, a tall, quiet, balding man. His job was more directly connected to making court assignments each day than to officiating disputes. So, even though Bellenger did come trotting onto the court, it was actually Farrar who Armstrong signaled for. He was the man in charge. He was the one who had the authority to reverse Armstrong's decision.

He didn't.

'In this case,' he said later, 'I had one goal: to get John back on the court and playing again. He wasn't going to win the argument, because it wasn't a judgment call. The racquet had cracked. I've dealt with him enough times to know that this wasn't going to be an easy one.'

McEnroe repeated his argument to Farrar, claiming again that he could still play with the racquet. Farrar kept shaking his head and telling McEnroe that the crack made the call automatic. Sitting in the chair, Armstrong listened impassively. Bellenger stood a few feet away, watching silently. Throughout the argument Pernfors stood on the baseline, holding the tennis balls, preparing to serve whenever McEnroe came back to play. By now, the crowd was whistling loudly, wanting the match to continue. McEnroe kept insisting that he could play with the racquet and it should still be 2–3, advantage Pernfors.

Farrar shook his head one more time and finally told Armstrong, 'Let's play.' With that he turned to walk back across the court to his seat. Bellenger headed back to the tunnel. McEnroe hadn't moved. By now, he was furious and a little bit scared. He was looking at a five-setter and, in his current mood, he didn't want that. Yet there went Farrar, walking off, confirming his sentence. In his mind at that moment, McEnroe was still *two* strikes from default. He had forgotten the new rule, had forgotten he had only one strike left. And so he decided to get in one last parting shot.

'Just go fuck your mother!' he shouted.

It wasn't whispered. It wasn't even spoken in a normal tone of voice. Five rows back in the stands, the profanity was audible. John Alexander, the ex-Australian Davis Cup player who was doing courtside commentary for Australian television, heard it clearly. 'John McEnroe has just used a terribly abusive profanity,' Alexander told his audience, adding, 'and I don't think Ken Farrar is going to let him get away with it.'

Farrar took two more steps before what he had heard sunk in. 'My first thought was, "Did he really say that?" Then I said, "Yeah, he *said* that." I turned around and went back to Gerry right away.'

Seeing Farrar turn around and walk back to Armstrong, McEnroe was disgusted – at least in part with himself. 'I thought, Oh God, the guy's going to give me a game penalty,' he said. 'I was upset with myself because I shouldn't have said what I said. I've gotten into the habit the last few years of using that kind of language, and when you do that, sooner or later it's going to come out when you don't want it to.'

Farrar had no intention of giving McEnroe a game penalty – especially since it no longer existed in the rules. But even under the *old* rules,

Farrar would have responded the exact same way. 'No player has ever spoken to me that way,' he said. 'Not John, not anyone. Not ever.

'Right there, that was gross misconduct under the rules. If he hadn't had a single strike against him at that point, the same thing would have happened.'

What happened was swift and shocking. Farrar called Bellenger back to the chair. 'Gerry,' he asked, 'did you hear that?'

Armstrong nodded that he had. 'If Ken hadn't heard it and hadn't come back, I would have called him back,' Armstrong said. 'My reaction was exactly the same as his.'

Having confirmed that his ears weren't playing tricks on him, Farrar turned to Bellenger. 'Peter,' he said, 'I think we're looking at a default here.'

Bellenger nodded. Farrar looked up at Armstrong one more time. 'Default him,' he said. And then he turned and walked quickly back across the court. He was halfway there when Armstrong made the announcement. 'Verbal abuse, audible obscenity, Mr McEnroe. Default. Game, set, and match, Pernfors.'

The whole thing – from McEnroe's profane outburst to Armstrong's announcement – took no more than twenty seconds. For a split second, no one in the place moved. It was as if they knew they had heard wrong. Few of the fans had any idea what the rules were. McEnroe had cursed, but so what? He had done that for years and had never been defaulted. Why was this different? How could a fourth-round match in the Australian Open be over *just like that*? There had to be a mix-up here; there had to be someone McEnroe could appeal to.

But there wasn't. Armstrong climbed down from the chair. Neither player had moved. Pernfors was still on the baseline, waiting to serve. McEnroe stood in the same spot where he had unleashed the fatal phrase. His hands were on his hips, a stunned smile on his face.

It was what his friends call his 'you cannot be serious' look, a combination of amazement, anger, and disbelief. They had all seen it before but never quite like this. Watching the incident on tape over and over several hours later at her home in Florida, Mary Carillo, McEnroe's one-time mixed-doubles partner and lifelong friend, would think to herself, He's standing there, thinking, 'I haven't even cleared my throat yet and I'm defaulted? You *cannot* be serious!'

In fact, they could not have been more serious.

The chaotic scene that unfolded in those first moments after McEnroe's default was a perfect metaphor for what professional tennis had become as the 1990s began. Tennis was in a period of turmoil and transition – again. The men were split politically, while the women had sponsor problems and were counting on a thirteen-year-old to replace the irre- placeable Chris Evert as both icon and girl next door.

The great irony of McEnroe's default was that the two men responsible, Armstrong and Farrar, were on opposite sides of the civil war being waged for control of the men's game. In 1989, both had been employed by the Men's Tennis Council, then the governing body for all of men's tennis. By 1990, the MTC no longer existed. Farrar was an employee of the International Tennis Federation, the group that ran the four Grand Slams – Wimbledon and the Australian, the French and US Opens. Armstrong was one of ten full-time umpires who worked for the new ATP (Association of Tennis Professionals) Tour.

The ATP Tour had replaced the MTC because the players were unhappy with many of the rules they were forced to follow. As a result, they now had control over all the non-Grand Slam tournaments, the week-in, week-out events that snaked endlessly around the world. The game's umpires were as divided as the bureaucrats and the players. Farrar, who had once hired Armstrong and all of his fellow full-time umpires, was now considered the enemy.

'There were a lot of hurt feelings,' Farrar said. 'I know they all felt I had let them down.'

On this Sunday, though, Armstrong and Farrar had found common ground: John Patrick McEnroe, Jr. For each of them and for the sport, his banishment from Australia was a crisis. It was the first time a top- ranked player had *ever* been evicted from a major tournament. And even though he had not won a Grand Slam title since 1984, McEnroe was still the game's most visible figure. It was bad enough that the angry crowd was shouting and gesturing furiously, demanding that the match begin again. The next day, the front page of virtually every newspaper in the world would carry the story. Every television station would be repeating images of McEnroe's ejection. This Australian Open, which for better or worse was the beginning of a new era in tennis, would now be remem- bered for one thing and one moment: 5.30 p.m. on 21 January 1990.

As soon as he had announced the default, Armstrong walked up the players' tunnel and found that he was completely lost in the maze of halls that run underneath the Flinders Park Stadium, since, in his haste to depart, he had come off-court on the wrong side. He had to ask for directions several times before he finally found his way back to the umpires' lounge.

'When I walked in, one of the Australian supervisors was talking to everyone in kind of a hushed tone,' he said. 'He was saying things like, "Everyone remain calm; don't answer questions and just go about your business." That was when it really hit me that something very drastic had taken place.'

The weight of it all hit Farrar more quickly. By the time he got off the court he was sweating profusely and he could hear his heart pounding. He walked back to his office and found his boss, Bill Babcock, sitting there staring at the television set. The cameras were still showing the stadium where the crowd had now broken into a chant of 'We want McEnroe!'

Babcock looked up when Farrar walked in and saw the pained look on his face. 'Ken, you had no choice,' he said. 'You did the right thing.'

Farrar sank into a chair. 'What a hell of a way to start a new job,' he said.

Babcock didn't even crack a smile.

Armstrong knew he had to call home. It was 7 a.m. in Eastbourne and his longtime girlfriend, Julie, and their four-month-old son would just be waking up. Soon, he knew, their phone would start ringing off the hook. What's more, Richard Kaufman, the most experienced of the full-time umpires and the man looked to as a mentor by almost all of his colleagues, was visiting Julie for the weekend. Kaufman was in a PhD program at the London School of Economics, two hours away by train.

When Julie answered the phone, Armstrong briefly explained to her what had happened and then asked to speak to Kaufman. When Kaufman picked up the phone, Armstrong cheerily asked, 'How are you, Rich?'

'Asleep,' Kaufman answered.

'Well,' Armstrong said, 'I've just had to default McEnroe.'

'*Now*,' Kaufman said, 'I'm awake.'

Since the tournament's junior competition would begin the next morning, the men's locker room was aswarm with teenage players, many of whom had stood watching as the wild scene unfolded on television. Just as

McEnroe began walking down the long hallway that led from the court to the locker room, one of the Australian junior coaches raced inside.

'Everyone out!' he screamed. 'I want every junior player out of this locker room right now!'

As McEnroe approached, a stream of juniors began piling into the hallway, all of them wishing, no doubt, that they had been allowed to stay and witness what was to come.

But the fury had passed for McEnroe. Seconds after Armstrong had left the court, he had walked to his chair to begin gathering his racquets and clothing. Pernfors, who was at least as stunned as McEnroe, walked up, put his arm on his back, and said, 'John, I'm really sorry.'

McEnroe didn't respond. He didn't even hear Pernfors. If someone had fired a cannon behind his back at that moment, he wouldn't have flinched. He was in the kind of shock people go into when they have been shot. McEnroe would not feel the pain until much later. By the time he reached the locker room, he was resigned to his fate. He tossed a few racquets – perhaps as a matter of principle – but that was it. His agent, Sergio Palmieri, who had been sitting in the stands with his client's wife, Tatum O'Neal, greeted him at the door. Palmieri knew his job right then was to listen to everything McEnroe said – whether it made sense or not – nod his head, and say, 'You're right, John, you're right.'

Twenty minutes after his default, McEnroe, escorted by a coterie of security guards, came into the pressroom. Photographers were literally climbing over one another, trying to take his picture. They kept snapping and flashing and yapping until McEnroe finally said, 'If they don't stop, I'm leaving.' The reporters screamed at the photographers to stop. Grudgingly, they did.

If John McEnroe has been consistent in anything throughout his career, it is his remorse in the aftermath of his worst on-court incidents. McEnroe has come into post-disaster press conferences and said, 'Bless me, father, for I have sinned' so many times that reporters who have been around him through the years have begun to feel a bit like priests in the Catholic confessional.

This confession was no different. McEnroe rambled – as always – and ruminated. At one point he said, 'It was just one little four-letter word. The guy could have let me off.' But in the end, he knew that wasn't true.

'In a way, this was inevitable,' he said. 'This is like the icing on the cake. This is a long story and now it culminates in me getting defaulted in a big tournament.'

He paused for a minute and shrugged. 'I can't say I'm surprised.'

There was more. McEnroe has never in his life cut a press conference short. He admitted to forgetting the rule change from four steps to three and very rationally conceded, 'In that sense, it was my fault.'

But not everything was so rational. All the rules in tennis, he said, had been made for him. This was proof, he added, that the players have no power. (Actually, it was the players who had created the new stricter rules because of concerns about their image.) He could have played, McEnroe insisted, with the cracked racquet.

'You know, it's really not fair,' he said. 'Everyone understands English. Pernfors could be cursing in Swedish and the guy would never know it.'

Also not true. Several years earlier, the umpires had put together a profanity cheat sheet that contained the key profanities in just about every language spoken on the tennis tour. Some knew the words by heart; others carried a copy of the cheat sheet with them so if they heard something that sounded familiar, they could check it out. If Pernfors had cursed at Armstrong in Swedish, Armstrong would have known.

McEnroe was flailing, knowing he had messed up and messed up badly. When he left the interview room, it was as if the entire tournament had stopped dead in its tracks. After a lengthy delay (brought on by the unruliness of the crowd), Rachel McQuillan was last on court. If she had won 6–0, 6–0 (she didn't), she *might* have gotten a sentence in the next day's newspapers.

With his arm around Tatum, McEnroe walked through the tunnel to the underground garage, where a car waited to take him away from the carnage he had left behind. Tatum looked neither right nor left as the photographers continued to snap away from every possible angle. McEnroe looked as if he had just come back from an afternoon practice session. His face was completely blank. He even paused to give the photographers an extra few seconds while he loaded his racquets into the trunk. Then he got into the backseat of the car and was gone.

McEnroe had left the building. The Australian Open was in tatters. Tennis's new era had begun.

Hard Courts, 1991

Tennis Personalities

MARTIN AMIS

I have a problem with – I am uncomfortable with – the word 'personality' and its plural, as in 'Modern tennis lacks personalities' and 'Tennis needs a new star who is a genuine personality.' But if, from now on, I can put 'personality' between quotation marks, and use it as an exact synonym of a seven-letter duosyllable starting with 'a' and ending with 'e' (and also featuring, in order of appearance, an 'ss,' an 'h,' an 'o,' and an 'l'), why, then, 'personality' and I are going to get along just fine.

How come it is always the old 'personalities' who lead complaints about the supposed scarcity of young 'personalities'? Because it takes a 'personality' to know a 'personality'? No. Because it takes a 'personality' to *like* a 'personality.'

Ilie Nastase was a serious 'personality' – probably the most complete 'personality' the game has ever boasted. In his memoir, *Days of Grace*, Arthur Ashe, while acknowledging that Nastase was an 'unforgettable personality,' also recalls that Ilie called him 'Negroni' to his face and, once, 'nigger' behind his back. Ilie, of course, was known as a 'clown' and a 'showman'; i.e., as an embarrassing narcissist. Earlier this year, his tireless 'antics' earned him a dismissal and a suspension as Romania's Davis Cup captain ('audible obscenities and constant abuse and intimidation'). Ilie is forty-seven. But true 'personalities' merely scoff at the passage of time. They just become even bigger 'personalities.'

Jimmy Connors: another total 'personality.' Imagine the sepsis of helpless loathing he must have inspired in his opponents during his 'great runs' at the US Open. There's Jimmy (what a 'personality'), orchestrating mass sex with the Grandstand Court. It's great for the mild-mannered Swede or Swiss up at the other end: he double-faults, and New York goes *wild*. Jimmy was such an out-and-out 'personality' that he managed to get into a legal dispute with the president of his own fan club. Remember how he used to wedge his racket between his legs with the handle protruding and mime the act of masturbation when a call went against him? *That's* a 'personality.'

Twenty-odd years ago, I encountered Connors and Nastase at some PR nightmare in a Park Lane hotel. Someone asked these two bronzed and seer-suckered 'personalities' what they had been doing with themselves in London. 'Screwing each other,' Nastase said, and collapsed in Connors' arms. I was reminded of this incident when, last fall, I saw an account of a whistle-stop tour undertaken by John McEnroe and Andre Agassi. Questioned about their relationship, Agassi described it as 'completely sexual.' Does such raillery inevitably come about when self-love runs up against mutual admiration? Or is it part of a bonding ritual between 'personalities' of the same peer group?

By turning my TV up dangerously loud, I once heard McEnroe mutter to a linesman (and this wasn't a Grand Slam event but one of those German greed fests where the first prize is something like a gold helicopter), 'Get your fucking head out of your fucking [personality].' Arthur Ashe also reveals that McEnroe once called a middle-aged black linesman 'boy.' With McEnroe gone, it falls to Agassi to shoulder the flagstaff of the 'personalities' – Agassi, the Vegas traffic light, the 'Zen master' (B. Streisand) who used to smash forty rackets a year. And I don't think he has the stomach for it, funnily enough. Nastase, Connors, McEnroe, and Agassi are 'personalities' of descending magnitude and stamina. McEnroe, at heart, was more tremulous than vicious; and Agassi shows telltale signs of generosity – even of sportsmanship.

There is a 'demand' for 'personalities,' because that's the kind of age we're living in. Laver, Rosewall, Ashe: these were dynamic and exemplary figures; they didn't need 'personality' because they had character. Interestingly, too, there have never been any 'personalities' in the women's game. What does this tell us? That being a 'personality' is men's work? Or that it's boys' work?

We do want our champions to be vivid. How about Pete Sampras, then – so often found wanting in the 'personality' department? According to the computer, Sampras is almost twice as good as anyone else in the sport. What form would his 'personality' take? Strutting, fist-clenching, loin-thrusting? All great tennis players are vivid, if great tennis is what you're interested in (rather than something more tawdrily generalized). The hare-eyed Medvedev, the snake-eyed Courier, the droll and fiery Ivanisevic, the innocent Bruguera, the Wagnerian (and Machiavellian) Becker, the fanatical Michael Chang. These players demonstrate that it is perfectly possible to have, or to contain, a personality – *without* being an asshole.

New Yorker, 1994

My Life with Gabriela Sabatini
ALISTAIR COOKE

It has been my privilege for many years, during the first week in April, to go down to Georgia to that marvellous botanical garden that masquerades as a golf course, and address the amateur dinner given by the Augusta National Golf Club to honour the reigning British and American amateur champions in the name of the greatest amateur of them all who founded the Masters tournament, Robert Tyre Jones.

At that dinner, everyone except me is or was an amateur golfer of deafening fame. Not quite as deafening as the fame of the humblest pro on the American tour, for the simple bleak reason that amateurs do not appear every weekend on national television. (By the way, the amateur champions of Britain and America are not always Britons or Americans. Last year, I recall, the British champ was a Dutchman. You will appreciate this embarrassment, I'm sure: you have been appreciating it in gentlemen's tennis for — what is it? — fifty-eight years!)[1]

Now these champions, however far flung their native land, are uniformly very young and very pink-cheeked. And I am there — you may have been wondering — to address them because I am the President of a world-wide organization: HOW — Hackers of the World. I tell them two things. One: do not mock or disdain us hackers, who are riveted to the box every Saturday and Sunday pathetically buying everything that's urged on us to improve our game (a new rubber grip, different balls, magical metal woods). It is we who make it possible for you to tap a very small ball into (as Winston Churchill put it) 'an even smaller hole' in order, on Sunday evening, to pick up a quarter of a million dollars. Secondly, I beg them not to turn pro, to resist the lust for a million dollars. There is more to life, I tell them, than golf. They haven't the faintest notion what I'm talking about.

This leisurely introduction is, you may have guessed, a way of postponing an answer to the awkward question: What am *I* doing here? I am not a 22-handicap tennis player. I can't quite imagine what that would be. I am not, indeed, a tennis player at all. I gave up the game forty years ago. I am too vain, I suppose, to share G. K. Chesterton's splendid philosophy, so simply expressed: 'If a thing's worth doing, it's worth doing badly.'

It must be, I decided, simply because I am an amateur, a lover. To be truthful, I am a lover (John Barrett is the only person here who knows this) of Gabriela Beatriz Sabatini! But I mean in the larger, purer sense. I love her tennis. (She is only the latest of the very many women of whom I have been an amateur.) I have been watching tennis, and watching the best, longer than most people here. That is not, believe me, a foolish or tasteless boast. It's just the unfortunate accident of the calendar. It's a dread reminder of something Mr Justice Blackman said last week when a reporter, a very pink reporter (couldn't have been a day over fifty) asked him why he was retiring. He said: 'My goodness! Eighty-five is very old.' So it is. The first tennis player I fell in love with was Mrs Lambert Chambers. The fact that I was only six at the time is no reason why you should smirk at my passion.

But I have gathered that you mean simply to honour me as a symbolic amateur, and if so I am touched and very grateful.

Now, John Barrett – in, I imagine, a sort of mild panic – fearing I might forget myself and talk exclusively about golf, phoned me to say he was sending by express mail two weighty volumes. The lighter one – Alan Little's *Wimbledon Compendium*, and his own 3 lb 4 oz tome (I took it with me on my bathroom scale). He apologized for imposing these encyclopaedias on me. And then he said a very sinister sentence: 'You'll be *needing them*, won't you?'

So that's what this was to be! I thought it was going to be a jolly dinner. But he made it clear with his meaningful stresses: it was to be also an examination! Well, I can tell you, and him, that I have done my homework. I have swatted away. I have boned up. *I* know who was the British general who said what he enjoyed most about Wimbledon was 'the man-to-man combat'. (He couldn't apparently bear the thought of the woman-to-woman combat and went home.) I don't need to be told about the mind-shattering third set of the 1937 men's singles semi-final, between Bunny Austin and the Baron von Cramm: 12–14! I was there. I know why the American champion, May Sutton, was born in Plymouth. The same reason, the same answer to a very puzzling question put to me when I was a very small boy: Why was the Welshman Lloyd George born in Manchester? The answer was: His mother happened to be there at the time! Same with May Sutton. How many veterans here know the name of the Sleeping Lineswoman? If you don't you'd better get John to send you his book. Better, buy it. The name? Of course, it was none other than Dorothy Cavis Brown. First round, 1964, court No. 3.

But, in this great work, I don't see a picture of Mr Tilden banging his racket on the ground. Rebukes, penalty. Conference of umpire, referee, officials. Play suspended, headlines in all the papers, it was in all the newsreels. As Othello said at the time: 'Chaos is come again.' John, will you please correct this in the second edition?

To be fair, I ought to say that John is to be applauded for his really staggering scholarship: diligent, unflagging, meticulous with minuscule details – splendid. And he bends over backwards to be objective. I think the most back-breaking sentence in the book is about the ladies' singles champion of 1961.[2] About her, he writes: 'She was sound more than spectacular.' (I'll bet he's never heard the last of that.)

I have been immensely fortunate to spend my life in the observation of two nations, two cultures. The main reward has been to double my interest in, my curiosity about, the human being. And, in a small way, I like to think that coming to tennis from golf lets you see some things in the game that the people preoccupied with it may not see. For instance, whenever I come, as I do, more or less directly from the United States Open (golf) championship to Wimbledon, I am always struck in the first days by the innocence, the naïvety, of tennis players considered as gamesmen. I was a good friend of Stephen Potter and associated with him in the furtherance of his mission: How to Win at Games Without Actually Cheating. That's the way we put it in the early days. It was later refined into the business of helping games players to lead a fuller, more deceitful, life. I expected that tennis players would know all about the Double Ploy, the Secondary Hamper, the Pour. But from my observation, gamesmanship in tennis is in its infancy.

Mary Carillo, watching Steffi Graf bounce the ball nine times instead of six, says: 'She's taking her time, *she's* going to dictate the tempo.' Pretty crude. Ivan Lendl has never got beyond examining his strings as he if he was playing with a harp. Though I have to recall that he once managed what Potter called an Oblique Huff, which put paid to Monica Seles's grunt for a week or two. Lendl didn't object to *her* grunt but to the grunt of the Las Vegas Lollipop – Andre Agassi.

Time out for the paramedics: the bandaging of non-existent injuries. That's good, though the question arises whether watching the clock doesn't generate more anxiety in the one being bandaged than in the opponent counting his strings. Boris Becker, I have to say, is the best gamesman alive at lounging in slow motion through $24\frac{3}{4}$ seconds.[3]

But so far, the only first-rate tennis gamesman I've seen is a gameswoman: Mary Pierce. I saw her a couple of weeks ago win the first set. She did something extraordinary, something she'd never done before. She lifted those heavy eyelids and smiled! In disbelief, suggesting it was a freak. Then she appeared to have lost her nerve. She lost five games in a row, and the second set. She was shattered. She shook her head. She paced the baseline. She tapped her left toe and her right in rhythm. She was plainly doomed and bedraggled. Which gave the cue for her opponent, Sanchez-Vicario, to go into her well-known Bouncing Midget act. Which immediately gave Mary Pierce *her* cue to abandon her masquerade and slaughter Sanchez-Vicario 6–love! Of course, Pierce does have the advantage of a cruel father. She invites sympathy, the crowd on her side, the moment she steps on to the court.

I do wish somebody would give Sabatini a kindergarten course in gamesmanship. I think that in the hands of a good gamesman coach, that second serve could become a great weapon. Time and again, I've thought – if only she'd read Potter and just make a point, at unpredictable times, of seeing that her second serve was no faster than twelve miles an hour! Imagine the effect on the opponent. Martina! – 'You kidding or something.' Could be as effective as Michael Chang's serving underhand to Ivan Lendl. Result: bewilderment, outrage and, of course, defeat. That, by the way, was the only masterful bit of tennismanship I've seen in the past few years.

Of course, you've noticed, I talk as a critic, a commentator, a never-challenged outsider. That's because most of my time watching golf or tennis is spent with critics and not with players. But I hope it's as true of tennis as it is of golf, that you don't need to be a great player to be a great critic or, for that matter, a great teacher. Look at John, again. I've never seen *him* play. I understand he *can* play. I don't care. He's a great teacher – he says.

But I have a cautionary tale for critics, either amateur or professional. Beware! Speak too often out of turn and you may be invited to demonstrate your expertise before experts. My tale is of a Lancashire and Yorkshire match in the long ago, in the late 1920s, I believe. Certainly, in those days, the Wars of the Roses had not ended. Whenever Yorkshire came to Old Trafford, the grounds could not contain the seething mob of Lancastrians come to see the Yorkshire snout rubbed in the mud. (Since the match was played in Manchester in midsummer there was every chance of actual mud.) Unfortunately, during most of that decade, it was Yorkshire that did the rubbing. But whether at their best or their worst, they were fair game for the Lancashire critics. Not least for the best cricket writer of his day, some say of any day: Neville Cardus.

Well, Lancashire had won the toss and gone in first, and were out at the end of the day with a modest score, thanks to the impressive bowling of Yorkshire's slow bowler, Emmott Robinson. Next morning, as always, Cardus had a long, eloquent and glowing piece, at the end of which he analysed the fine work of Emmott Robinson. While allowing him all due praise, he did suggest that if he paid closer attention to the flight of the ball, a touch more flexible with the wrist at the top, he'd be not just a very good bowler but a great one.

In mid-morning of that second day, an old friend spotted Robinson sitting on a bench in the pavilion watching his side bat. The man moved down and sat next to him. He said: 'Did you see what Cardus wrote about ya this mornin'?' Robinson said: 'Aye – ' (*long pause*) – 'Ah'd lahk t' bowl at bugger.'

All fun and gamesmanship aside, I can't end without telling you of my one brave effort to cure a very sore spot in championship tennis. It happened, oh, maybe ten, a dozen years ago, at a time anyway when the tennis world alternated between marvelling at McEnroe's magical skill and shuddering at his loutish manners. I had a head-shaking session about this with a very famous golfer – well, since it won't go beyond these four walls – it was Jack Nicklaus. He said at once: 'The guy to blame is the father. When I was about eleven years old, I threw a club. My father said: "Jack, if you do that again, you won't play golf for another six months." I sulked and went off to my room. He came after me, opened the door and said: "What would Mr Jones think?" – Bobby Jones was my dad's idol. I never threw another club.'

Well, it gave me an idea. I remembered a sentence. I wrote to Mr McEnroe, Senior. I said: 'Here is a sentence once written by the immortal Bobby Jones. I thought you might like to have it done in needlepoint and mounted in a suitable frame to hang over Little John's bed.' It says: 'The rewards of golf – and of life, too, I expect – are worth very little if you don't play the game by the etiquette as well as by the rules.' I never heard from Mr McEnroe, Senior. I can only conclude that the letter went astray.

Speech given before the All-England Lawn Tennis and Croquet Club, 1994

1 The last British Wimbledon singles champion was Fred Perry, in 1936.
2 Angela Mortimer – Mrs John Barrett.
3 At Wimbledon in 1994 he proved – with one or two crude ploys – that he didn't know the difference between gamesmanship and cheating.

Acknowledgements

Grateful acknowledgement is made to the following for permission to reprint previously published material:

"Tennis Personalities" by Martin Amis (originally published in *The New Yorker*, Sept. 5, 1994). Reprinted by permission of The Wylie Agency (UK) Limited, London, on behalf of the author.

Two excerpts from *Days of Grace* by Arthur Ashe and Arnold Rampersad, copyright © 1993 by Jeanne Moutoussamy-Ashe and Arnold Rampersad. Reprinted by permission of Alfred A. Knopf, Inc.

"Chris Evert: The Cold and Absolute Fire" from *The Courts of Babylon* by Peter Bodo (Scribner, New York, 1995), copyright © 1995 by Peter Bodo. Reprinted by permission of Carol Mann Agency.

"Grooming Monica" from *My Aces, My Faults* by Nick Bollettieri and Dick Schaap, text copyright © 1996 by Nick Bollettieri Tennis and Sports Academy, Inc., and Dick Schaap. Reprinted by permission of Avon Books, Inc.

"Becker" by Gordon Burn (*Esquire* magazine, British edition), copyright © 1992 by Gordon Burn. Reprinted by permission of Gillon Aitken Associates Ltd., London.

"My Life with Gabriela Sabatini" by Alistair Cooke (a speech given at the All-England Lawn Tennis and Croquet Club, April 14, 1994). Reprinted by permission of the author.

Index

Figures in **bold** indicate authors in the anthology

Stevenson, Alexandra, 150
Stewart, Hugh, 95
Stich, Michael, 265, 267, 268
Stockholm, 135
Stoefen, 82
Stove, Betty, 178, 179, 192
Stranahan, Frank, 96
Streisand, Barbra, 276, 308
Sturgess, Eric, 122, 123
Sukova, Helena, 255
Summers, Pops, 89
Sundstrom, Henrik, 136
Superstars competition, 187
Sutherland, Duke of, 40
Sutton, May, 310
Sweden (Masters tournament), 134
Swiss Army, 281
Swiss International Championships, 126–9
Sybase Open, 279, 280, 281

Tampa, 185
Tate, Thomas J., 27
Taylor, Elizabeth, 226
Taylor, Fred, 22, 23, 27
tennis balls
  Ayres, 19, 22, 25–6
  flannel cover, 5, 11
  Peck and Snyder, 25, 26
  'Regulation', 19, 21
  rubber, 5
  size, 9, 10, 19, 21, 26
  weight, 9, 10, 11, 14, 21, 26
  Wright and Ditson, 26
Tennis Committee of the Riviera, 40
Tennis magazine, 111, 190, 238, 254, 266
Thompson, Bertha ('Too Mom'), 258, 259, 260, 262–3
Thorpe, Jim, 93
'throwing a point', 288–9, 294
Thurber, James, 46–50
ticket prices, 39
Tilden, Bill, xii, 35, 39, 61–73, 81, 91, 92, 310–11
  Match Play and the Spin of the Ball, 64
  My Story, 66
Tinling, Teddy, 61–8, 178, 226, 228, 232
Tiriac, Ion, 134, 266–70
Tolley, Cyril, 40
Topping, Tom, 38
Towle, Sir Francis, 40
Toyota Series Championships, 212
Trabert, Tony, 99–100, 103, 105, 183
Triple-A Pacific Coast League, 171
Tropicana hotel, Las Vegas, 273, 274
Tuero, Linda, 144
Tunis, John, 33, 34, 36, 37, 38, 40
Tuohy, Ferdinand, 31, 55–7
Turnbull, Wendy, 184, 216

umpires, the first, 12
United States of America
  early history of lawn tennis in, 16–21
  women players, 168
United States Championship (United States Open from 1968)
  Austin's record, 251
  the first Championships, 21–8
  the Four Musketeers, 68
  Graebner-Leschly match (1966), 293, 295
  Lacoste-Tilden match (1927), 69–73
  Lenglen-Mallory match (1921), 65, 75
  Shriver-Navratilova matches, 218–19
  ticket prices, 39
  Wills-Jacobs matches, 73–80
  Wills-Mallory match (1921), 32, 35, 65
United States National Lawn Tennis Association (USNLTA), 20, 25, 51, 75, 130
  and the amateur code, 93–4
  and the Diamond Racket, 24
  first President, 19
  inaugural meeting (1881), 19, 22
  Virginia Slims tour, 142
United States Tennis Association (USTA), 157–8
  Tilden and, 66, 67, 68
  USTA tour, 142
  women's circuit, 243, 244, 246
University of California at Los Angeles, 93
University of Kentucky, 93
Updike, John, 271
US Pro Championship, Boston, 293–4

Van der Meer, Dennis, 189, 224–5, 229
Van Ryn, John, 82
vantage sets, 15, 23–6
Vilas, Guillermo, 268
Vincent, Tony, 95
Vines, Ellsworth, 82, 83, 89, 91, 92
Virginia Slims Championships, Madison Square Garden, 234
Virginia Slims tour, 142, 178, 190, 228, 229, 230, 243–4, 246
Vitale, Dick, 108
Vittel, France, 103
Vlasto, Didi, 50, 51, 57
volleying, 205
  early, 12, 13, 15–16, 20, 21, 22
  women and, 165–6
volunteer administrators, 66
Volvo Championship, 280
Von Cramm, Baron Gottfried, 89, 117, 118, 310

Wade, Virginia, 142, 178
Wallace, Marjorie, 248
Walsh, J. H., 9
Walsh, Sharon, 145, 184
Warhol, Andy, 248